The Trinity
and the Paschal Mystery

A Development
in Recent Catholic Theology

Anne Hunt

A Michael Glazier Book

THE LITURGICAL PRESS
Collegeville, Minnesota

NEW THEOLOGY STUDIES
General Editor: Peter C. Phan
*
Editorial Consultants:
Monika Hellwig
Robert Imbelli
Robert Schreiter
*
Volume 5: The Trinity and the Paschal Mystery

Cover design by David Manahan, O.S.B.

A Michael Glazier Book published by The Liturgical Press

1	2	3	4	5	6	7	8

Library of Congress Cataloging-in-Publication Data

Hunt, Anne, 1952–
    The Trinity and the paschal mystery : a development in recent
Catholic theology / Anne Hunt.
        p.   cm. — (New theology studies ; v. 5)
    "A Michael Glazier book."
    Includes bibliographical references and index.
    ISBN 0-8146-5865-2
    1. Trinity—History of doctrines—20th century. 2. Paschal mystery—History of doctrines—20th century. 3. Catholic Church—Doctrines—History—20th century. I. Title. II. Series.
BT111.2.H85   1997
231'.044—dc21   97-20143
                                                        CIP

Contents

Editor's Preface

This series entitled *New Theology Studies* is an attempt to answer the need felt by professors and students alike for scholarly yet readable books dealing with certain Catholic beliefs traditionally associated with dogmatic theology. The volumes in the series treat of fundamental theology (revelation, the nature and method of theology, the credibility of the Christian faith), trinitarian theology, christology, ecclesiology, anthropology, and eschatology.

There has been, of course, no lack of books, published singly or in series, both in this continent and elsewhere, which are concerned with these central truths of Christianity. Nevertheless, there is room, we believe, for yet another series of texts on systematic theology, not because these offer entirely novel insights into the aforementioned teachings, but because it is incumbent upon Christians of every age to reflect upon their faith in light of their cultural and religious experiences and to articulate their understanding in terms accessible to their contemporaries.

Theology is traditionally described as faith in search of understanding, *fides quaerens intellectum.* The faith to which the contributors to this series are committed is the Christian faith as lived and taught by the (Roman) catholic church. It is, however, a faith that is ecumenically sensitive, open to ways of living and thinking practiced by other Christian communities and other religions. The understanding which the series seeks to foster goes beyond an accumulation of information, however interesting, on the Christian past to retrieve and renew, by means of the analogical imagination, the Christian tradition embodied in its various classics. In this way, it is hoped, one can understand afresh both the meaning and the truth of the Christian beliefs and their multiple interconnections. Lastly, the contributors are convinced that theology is a never-ending quest for insights into faith, a *cogitatio fidei.* Its ultimate purpose is not to provide definite and definitive answers to every conceivable problem posed by faith, but to gain an understanding, which will always be imperfect and fragmentary, of its subject, God the incomprehensible Mystery. Thus, theology remains an essentially unfinished business, to be taken up over and again in light of and in confrontation with the challenges found in every age. And our age is no exception, when, to cite only two examples, massive poverty and injustice structured into the present economic order, and the unprecedented meeting of religious faiths in new contexts of dialogue, have impelled theologians to reconceptualize the Christian faith in radical terms.

Contrary to some recent series of textbooks, *New Theology Studies* does not intend to advocate and advance a uniform or even unified viewpoint. Contributors are left free to present their own understanding and approach to the subject matter assigned to them. They are only requested to treat their themes in an integrating manner by situating them in the context of Tradition (highlighting their biblical, patristic, medieval, and modern developments), by expounding their theological meaning and function in light of current pronouncements of the Magisterium, by exploring their implications for Christian living, and by indicating possible different contemporary conceptualizations of these doctrines. The goal is to achieve some measure of conprehensiveness and balance by taking into account all the important issues of the subject matter under discussion and at the same time exhibit some thematic unity by means of a consistent method and a unifying perspective.

The eight volumes are intended primarily as resource books, "launching and landing bases," for upper-division theology courses in Catholic colleges and seminaries, but it is hoped that they will be useful also to people—priests, permanent deacons, religious, and educated laity, inside and outside of the Roman Catholic communion—interested in understanding the Christian faith in contemporary cultural and ecclesial contexts. We hope that these volumes will make a contribution, however modest, to the intellectual and spiritual life of the Christian Church as it prepares to enter its third millennium.

Peter C. Phan
The Catholic University of America

Foreword

Trinitarian theology is enjoying something of a renaissance in contemporary theology. After so long a period in which trinitarian theology featured almost not at all, as if it were almost peripheral to the major tracts of theology or perhaps because it was considered that everything that could be said about this ineffable mystery had been said by Thomas Aquinas in his monumental *Summa Theologiae*, this renaissance is most welcome. After all, it is the Trinity that lies at the core of our faith, as both the formula of baptism and the Nicene Creed attest.

Yet on another level this renaissance is a rather strange phenomenon, for it is hardly as if an understanding of or devotion to the Trinity is deeply embedded in the faith-life of most members of the Christian community. Though we regularly recite the *Gloria in excelsis* and the Nicene-Constantinopolitan creed and begin and end our prayers with the sign of the cross and the words "In the name of the Father and of the Son and of the Holy Spirit," and though we offer the trinitarian doxology (Glory be to the Father and to the Son and to the Holy Spirit, as it was in the beginning is now and ever shall be, world without end), our trinitarian expressions of faith seem to make little real impression on us as believers. As Karl Rahner commented, it would seem that it would actually make very little if any difference to the person in the pew were it to be announced from the pulpit that the doctrine of the Trinity was to be revoked.

Is it not also somewhat paradoxical that we make that prayer "In the name of the Father and of the Son and of the Holy Spirit" while at the same time tracing on our ourselves the sign of the cross? In our prayer, *lex orandi*, the cross and the Trinity are in this very concrete way intimately and inextricably connected and yet, when we turn to study the classical expressions of trinitarian theology, the *credenda*, as expressed in the Augustinian-Thomistic synthesis at the apogee of Latin trinitarian theology, we find no direct or explicit connection at all between the Trinity and the Easter events of Jesus' death and resurrection, even though it was through precisely those events that Jesus' disciples came to proclaim that Jesus is Lord and that God is Father, Son, and Holy Spirit. The *redemptive* significance of Jesus' death and resurrection was clearly recognized, but not its *revelatory* significance. Instead classical trinitarian theology was fashioned, admittedly with superb elegance and rigor, in refined philosophical terms, but oddly abstracted from the events of salvation history.

Christians have been making the sign of the cross and reciting the trinitarian formulae for centuries, yet now, almost two thousand years after the death and resurrection of Jesus, theologians (only a few to date) are starting to make a *direct* connection between the Trinity and Jesus' paschal mystery, his passover from death to resurrection and new life as the Risen Lord. The trinitarian theology that emerges from this interconnection is startling in its vitality and dynamism, and a comparison of this theology with the classical treatment is fascinating. My aim in this study is to examine and assess this new development in relation to the classical tradition of trinitarian theology and to offer a perspective from which to understand it. What does this development contribute to trinitarian theology? What does it mean for theological method? Why has this extraordinary innovation arisen at this stage in the tradition?

Alas, I cannot promise the reader an easy or effortless journey into the realms of trinitarian theology. Even Augustine, great theologian that he was, observed that nowhere else is a mistake more dangerous or the search more laborious. I do promise an exhilarating and invigorating journey into that most central of the Christian mysteries, our triune God.

Why is it important to make the strenuous effort to explore this link between God and the paschal mystery? It is important because if God is our ultimate concern it matters greatly that we perceive, understand, and know God as much as revelation and the limitations of our knowledge allow. Moreover, it matters greatly not only for what we know of God and for our understanding of all the mysteries of faith, but no less importantly for what we know of ourselves, the life we lead, our relationships with each other, the Church in which we live, and the ministries we exercise—indeed, for the ways in which we exercise those ministries. If this new development in trinitarian theology enhances our understanding of God, if it more adequately meets contemporary exigences and our search for meaning, if it fosters the emergence of more authentic humanity, then it is vitally important that we attend to this development and contribute to its advance. As Augustine added to his note of caution in regard to trinitarian theology, nowhere else is the discovery more advantageous.

My great thanks go to my esteemed teacher and friend, Tony Kelly C.SS.R., President of Yarra Theological Union, Melbourne, for his generous assistance at numerous points along the way and his ongoing interest in the study. It was he who first quickened my fascination for theology in general and for our three-personed God in particular. My gratitude is owed also to the many fine teachers who over the years have led me more deeply into the tradition of Christian thought, and especially to Zachary Hayes, O.F.M. of Catholic Theological Union, Chicago. My family and friends have been unfailing in their encouragement, patience, and support, in ways to numerous to count. The Institute of the Blessed Virgin Mary, founded by that extraordinary woman, Mary Ward, has graciously allowed me the freedom to pursue my love for theology while continuing my work in the school. My thanks go also to my delightful extended family, the school community of Loreto Mandeville Hall, for its generosity in granting a semester's leave in order to bring this study, so dear for so long to my heart and my mind, to completion. Finally, my thanks to Linda Maloney, editor, and the staff of The Liturgical Press for their diligence, good humor, and encouragement in preparing the manuscript for publication.

Anne Hunt
Trinity Sunday, 1996

Introduction

Something new has been happening in Catholic trinitarian theology. The mystery of the Trinity is now being approached by some theologians from the perspective of its interconnection with the paschal mystery of Jesus' death and resurrection. This approach stands in considerable contrast to the traditional treatment of the mystery. It highlights the absence of any direct reference to the paschal mystery in the traditional approach and it prompts numerous questions as to what this new approach achieves in the history of trinitarian thinking and, indeed, why it has occurred at this stage in the theological tradition.

Classical trinitarian theology took shape with the great trinitarian controversies and the ecumenical councils of the fourth century.[1] In the face of the Arian crisis the central role Christian faith accorded to Jesus demanded a clear and unambiguous answer to the question whether he was himself Lord and God or only a created intermediary between God and humankind. In response to this question the first ecumenical council employed the non-biblical term *homoousios* (of the same substance) to proclaim that the Son was truly God. This was a most significant step forward in Christian theology. Not only did it settle the question of Jesus' ontological status, it endorsed

---

[1]For surveys of classical trinitarian theology, see Bertrand de Margerie, *The Christian Trinity in History*. Studies in Historical Theology I. Translated by Edmund J. Fortman (Petersham, Mass.: St. Bede's Publications, 1982); Edmund J. Fortman, *The Triune God: A Historical Study of the Doctrine of the Trinity* (London: Hutchinson, 1972); William J. Hill, *The Three-Personed God: The Trinity as a Mystery of Salvation* (Washington, D.C.: Catholic University of America Press, 1982); J.N.D. Kelly, *Early Christian Doctrines* (rev. ed. New York: Harper and Row, 1960, 1965, 1968, 1978); T. F. Torrance, *The Trinitarian Faith* (Edinburgh: T & T Clark, 1988); Basil Studer, *Trinity and Incarnation: The Faith of the Early Church*, ed. Andrew Louth. Translated by Matthias Westerhoff (Edinburgh: T & T Clark, 1993); Thomas Marsh, *The Triune God: A Biblical, Historical and Theological Study*. Maynooth Bicentenary Series (Blackrock, Co. Dublin: Columba Press, 1994).

the use of non-biblical terminology in theology and effectively introduced metaphysical conceptuality into theological reflection.

What is particularly interesting to note here is that trinitarian doctrine took shape before christology. The conciliar form of trinitarian doctrine was virtually settled before the Council of Chalcedon in 451 and its christological deliberations. In other words, the first theological questions and reflections to arrive at conciliar formulation were those concerning God and Jesus' relationship to God. They grew out of the christological question: Is Jesus fully God? However, the council's affirmation that the Son is fully God led to questions as to how this could be understood and so focused attention on the godhead. Although grounded in the theology of redemption, consideration at this stage concerned the divine being *ad intra*. Christological considerations of the person of Jesus came later. When they did emerge the philosophical framework in which they would be addressed was already set in place, trinitarian doctrine effectively providing a normative framework for christology. Hence christology, like the doctrine of the Trinity, was expressed in the metaphysically fashioned categories of "person" and "nature".

In terms of trinitarian theology Jesus' death and resurrection, even at this very early stage, were evidently deferred, as it were, as a kind of "empirical residue,"[2] data that are not perceived to be immediately relevant, at least in a direct sense, to reflections on the mystery of the Trinity as such. The doctrine of the Trinity was thus crystallized without any direct reference to the events of salvation history. But what we find in recent times is that what had been deferred is now appearing, emerging indeed as essential data, even of basic analogical importance for trinitarian thinking. The mysteries are being interconnected in startlingly fresh and inspiring ways. The death and resurrection of Jesus are being raised to the level of properly "theological" meaning and significance.

Certainly the proclamation of *homoousios,* the consubstantiality of the Son and Father, by the Council of Nicea in 325, and later that of the Holy Spirit by the Council of Constantinople in 381 solved the problem as to what constituted orthodox doctrine in regard to the Trinity. However in the process it undoubtedly contributed to a shift in theological reflection away from a consideration of what God does to what God is, and thus from soteriology to ontology. It prompted new questions: How was the consubstantiality of Father, Son, and Holy Spirit to be understood? How can the Three be consubstantial,

---

[2]In Lonergan's terms, "empirical residue" is "the class of matters of fact which have no immanent intelligibility." The element of anticipating an intelligibility is missing; there is no expectation of intelligibility in the data. See Lonergan, *Collection.* Collected Works of Bernard Lonergan 4, Frederick E. Crowe and Robert M. Doran, eds. (2nd rev. and augmented ed. Toronto: University of Toronto Press for Lonergan Research Institute of Regis College, 1988) 58, 206, 287–289. Admittedly it is not that there is no anticipation of intelligibility at all in Jesus' death and resurrection but that this is not in direct relation to trinitarian theology.

identically the same God and one in substance? How can they be truly distinct in their consubstantiality?

Addressing these kinds of questions Augustine of Hippo, although much indebted to the work of the Cappadocians in the East, brought a new level of conceptuality to trinitarian theology and profoundly influenced the development of Latin theology. Most remarkable of all his contributions to trinitarian theology are his psychological analogies.[3] Rooted in the biblical understanding of the human person as created in the image of God his search for trinitarian analogies, all drawn from reflection on the self-conscious subject, passed through memory, knowledge, and love *(mens, notitia, amor)*[4] to memory, knowledge, and love of self *(mens meminit sui, intelligit se, diligit se)*[5] and culminated in the image of the human self in the dynamic activity of remembering God, understanding God, and willing or loving God *(memoria Dei, intelligentia Dei, amor in Deum)*.[6] As Augustine explains: "Now this trinity of the mind is God's image, not because the mind remembers, understands, and loves itself, but because it has the power also to remember, understand, and love its Maker."[7] Augustine also considered the triad of the loving subject, the object loved, and the relation of love that unites them.[8] Although he does not pursue this analogy to any great extent the twelfth-century monastic theologian Richard of Saint Victor would later explore it in considerable depth.[9]

Augustine's analogies exercised a decisive influence on Latin theology. They were transmitted in succinct form to the Middle Ages by Peter Lombard, who gathered them together in his *Liber Sententiarum,* and became a required subject of theology. However, the influx of the new Aristotelian science and philosophy allowed a far greater logical rigor and conceptual precision than the older, more intuitive and subjective interior approach. In Aquinas's hands Augustine's richly experiential and subtle analysis of the mystery of the Trinity was transposed into a comprehensive systematic framework and reached a highly refined level of technical expression and precision. Later, with the emergence, indeed dominance of system in neo-scholasticism there would be a drastic attenuation of the existential reference that is so strong a characteristic of Augustine's treatment.

For Aquinas as for Augustine consideration of the Trinity follows a prior consideration of the unity and perfections of the divine nature. However, we find a reversal of order in Aquinas's synthesis of trinitarian theology. Augustine, taking a more historical approach, begins with the missions of Son

---

[3] See *De Trinitate* (hereafter referred to as *DT*) books IX–XI, XIV.
[4] *DT* IX, 1–7.
[5] *DT* X, 17–19.
[6] *DT* XIV, 11-21.
[7] *DT* XIV, 15. See Walter H. Principe, "The Dynamism of Augustine's Terms for Describing the Highest Trinitarian Image in the Human Person," *Studia Patristica* 18 (1982) 1291–1299.
[8] *DT* VIII, 14; IX, 2; XV, 10.
[9] See Ewert Cousins, "A Theology of Interpersonal Relations," *Thought* 45 (1970) 56–82.

and Spirit. In contrast, Aquinas's exposition passes from consideration of the processions and the relationships of the divine persons *ad intra* to their missions *ad extra*. Concerned for systematic intelligibility, Aquinas adopts the *via disciplinae,* not the *via inventionis,* the way of discovery. He begins with the supra-historical, intra-trinitarian processions and moves from consideration of the immanent to the economic. Augustine's psychological analogy in terms of word and love is taken up into a metaphysical understanding of God as the perfection of spiritual being. In God as Pure Act of Being, to be, to know, and to love coincide. An understanding of the divine processions is then expressed in terms of the Aristotelian categories of intellect and will. In this way Aquinas arrives at an analogy for the divine processions in terms of the acts of knowing and loving, which are proper to the Pure Act of being.[10] He thus moves from psychological acts to a consideration of being and grounds the innertrinitarian relationality in being itself. The psychological analogy is then metaphysically grounded and the resultant relationality is ontological. But see how very remote these trinitarian reflections are from the biblical data concerning the actual events of salvation history at this point.

Only after a consideration of the processions and relations of the divine persons *ad intra* does Aquinas move to their missions *ad extra*. He carries forward Augustine's understanding of the missions in relation to the processions: the temporal mission of a divine person includes the eternal procession of that person and adds a temporal effect.[11] Like Augustine he considers both the visible and the invisible missions.[12] In the visible missions the Son becomes incarnate and the Spirit is given at Pentecost. The visible mission reveals the invisible mission and is ordered to it. In the invisible missions created consciousness *(rationalis creatura)* is conformed to God, configured to the divine persons in the love of the Spirit and in the wisdom of the Word.

Aquinas grounds the invisible missions of wisdom and love in "the common root of grace,"[13] that is, in the one basic reality of God's self-communication. However, in his treatment of the visible missions Aquinas does not clearly bring the missions together under a single aspect as he does with the invisible missions. The visible missions are thus not clearly connected within the one mystery. Moreover, his treatment of the visible missions is relatively limited, with no explicit reference to Jesus' death and resurrection. The visible missions are clearly not as disclosive in the Thomistic treatment as the biblical data imply. Indeed, more detailed attention is given to the invisible missions.

The omission of any direct connection between the Trinity and Jesus' death and resurrection is all the more intriguing when one returns to consider Aquinas's understanding of our knowledge and naming of God, expounded a

[10]*ST* Ia 27.
[11]*ST* Ia 43, 2 ad 3.
[12]*ST* Ia 43.
[13]*ST* Ia. 43, 5 ad 3.

little earlier in the *Summa Theologiae*.[14] There he explains that we know God through God's effects or works

> Although in this life revelation does not tell us what God is, and thus joins us to him as to an unknown, nevertheless it helps us to know him better in that we are shown more and greater works of his and are taught certain things about him that we could never have known through natural reason as for instance that he is both three and one.[15]

It seems that Aquinas does not give consideration to the death and resurrection of Jesus as part of God's "works" in the economy, yet later in the *Tertia Pars* of the *Summa Theologiae,* in response to the question whether the passion and death of Jesus Christ add to what was achieved in the incarnation, Aquinas attributes to the passion a particular and irreplaceable role in the economy of salvation, having a special effect. There he writes: "Christ's passion had one effect that his previous merits had not. Not that the passion indicated a greater love, but it was the kind of a deed suited to produce such an effect."[16]

Similarly, Aquinas accords great significance to the resurrection. In a scriptural commentary he writes: "There are many things to be meditated on in him [Christ] but especially the resurrection. Everything is ordered to it, particularly the whole economy of the Christian religion."[17]

Why then is the Trinity not considered in terms of Jesus' death and resurrection? In retrospect it seems an astonishing omission in classical trinitarian theology. Apparently the interconnection of the Trinity with Jesus' death and resurrection is simply not a question at this stage in the tradition. The Trinity, although known only through revelation, is elaborated by Aquinas in refined metaphysical terms in *Prima Pars* of the *Summa Theologiae* while the death and resurrection of Jesus Christ are treated in *Tertia Pars* under the rubric of the return of the rational creature to God *(motus rationalis creaturae in Deum)*. Clearly Aquinas's emphasis is on the redemptive effect rather than the revelatory aspect of Jesus' death and resurrection.

Aquinas's synthesis was a monumental achievement of logical coherence, scientific precision, and systematic rigor. With it we have what became the classical form and *ordo doctrinae* of trinitarian teaching for centuries to come. The experiential component that was the Augustinian inheritance was set aside, as was the analogy of love developed by Richard of Saint Victor. With little variation trinitarian theology in the neo-scholastic period followed the metaphysical framework established by Aquinas. We do, however, find in the

[14]*ST* Ia. 12–13.
[15]*ST* Ia. 12, 13 ad 1.
[16]*ST* 3a. 48, 1 ad 3.
[17]In epist. 2 ad Tim. 2 lect. 2. *Super Epistolas S. Pauli Lectura* 2, ed. Raphael Cal (7th rev. ed. Rome: Marietti, 1953).

mid-nineteenth century, in the work of Matthias Scheeben, one hint of a new development that was to come in the second half of the twentieth century when trinitarian theology would return to the biblical data and to a consideration of the paschal mystery in particular. Scheeben's treatment of the cross to some degree anticipates the contemporary emphasis on the place of the cross in trinitarian life. Suggesting that "the idea of Christ's sacrifice thrusts its roots deep into the abyss of the Trinity,"[18] Scheeben describes "Christ's sacrifice in the very form in which it was actually offered, namely in the shedding of His blood to the last drop, as the highest expression of the Trinitarian relations and the most perfect vehicle of their extension to the outer world."[19] Scheeben thus recognized the *double* significance of the sacrifice of the cross, that the death and resurrection of Jesus are both the consummation of the act of the divine relationality *and* the act by which creation is incorporated within the inner-trinitarian life.[20]

Nevertheless an exploration of the interconnection of the Trinity and the cross, indeed the whole paschal mystery, was to be a long time in coming to light. It would be the biblical renewal movement that would finally prompt a return to the sources of Christian faith. Meanwhile in the mid-twentieth century the distinction between what came to be referred to as the immanent and economic Trinities (as distinct from previous considerations in terms of God *ad extra* and *ad intra*) came to the fore in trinitarian theology, together with questions regarding the relationship between the two. The issue was catapulted to prominence by Karl Rahner and his contentious *Grundaxiom* that the economic Trinity is the immanent Trinity and vice versa.[21] In a sense the *Grundaxiom* was itself indicative of the separation that had developed between economic and immanent considerations in trinitarian theology.

This, then, is the context in which a very different approach to the mystery of the Trinity emerges in recent theology, both Catholic and Protestant. In this new development the mystery is not approached by way of the Thomistic *ordo doctrinae*. In fact, a deep dissatisfaction with traditional Augustinian-Thomistic trinitarian theology prompts the development. Instead the mystery of the Trinity is approached by reflection on the biblical data concerning the paschal mystery of Jesus' death and resurrection.

---

[18]Matthias J. Scheeben, *Mysterien des Christentums* (1865). English: *The Mysteries of Christianity*, translated by Cyril Vollert (London: B. Herder Book Co., 1947) 446.

[19]Ibid., 445.

[20]Hans Urs von Balthasar discusses Scheeben's theology in *The Glory of the Lord: A Theological Aesthetics. 1. Seeing the Form*, ed. Joseph Fessio s. j. and John Riches, translated by Erasmo Leiva-Merikakis (San Francisco: Ignatius Press, 1982) 104–117. Describing Scheeben as "the greatest German theologian to-date since the time of Romanticism" (104), von Balthasar says that Scheeben "did us the service of replacing the 'aesthetic theology' of Romanticism with the outlines of a methodically founded 'theological aesthetics.'" (105)

[21]Karl Rahner, *The Trinity*, translated by Joseph Donceel (London: Burns and Oates, 1970) 21–24.

Admittedly, "paschal mystery" is not itself a biblical term. Although the link between Jesus' death and resurrection is clearly evident in scriptural understandings the origins of the term "paschal mystery" lie in the Christian liturgy of the *Sacrum Triduum,* the ritual enactment of the historical events as distinct from the events themselves. The term "paschal mystery" is, however, relatively new to Christian theology as such, having emerged in the liturgical renewal of the twentieth century and having risen to some prominence in the Second Vatican Council, where it is referred to in a number of council documents.[22]

This new approach is an extraordinary development in Christian theology in many ways. It raises numerous questions concerning the relationship between the mystery of the Trinity and the paschal mystery. Highlighting the fact that trinitarian theology has developed in relative isolation from a consideration of the life, death, and resurrection of Jesus despite the fact that it was as a result of those Easter events that the disciples of Jesus were led to proclaim that Jesus is Lord and that God is Father, Son, and Holy Spirit, this approach also raises questions concerning the development of classical trinitarian theology and of theological method more generally. Moreover it leads us to ask why this striking development has arisen at this stage in the tradition.

Our study examines and assesses this new development in recent trinitarian theology whereby the mystery of the Trinity is approached from the perspective of its interconnection with Jesus' paschal mystery. By the term "paschal mystery" I mean essentially the Easter events of Jesus' death and resurrection, the events of his passover to new life as the Risen Lord. Our questions concern what trinitarian theology emerges when it is based on a consideration of Jesus' paschal mystery. What does this development contribute to trinitarian theology in comparison with its classical antecedent? What methodological shifts does it involve? Most importantly of all, is this new approach to be commended?

Method

In order to offer a manageable and constructive contribution to the question I shall first confine my focus in this study to recent Roman Catholic theology, though this new development has arisen in the Protestant as well as the Catholic tradition.[23] Second, we shall examine the work of four theologians:

---

[22]See *Sacrosanctum Concilium* (Constitution on the Sacred Liturgy) 5, 6, 61, 104, 106; *Gaudium et Spes* (Pastoral Constitution on the Church in the Modern World) 22, 38, 52; *Optatam Totius* (Decree on Priestly Formation) 8.

[23]See, for example, Jürgen Moltmann, *The Crucified God,* translated by R. A. Wilson and John Bowden (London: SCM, 1974); idem, *The Trinity and the Kingdom of God: The Doctrine of God,* translated by Margaret Kohl (London: SCM, 1981); idem, *History and the Triune God,* translated by John Bowden (London: SCM, 1991). See also Eberhard Jüngel, *The Doctrine of the Trinity: God's Being is in Becoming,* translated by J.C.B. Mohr (Edinburgh: Scottish Academic Press,

François Durrwell, c.ss.r., Ghislain Lafont, o.s.b., Hans Urs von Balthasar, and Sebastian Moore, o.s.b. Each addresses quite explicitly the interconnection of the paschal mystery and the mystery of the Trinity. All stand firmly in the Latin Catholic tradition and share in its Greek philosophical and subsequent scholastic inheritance. Each expresses dissatisfaction with classical Latin trinitarian theology and seeks a more adequate explication of the mystery. Alsatian biblical scholar François Durrwell approaches the connection from the perspective of biblical theology. Concerned that traditional trinitarian theology does not accord well with the biblical data, he insists that theology return to the data. French theologian Ghislain Lafont addresses the interconnection from the perspective of systematic theology in the Thomistic tradition. He is particularly concerned for the way the divine persons are traditionally designated and seeks a more dynamic rendering of the Three. Swiss theologian Hans Urs von Balthasar approaches the question from an entirely different perspective again. For him faith is first an act of perception, an aesthetic act. He addresses the interconnection by way of a theological aesthetics in which Jesus in his paschal mystery is the "form" *(Gestalt)* of God's love. English Benedictine Sebastian Moore looks at the interconnection from a distinctly psychological perspective. His concern is not in the first instance for trinitarian theology as such but for the process of religious conversion itself. By means of an imaginative reconstruction of the disciples' experience he seeks to describe the "grass-roots derivation of the theology of Trinity."

Admittedly, at least at first sight these four writers are rather strange theological bedfellows. Francophone theologians Durrwell and Lafont are not well known in the English-speaking world although they deserve to be, especially in regard to the topic of interest to us here. Moore may seem a particularly dubious inclusion. His theology has a rather sketchy character about it: the volumes are slim, the chapters short, with pithy sentences and the occasional break into poetry, and his treatment of the interconnection of these mysteries is addressed not to questions of *divine* intersubjectivity but *human* subjectivity. The point, however, is that each of these writers, including Moore, addresses the specific question of the interconnection between Trinity and paschal mystery. We therefore have a clear thematic link between them although they demonstrate very different approaches and even though they focus on different aspects of the mystery. Moreover, that they address the interconnection from different perspectives sheds light on developments in theological method in light of the Augustinian-Thomistic tradition. The different perspectives provide valuable data for us in posing deeper kinds of

---

1976); idem, *God as the Mystery of the World: On the Foundation of the Theology of the Crucified One in the Dispute between Theism and Atheism*, translated by Darrell L. Guder (Grand Rapids: Eerdmans, 1983). Interestingly, it seems that this development in trinitarian theology is presently occurring only in western Christian thinking. I have to date found no evidence of a connection between the Trinity and the paschal mystery in the eastern tradition.

methodological questions. They enable us to attend to the significance of this new development for theology more generally.

It may at first seem surprising that such influential theologians as Karl Rahner, Walter Kasper, Yves Congar, Edward Schillebeeckx, and Leonardo Boff, and the recently published trinitarian theologies of Elizabeth Johnson and Catherine LaCugna are not included in our study. They simply do not treat this interconnection of the mysteries. This indeed serves to throw into even stronger relief the rather startling originality of this new development.

The aim of our study

This examination of the interconnection of the paschal mystery and the mystery of the Trinity has both thematic and methodological interest in this development. Thematically, I will examine the development in the light of traditional Latin trinitarian theology and assess the gains this new approach yields. What new meaning does it afford? In what ways does it enhance our understanding of the mystery of the Trinity? How does the understanding of the Trinity that results from this new approach compare with the traditional understanding and explication of the mystery of the Trinity? Methodologically, the study is an effort to document and evaluate the significance of this development for theological method. I will be concerned not only for what each author has to say about the interconnection itself and what it yields in terms of an understanding of the mystery of the Trinity, but also for the approach and method each author adopts. How does this new development compare methodologically with the traditional *ordo doctrinae?* What methodological shifts emerge in our authors' works? I will assess the thematic yields and observe the methodological shifts against the background of traditional Latin trinitarian theology, particularly the contributions of Augustine of Hippo and Thomas Aquinas.

No doubt not all would agree that this new development represents a genuine theological advance in trinitarian theology, for example in regard to the work of François Durrwell or Sebastian Moore or perhaps even Hans Urs von Balthasar. Indeed, I suspect that one of the reasons why von Balthasar's theology has remained largely peripheral to contemporary mainstream Catholic theology until recently is that few have recognized and adverted to the place of his work methodologically. Such is the level of confusion as to how and where to place his work that we find him referred to as pre-modern,[24] unmodern,[25] and post-modern.[26] Von Balthasar's extraordinary corpus is dense,

---

[24]See, for example, McDade's comments on Hans Urs von Balthasar in his article, "Catholic Theology in the Post-Conciliar Period," in Adrian Hastings, ed., *Modern Catholicism: Vatican II and After* (London: SPCK, 1991) 426–429.

[25]John Saward, *The Mysteries of March: Hans Urs von Balthasar on Incarnation and Easter* (London: Collins, 1990) vii.

[26]See, for example, Jean-Luc Marion, *God Without Being: Hors-Texte,* translated by Thomas A. Carlson, with a foreword by David Tracy (Chicago: University of Chicago Press, 1991). See also

complex, and from a traditional systematic perspective, seems rather unsystematic and disordered. Indeed, John J. O'Donnell comments that there is "a certain capriciousness in Balthasar's method,"[27] while O'Hanlon refers to "the glorious disorder of his theological style."[28] Similarly, without a methodological framework that situates his endeavors within the realm of the psychological consciousness of the existential subject Sebastian Moore's work risks being relegated to the margins of theology, as "spiritual theology" to be dismissed as peripheral to the main work of theology. Without an adequate and appropriate methodological framework these theological explorations we have before us are, at best, left to be considered as belonging to what in Lonergan's terms is the functional specialization of Communications, but not Systematics. Ultimately, then, our question concerns whether this recent development in trinitarian theology effects a genuine advance in properly systematic theology.

Jeffrey Kay, "H. U. von Balthasar, Post-Critical Theologian?" *Concilium* 141–146 (1981) 84–89; and Cyril O'Regan, "Von Balthasar and Thick Retrieval: Post-Chalcedonian Symphonic Theology," *Gregorianum* 77 (1996) 257.

[27]John J. O'Donnell, "Truth as Love: The Understanding of Truth according to Hans Urs von Balthasar," *Pacifica* 1 (1988) 210.

[28]Gerard F. O'Hanlon, "Legacy of Hans Urs Von Balthasar," *Doctrine and Life 41* (1991) 405.

CHAPTER ONE

François X. Durrwell:
The Resurrection Rediscovered

In classical trinitarian theology the mystery of the Trinity is considered quite separately from any direct consideration of the paschal mystery. Jesus' death and resurrection are treated in terms of a theology of redemption, as the means by which our salvation was achieved. The traditional theology of redemption developed in such a way that Jesus' salvific work was seen to consist of his incarnation, his life, and his death on the cross. It was not the resurrection but the reparation, satisfaction, and merit of the life and death that were stressed. When and if the resurrection was mentioned it was not in terms of its role in effecting our salvation, but more as addendum or validation. This is the context in which François Durrwell's study of the resurrection emerged to break new ground.[1]

That such theologies of redemption had gained currency in the West was due in no small measure to Anselm's stress on the notion of satisfaction. If redemption equals satisfaction then the resurrection, which is seemingly not a work of satisfaction, is not redemptive in any intrinsic manner. From this perspective the resurrection seems almost incidental to the work of redemption. Aquinas's view, however, was an exception. In a deft treatment of redemption as satisfaction he went beyond Anselm and attributed an efficient causality to the passion, death, and resurrection in achieving our salvation.[2] Instead of constructing a theory of divine justice within which to *insert* Christ's passion and death as perfect satisfaction Aquinas interpreted the passion as an expression

---

[1] See Charles Davis's "Introduction" in *The Resurrection: A Biblical Study,* translated by Rosemary Sheed (London: Sheed and Ward, 1960) xiii–xx.
[2] *ST* 3a. 56, 1–2.

of a voluntary human action, a perfect act of love.[3] Nevertheless later theology truncated the dimension of divine love and shifted emphasis to the juridical dimension.

A persistent failure to recognize the theological significance of the resurrection contributed to the "parceling out" of theology into discrete tracts as a sense of the interconnection of the mysteries of Christian faith was overshadowed. The result was that theologies of redemption were based on theories of reparation, atonement, or satisfaction. All essentially juridical in tone, they necessarily found their focus in the life and death, as distinct from the resurrection, of Christ. In such satisfaction-fashioned theologies Jesus' loving obedience constitutes the formal element by which the divine demand for justice is satisfied. In this way other aspects of redemption and of Jesus' paschal mystery, most particularly the resurrection, came to be regarded as peripheral to the essentially juridical problem of redemption itself.

A "truncated" theology of redemption disconnected from the resurrection prevailed. If the resurrection was redemptive at all it was only in the sense and to the extent that it constituted a motive of credibility. The resurrection was thus effectively left to be considered almost exclusively from an apologetic perspective. It was relegated to a lesser role than the death of Jesus, a kind of epilogue or supplement or apologetic proof in regard to a fullness of redemption that was understood as essentially external to it. Thus was the resurrection shorn of its theological significance.

The first protest against this truncated theology of redemption and its treatment of the resurrection came from biblical scholars, not least among them Durrwell, who recognized that such a theology is defective and does not do justice to the New Testament data. Scripture, Durrwell observes, sees our salvation quite differently. The good news the apostles proclaimed is not that pardon has been accorded or that a debt has been settled, but that Jesus is risen and is sent to us: it is not primarily a message of reparation or satisfaction. Instead Scripture speaks of communion and of the resurrection as *parousia,* the coming of the Lord that permits this communion.[4] In the New Testament, therefore, the resurrection is no mere epilogue or supplement to the mystery of our salvation; rather, in and through the resurrection, in the fullness of Jesus' paschal mystery, our salvation is effected by the triune God.

Observing that the resurrection was indeed source and center of theology in apostolic times, Durrwell maintains that it soon lost is central place because it was not recognized as the eschatological event, the plenitude of salvation.

---

[3]See Bernard Catão's study of Aquinas's theology of redemption, *Salut et rédemption chez S. Thomas D'Aquin,* Théologie études publiées sous la direction de la Faculté de Théologie S. J. Lyon-Fourvière 62 (Paris: Aubier, 1965). Catão observes that Aquinas employs the categories of merit and satisfaction of his time but explicates the instrumental efficacy of the actions of Christ in the work of salvation in a way that is unique (xiv).

[4]Durrwell, "Mystère pascal et Parousie: L'importance sotériologique de la présence du Christ," *Nouvelle Revue Théologique* 95 (1973) 253–278, especially 268–270.

Juridically-styled theologies of redemption resulted.[5] Consequently redemption was not considered as a trinitarian event but instead as a work of the God-man. God was portrayed in terms of infinite justice rather than as the Father who, in the Holy Spirit, engenders the Son in the world and leads him, through his life and death, to his glorious filial plenitude. In this way the death of Jesus came to be considered as a payment in satisfaction of a debt and not as entrance into communion. It was disconnected from the resurrection and had a redemptive role imputed to it alone. Moreover, not only was an understanding of the role of the resurrection impoverished but the person of the Holy Spirit was particularly difficult to situate in such juridically-fashioned theologies. Durrwell accounts in this way for the fact that a treatment of the Holy Spirit is almost absent from theology in recent centuries.[6]

Recognizing that the theological import of the resurrection had been lost in more juridically-styled theologies of redemption, Durrwell in his foundational study *La Résurrection de Jésus, mystère de salut. Etude biblique,*[7] published in 1950, presented a comprehensive synthesis of the biblical texts that deal with the resurrection of Jesus Christ. He attempted to reclaim the properly *theo*-logical significance of the paschal mystery, and particularly of the resurrection, by means of a return to the biblical data. Indeed, the very notion of the death and resurrection as "two aspects of the one paschal mystery"[8] emerged with unprecedented clarity in his study,[9] in fact foreshadowing Vatican II's rediscovery of the paschal mystery.[10] The result of Durrwell's study was a strongly revelation-centered and resurrection-centered theology that stood in stark contrast to the prevailing theologies of redemption in which Jesus' death had the primary focus: in Durrwell's work the significance of the resurrection is rediscovered.

The fruit of a refined biblical scholarship, *The Resurrection* also represented a new method of scriptural inquiry and a significant shift in theological method. As a work of "biblical theology" it effectively lies somewhere between exegesis and systematics.[11] Though it is less critical and technical in its style compared to current exegetical procedures it is more ambitious in its

---

[5]Ibid. 277–278.

[6]Durrwell, *L'Esprit du Père et du Fils* (Paris: Médiaspaul, 1989). English translation by Robert Nowell: *The Spirit of the Father and of the Son: Theological and Ecumenical Perspectives* (Middlegreen, Slough: St Paul Publications, 1990) 8. I will hereafter, unless otherwise indicated, refer to the English translation, and abbreviate it in the notes as *SFS*.

[7]I will hereafter refer to the English translation, *The Resurrection: A Biblical Study.*

[8]*L'Esprit du Père et du Fils* 58.

[9]Certainly, as noted in the Introduction, the notion of the paschal mystery was well established in Christian tradition but its use, in both the eastern and western traditions, was largely confined to liturgical reference. Durrwell's introduction of the notion into theology as such marked a new development.

[10]As noted in the Introduction, n. 22.

[11]For current reflection on the method of biblical theology, see Gerard S. Sloyan, "Biblical Theology," in Joseph A. Komonchak, Mary Collins, and Dermot Lane, eds., *The New Dictionary of Theology* (Wilmington, Del.: Michael Glazier, 1987) 118–129.

systematic effort. At the same time it is more fully biblical than the traditional trinitarian schemes and eschews philosophical categories or systems. As Durrwell himself explains:

> Have they [Sacred Scriptures] not been inspired by the Christian mystery itself, and are they not thus the most faithful conceptual expression of it? My wish was to let myself be wholly guided by them, in the Church's faith and free from all preconceived systems. Whereas theology usually reasons about God according to concepts of essence or nature, a legacy of Greek philosophy, or according to juridical concepts on questions about redemption, the Scriptures have taught us to favour, in all reflection on God and salvation, the mysterious reality of *the person*. Just as faith is an encounter with Someone, theology is research on the part of the intellect into a mystery that is personal.[12]

Although Durrwell is familiar with a number of patristic sources and various elements of the tradition, *The Resurrection* (together with Durrwell's later explorations) thus remains largely within the biblical frame of reference. Durrwell seeks to say positively what images, concepts, and categories are given in the New Testament data, and negatively to challenge traditional theology where it does not accord closely with the biblical data.

The eschatological plenitude of the resurrection

Utterly fundamental to Durrwell's interconnection of the paschal mystery and the Trinity is what he describes as *"la plénitude eschatologique de l'événement pascal,"*[13] the eschatological fullness and completion of the paschal mystery. In the resurrection the Son is raised to the fullness and glory, the very plenitude of divine sonship. All the eschatological attributes of Christ, such as lordship of the universe, are a reality from the moment of the resurrection onwards.[14] All power is given to him. Salvation is entirely accomplished in the resurrection. The kingdom of God is established in him. The Spirit, the eschatological gift, is completely communicated through him and henceforth all the gifts of the Spirit come from him.[15] The resurrection of all the dead is contained in him. The last judgment is already present in him

---

[12]Durrwell, *L'Esprit Saint de Dieu* (Paris: Éditions du Cerf, 1983). English translation by Benedict Davies: *Holy Spirit of God: An Essay in Biblical Theology* (London: Geoffrey Chapman, 1986) viii. I will hereafter refer to the English translation, and abbreviate it in the notes as *HSG*.

[13]Durrwell, "Liminaire: La Pâque du Christ selon l'Écriture," in *La Pâque du Christ, Mystère de Salut: Mélanges en l'Honneur du Père Durrwell* (Paris: Éditions du Cerf, 1982) 13.

[14]See "The Effects of the Resurrection in Christ" in *The Resurrection* 108–150; also "Liminaire: La Pâque du Christ selon l'Écriture" 12; and Durrwell, "Resurrection of Christ, 2. Theology of," *New Catholic Encyclopedia* (1967) 12.410–419.

[15]*The Resurrection* 103–105.

at the heart of the world. In Jesus' resurrection the summit of salvation history is achieved. On this basis Durrwell recognizes that the lordship and plenitude accorded to Christ in the resurrection make the resurrection *the* eschatological event.[16]

Logically and theologically there is nothing more to be added to this eschatological plenitude of the risen Christ! He is raised to the fullness of the glory and power of the divine Son. There is nothing more to be added to it, for nothing can be added to plenitude. It is in this way, then, that Durrwell speaks of the "eschatological" character of the resurrection and of the resurrection as *the* eschatological mystery. It is thus that he can say not only that the resurrection is the anticipation of eschatology but that the paschal Christ is eschatology itself.

The permanent actuality of the resurrection

Since nothing can be added to the moment when Christ is accorded the fullness of glory and plenitude Durrwell can say that the resurrection knows no tomorrow in Jesus.[17] Jesus advances no farther than the first moment of his glorification, for that is his fullness, perfection, and goal. He no longer grows old but lives today and forever, eternally, in this moment of glorification. Durrwell therefore recognizes that this eschatological plenitude of the paschal event is effectively synonymous with its permanent reality and what he describes as its eternal (that is, ever-present) actuality.[18] Because it is the action of divine plenitude the resurrection remains ever present, ever actual. It remains forever in act. Hence Durrwell speaks of the "eternal" character of the resurrection and of the glorification of Jesus as a permanent actuality. He explains: "We must take it that Christ will never grow any older than he was at the Resurrection, that his life remains new, that his body, new-born in the Spirit, never grows beyond the moment of his Easter birth and therefore that the Father's action in raising Christ continues eternally in its single moment."[19]

While the work of our redemption has taken place in our past, in Christ it remains already and for always and in this sense "eternally" in the present actuality of its full accomplishment. Though it belongs to one precise moment of our time it has an eternal actuality because Jesus never for an instant leaves the moment of redemption, the moment of death in which he is raised and glorified. He lives eternally in its single moment of plenitude. The resurrection is thus to be understood as a permanent and eternal divine action. Durrwell writes: "God's act of raising is a permanent lasting reality. We must . . . see

[16]Ibid. 12.
[17]Ibid. 131.
[18]"Liminaire: La Pâque du Christ selon l'Écriture" 13.
[19]*The Resurrection* 130.

the Resurrection as both an event preceded and followed by others and a divine action outside history."[20] The resurrection is a permanent actuality both inside and outside of time as we know it.

The resurrection as a divine generation

Reflection on this permanent actuality of the resurrection, its eternal character, leads Durrwell to the inner-trinitarian mystery of the Father's generation of the Son. Thus he arrives at an understanding that the resurrection proceeds from the mystery of the eternal generation of the Son by the Father in the Spirit: "The Resurrection brought Christ wholly to birth in the life of the Son, extending to his whole being the glory of his eternal generation. And in that birth, there is no 'tomorrow.' Alongside our ancestor Adam, the old man, who continues to decay within us (2 Cor. iv. 16), here is the young Adam, the new man, Son of God, in the everlasting newness of his sonship."[21]

In the resurrection God takes Jesus, in his humanity, into the fullness of the eternal begetting of the Son. The resurrection corresponds to the divine generation by the Father of the beloved Son. Quoting Acts 13:32-33,[22] which serves as a key text for Durrwell in understanding the resurrection as the eternal generation, Durrwell writes, for example:

> Then the Father took him to himself, and introducing him totally into the secret of his divine being, into that embrace which confers sonship, he abolished in him the "condition of a slave" and brought his whole, once mortal, humanity into the eternal origins of the life of sonship, into the instant of divine generation. He generated him as Son of God in his entire being, saying in the act of glorifying him: "Thou art my Son, this day have I begotten thee."[23]

In this way Durrwell recognizes that the Father's action of raising Jesus is a divine generation. In the resurrection, in this "birth in eternity"[24] Jesus is reborn into the life of the Son of God. The resurrecting act of the Father is thus a divine begetting; it corresponds to the Father's generation of the Son in the inner-trinitarian mystery of God. Ultimately this means that trinitarian being and relationality are therefore not only *revealed*, but *realized* for us in creation in the resurrection of Jesus Christ.

---

[20]Ibid. 131.

[21]Ibid.

[22]"And we bring you the good news that what God promised to our ancestors he has fulfilled for us, their children, by raising Jesus; as also it is written in the second psalm, 'You are my Son; today I have begotten you'" (Acts 13:32-33).

[23]Durrwell, *In the Redeeming Christ*, translated by Rosemary Sheed (London: Sheed and Ward, 1963) 329.

[24]Ibid. 328.

Four very significant points emerge from Durrwell's reflections on the resurrection of Jesus as the divine generation of the Son:

1. Jesus' humanity is interior to the trinitarian mystery

Durrwell stresses that in this divine generation Jesus is brought "wholly to birth in the life of the Son."[25] *As human,* Jesus is raised into the permanent actuality of the resurrection, the eternal moment of glorification. "The whole of his human being is woven, by the Spirit, into his eternal filial origin."[26] In that ever actual moment of glorification, his *whole* being is interior to the trinitarian mystery where God engenders the Son. His humanity is thus interior to the trinitarian mystery. Henceforth a human person is raised to the level of God, taken into the mystery of the Trinity.[27]

2. The stigmata of death remain in the resurrection

In this glorification the stigmata of Jesus' suffering and death remain. Christ is not healed of his mortal wounds. The resurrection is evidently no antidote or corrective to his suffering and death. Just as the glorification of Christ is a permanent actuality, so too is his death.[28] In other words, the permanent actuality of the glorifying action of the Father in the resurrection maintains Christ in the instant when he submits himself to glory: he is glorified precisely in his dying, the summit of his self-giving. Jesus Christ is forever the Slain Lamb.[29] Death and resurrection are thus revealed as the essential and complementary dimensions of the one paschal mystery: "it is the mystery at once of death and resurrection and final coming."[30] Note that in contrast to its role in juridically-fashioned theologies, here the death of Jesus is essentially related to his glorification, without which indeed it would have no redemptive meaning.

Note too that though the role of death in the paschal mystery is crucial it is quite different from the part it plays in juridically-fashioned theologies of redemption. The paschal mystery of death and resurrection reveals that it is through death that Christ opened himself to the infinite gift of new life. Death is the vital passage, a way of utter "*disponibilité,*"[31] self-surrender. It is the door that opens to the infinite reception of eternal glory.[32] The death itself is a

---

[25]*The Resurrection* 131.

[26]*HSG* 43.

[27]"Mystère pascal et Parousie" 268.

[28]*The Resurrection* 149–150.

[29]This is a powerful image in Durrwell's theology and recurs frequently. He stresses: "He is not only like a lamb, He is the Lamb." See Durrwell, "Lamb of God," *New Catholic Encyclopedia* (1967) 8.338–340.

[30]"Mystère pascal et Parousie" 278.

[31]Ibid. 272.

[32]Ibid. 268–269.

birth or passover. Durrwell writes: "For Christ and his faithful, death is the
birth of completeness; it is the sublime movement carrying them out of this
world to God."[33] In this sense death is to be found at the heart of the divine
plan of creation. The creative, salvific action of the Spirit culminates in it. It
is the necessary passage or passover to life in communion in the triune God.

3. Creation enters into the trinitarian mystery

It is for our sake that Jesus in his humanity is taken into the mystery of the
Trinity; it is for us that God begets this human person divinely. Henceforth in
union with Christ we become subject to and are incorporated into the same divine generation. Raised with him, we too are fixed at the moment of eternal
birth. In him we are born of God in the Holy Spirit and share fully in the divine birth that is Christ's.[34]

Moreover not just humankind but all creation is involved. In communion
with Jesus, it too becomes interior to the trinitarian mystery where God engenders the Son. Creation, the whole cosmos, thus enters into the eternal
begetting of Christ. Through the resurrection the universe is drawn into the
trinitarian mystery of God. As Durrwell explains: "In Christ who inhabits the
Trinity, this creation is 'within' God; at its height and in its roots, it enters into
the eternal begetting of Christ."[35] In Christ all creation therefore becomes filial, sharing in the mystery of the eternal generation of the Son. This, in
Durrwell's theology, is salvation. It is not the distribution of merits or the redemption of a debt, but Jesus in person, the Savior in his gift of self. To be
saved is to be incorporated into Christ's filial being. It is to be raised with him
into the mystery of his resurrection. It is birth into the trinitarian communion.

4. The Father's begetting of the Son is accomplished in creation

In the resurrection God becomes in creation what God is eternally in the
mystery of the Trinity, the Father who begets the Son in the love of the Holy
Spirit. The eternal begetting of Jesus is thus accomplished within creation. It
is immanent within the world as its fulfilment. "The resurrection is the synthesis and the climax of creation, beyond which one cannot go, in the permanent today of the Easter birth of Christ (cf. Acts 13:33). *Henceforth the eternal
begetting of the Son in the Spirit is immanent within the world:* the world is
steeped, at this its own climax, in the eternal trinitarian movement."[36]

[33]*HSG* 121.
[34]See, for example, *In the Redeeming Christ* 328–336.
[35]*HSG* 140. See also *The Resurrection* 290–293.
[36]*HSG* 131. "Salvation history has progressed to the rhythm of God's mystery in the world. It
reaches its climax in Christ's passover, when the mystery becomes immanent in creation as it has
ever been in eternity." Ibid. 74.

Here is the crux of Durrwell's theology: the paschal mystery is the eternal divine mystery of the Father's generation of the Son in the Spirit, enacted ("en-acted" as in the enactment of the divine act of being) in the world. In other words we have not only the revelation but the accomplishment of the eternal inner-trinitarian begetting of the Son by the Father in the Spirit in creation. The eternal trinitarian movement of God *ad intra* is thus realized *ad extra*. Hence Durrwell, having set out to retrieve the eschatological and eternal character of the resurrection, establishes an understanding of the resurrection as the Father's act of generation of the Son and then implicates the eternal inner-trinitarian mystery of Father, Son, and Holy Spirit. He recognizes that the paschal mystery is not just redemptive or salvific but revelatory of what God is in God's own eternal being.[37]

The paschal mystery as Christ's personal mystery

An understanding of the interconnection of the paschal mystery and the mystery of the Trinity is further advanced by Durrwell's recognition of the paschal mystery as Christ's *personal* mystery. He notes that Scripture gives the death of Jesus what initially appear to be two barely reconcilable interpretations: that Christ "died for us" and that Christ died in order "to enter into his glory."[38] Durrwell observes that those theologies that are developed on the basis of the first interpretation, that Christ "died for us," and that give little attention to the second tend to be expressed in juridical style and language. Redemption is understood in terms of the payment of a debt by which the Son "satisfies" the exigencies of divine justice. Admittedly Jesus' identity as the incarnate Son of God gives the necessary infinite value to the debt paid, but the death is not seen as a reality intrinsic to his person. Consequently such theologies lose sight of the paschal mystery as the *personal* mystery of Jesus Christ. Salvation is understood as *obtained* by him rather than as *realized* in him. It consists in a merit achieved or a price paid. The death of Jesus is thus effectively reduced to *a work* through which he obtains the reconciliation of humanity to God. It is the *action* of Jesus, *an effect essentially exterior to himself,* that is seen as salvific, not the *person.* Durrwell insists, however, that while the metaphor of a price paid is biblical this use of it is not. The biblical data, he argues, do not indicate that a ransom was paid to the Father for our redemption. Rather God gives the only Son, making him the redemption of the world, and through him reconciles the world to God. In this sense Christ did not *acquire* salvation. Through the Father and in the Spirit he himself *became,* in person, the mystery of our salvation.

However, when emphasis is given to the second interpretation (that Christ died in order "to enter into his glory") a very different theology emerges, one

---

[37]"Liminaire: La Pâque du Christ selon l'Écriture" 13.
[38]"Mystère pascal et Parousie" 266–270.

in which the paschal mystery is recognized as Christ's *personal* mystery, his self-realization, expressive of the dynamics of his filial existence.[39] The work of salvation is consubstantial with the person. Salvation, from this perspective, is an intrinsically personal drama. It consists in Christ's entry into his own filial glory. The work of salvation is thus identical with the filial dynamism of Christ, proper to and expressive of his identity as Son. Not an action or an example or even a gift to God, it is the personal mystery of Christ, Son of God, who through his death and resurrection himself becomes the event of salvation in person.

Durrwell's emphasis is thus that Christ's death is not a gift made or a debt paid to God in order to obtain redemption. Certainly Christ gives himself, and entirely, but by unlimited and active receptivity. His infinite merit is to receive without limitation or reservation the fullness of divinity, and thus to enter into full communion with the Father. His death is total submission *(soumission)*, a complete and utter surrender *(disponibilité)* to the divine plenitude.[40] The purpose of his suffering and death was to prepare for this reception. Through his death Jesus opened himself to the infinite gift.[41] Note again how this understanding differs from satisfaction theories in which Jesus' obedience functions as the formal element by means of which the demand for justice is satisfied. Here his obedience is essentially expressive of his personal identity as the Son. In his obedience he is, and shows himself in creation to be, the Son.[42] Moreover we also see that, in contrast to a juridical theology in which Jesus Christ *must* be the Son of God in order to give infinite value to his work of reparation, in a theology of the paschal mystery the glorification of Jesus *shows* that the death was that of the Son of God.[43] It is the revelation and realization, the enactment in the realm of creation, of his divine sonship.

The person, hypostatic characteristics, and procession of the Holy Spirit

Durrwell's exploration of the theological meaning of Jesus' paschal mystery ultimately leads him to an even more explicitly trinitarian frame of reference. Some decades after the publication of *The Resurrection* his reflections resulted in the publication of *L'Esprit Saint de Dieu* and *Le Père: Dieu en son Mystère*.[44] Most recently he has returned to a study of the Holy Spirit in

---

[39]Ibid. 268.
[40]See Durrwell's summary of the relationship between death and resurrection in "Resurrection of Christ, 2. Theology of," *New Catholic Encyclopedia* (1967) 12.410–419.
[41]"Mystère pascal et Parousie" 268.
[42]*SFS* 50.
[43]"Mystère pascal et Parousie" 268, n. 46.
[44]*Le Père: Dieu en son Mystère* (Paris: Éditions du Cerf, 1988).

L'Esprit du Père et du Fils[45] where he develops a trinitarian theology in which, on the basis of the biblical data, he concludes that the Holy Spirit proceeds from the Father and the Son. Because of the division between East and West over the vexatious *filioque* controversy the issue of the procession of the Holy Spirit is of particular concern to Durrwell.[46] Here too, in the vitally renewed sense of the person of the Holy Spirit that emerges so strongly, his theology stands in contrast to prevailing theologies of his time in which reference to the Spirit is relatively scant. However, as he explains, when juridical concerns predominate not only is a sense of the mystery of our redemption as a mystery of love lost but the role and person of the Holy Spirit are also eclipsed. On the other hand Durrwell's exploration of the resurrection as the mystery of our salvation results in a vividly trinitarian theology, one in which the role and person of the Holy Spirit emerge with remarkable clarity and vitality.

Before turning directly to the mystery of the procession of the Holy Spirit Durrwell first analyzes the characteristics and role of the Holy Spirit as revealed in the biblical data, explaining that "the key to the problem of the procession of the Spirit is to be found in the mystery of the Spirit itself."[47] In shedding light on the characteristics of the person of the Holy Spirit the New Testament leads to an understanding of the manner of the procession of the Holy Spirit.

Durrwell first observes that the New Testament identifies the Spirit with the power of God.[48] It is the Father who raises and glorifies the Son. It is the Son who is raised. The Holy Spirit is evidently neither the one who glorifies nor the one who is glorified, but rather the power of the resurrection, the operating power of God, the divine action itself. We must conclude, Durrwell argues, that the Holy Spirit is, in person, the divine begetting:

> The resurrection of Jesus, which is the realization in the world of the eternal mystery of the Father and Son, reveals that *it is in the Spirit that God is father,* that the Spirit is the eternal action, the power, the holiness, the love and the glory in which God begets his Word. That is why we thought we could say that he is *in person* the eternal begetting. He is the mystery proper to the Father and the mystery proper to the Son. Without being either the beginning or the end of the trinitarian movement, he is at the beginning and at the end, acting in the Father as father, in the Son as son, and it is he who brings about the union of them both. All is accomplished in him who is love, infinitely powerful, the single action of the Father and of the Son.[49]

[45]*L'Esprit du Père et du Fils;* see also "Pour une Christologie selon l'Esprit Saint," *Nouvelle Revue Théologique* 114 (1992) 653–677. For a discussion of Durrwell's theology of the Holy Spirit see Gérard Remy, "Une Théologie pascale de l'Esprit Saint," *Nouvelle Revue Théologique* 112 (1990) 731–741.
[46]*SFS*, Foreword 7–11.
[47]*SFS* 15.
[48]*SFS* 17–23; *HSG* 8–11.
[49]*HSG* 162.

The trinitarian names follow: in God there is the Begetter *(Le Géniteur),* the Begotten *(L'Engendré),* and the act and power of Begetting, the generative power *(L'Engendrement).*[50] Note that in Durrwell's understanding both the Son and the Spirit proceed from the Father in his paternity, one as begotten, the other as the begetting.

Second, an exploration of the paschal mystery as a mystery of love leads Durrwell to a complementary notion: the Holy Spirit is love.[51] The Holy Spirit is not only the power in person but love hypostasized. Here Durrwell takes up Augustine's triad of "he who loves, he who is loved, and love."[52] The Spirit is love in person. At this point Durrwell also invokes an argument on the basis of the divine *perichoresis,*[53] for it is thus that this *perichoresis* obtains, he explains: "The Father is the Father in Love; the Son is the Son in Love; . . . without being the beginning or the end, the Spirit is at the beginning and at the end. It is the womb where everything is achieved."[54]

Durrwell concludes that the notion in classical Latin theology according to which the Father begets the Son by way of intelligence should be discarded, for the Father begets by *loving* the beloved Son.[55] The Father accomplishes his unique activity, the begetting of the Son, in love. Both processions are processions of love. Indeed, Durrwell explains, "in speaking of the Holy Spirit as hypostasized love one is suggesting that no psychological analogy is capable of plumbing the depths of the mystery of the one who is love itself."[56]

Third, Durrwell considers the Holy Spirit as the bond of communion, the bond of unity, between Father and Son.[57] Scripture, he observes, does not speak of a common nature but of *the communion of the Holy Spirit.* Whereas human beings possess a common nature that is dispersed in innumerable realizations the Father and the Son are one in the most absolute unity which *is that of a person who is common to them.* They are one in the inseparable unity of a third person, the Spirit, who abides in them both and in whom they are Father and Son. Durrwell explains:

[50]*SFS* 20; see also "Pour une Christologie selon l'Esprit Saint" 663.

[51]*SFS* 26–29; *HSG* 15–17.

[52]See the Introduction above, n. 8.

[53]Here, with the use of *"perichoresis,"* Durrwell introduces one of the few strictly non-biblical terms that he employs. It is interesting to note that he does not use the biblical category of *koinonia.*

[54]*SFS* 29. The Council of Florence (1438–1445) set forth the doctrine of *perichoresis* or circumincession, the coinherence or mutual indwelling of the divine persons, as an explication of the true identity of substance in the Trinity (*DS* 1331). The Greek word *perichoresis* has a double meaning and both Latin words, *circumincessio* (from *incedere,* to permeate and interpenetrate) and *circuminsessio* (from *sedere* and *sessio,* to be seated) were used to translate it. The former conveys a more active and dynamic indwelling and tends to be the preferred Latin form.

[55]*SFS* 28. Durrwell writes: "It seems that we should resolutely avoid an opinion found in one school of Latin theology according to which the Father begets the Son by way not of love but of intelligence." See also *SFS* 29–30, nn. 10 and 12, and 59–60.

[56]*SFS* 30 n. 10.

[57]*SFS* 32–38; "Pour une Christologie selon l'Esprit Saint" 665–669.

It is . . . in the Holy Spirit, that is to say, in the infinite begetting, that the Father is, that he is the person of fatherhood; it is in it, in the begetting in its infinite reception, that the Son is, that he is the person of sonship. It is there that their divine nature is found, their way of being the essential, infinite God the Father, the essential, infinite God the Son. In God, everything assumes the dignity of the person, just as the theological concept of divine nature tries to express.[58]

In this way the Holy Spirit emerges as "principle of personalization."[59] It is in the Holy Spirit that the Father is Father, the paternal person. It is in the Holy Spirit that the Son is Son, the filial person. In the realm of the economy Durrwell observes that the Holy Spirit is the spirit of incorporation. Through the Holy Spirit creation is incorporated into the person of Jesus Christ and shares in the eternal filial mystery of his death and resurrection. Moreover the attributes of God are made personal, are hypostasized in the person of the Holy Spirit: the eternal action, the eternal life, the holiness, the infinite love, the power, the glory in which God begets the Son. Indeed, all that the traditional notion of the divine nature evokes is personified, hypostasized, in the Holy Spirit.[60] In this somewhat novel sense Durrwell speaks of the Holy Spirit as the divine nature. He writes:

There is a theological tradition which distinguishes between a divine nature, which is one, and the three Persons constituted after this nature. Unity, holiness, power, and love are the "attributes" enumerated as belonging to this nature . . . . Such a distinction makes it easier to talk about God, but it does not correspond to the reality revealed in Jesus, and it ignores the central role of the Spirit. *In God there is no nature which becomes fruitful in Persons:* there are three Persons, *it is God's nature to be Trinity.* Of these three Persons one is the Holy Spirit in whom God begets; he is the "common property" and the bond of unity between the Father and the Son; *in him the attributes of God are personified.*[61]

On the basis of this biblically-based understanding of the Holy Spirit Durrwell proposes that theology should "transcend the opposition between essentialist and personalist theologies"[62] whether in trinitarian theology, where we traditionally distinguish between the divine nature and the three persons, or in christology, where we speak of the two natures in the one person. Although not rejecting or contradicting the classical formulations Durrwell is

---

[58]*SFS* 38.

[59]*SFS* 46 n. 6.

[60]*SFS* 47; *HSG* 148; "Pour une Christologie selon l'Esprit Saint" 667–669.

[61]*HSG* 148. Certainly Augustine taught that the Holy Spirit possessed in person what the other divine persons possessed by virtue of the divine nature (*DT* XV, 37). Durrwell, however, virtually collapses the notion of the divine nature at this point.

[62]See *SFS* 40 n. 19.

acutely aware of their limitations. In his assessment the doctrinal definitions fail to convey the *personal* mystery that lies at the heart of theology.

Finally Durrwell arrives at the question of the inner-trinitarian mystery of the procession of the Holy Spirit.[63] Having surveyed the biblical data in regard to the characteristics of the Spirit he concludes that the procession of the Holy Spirit necessarily involves the Son. He argues that if the Holy Spirit is the divine begetting, the love in which the Son is begotten, and the bond of unity between Father and Son, then one cannot speak of the procession of the Spirit from the Father unless also in relation to the Son. We briefly turn to consider his thought in this regard.

Durrwell understands that the Spirit proceeds in a primordial manner from the Father. As the divine begetting, the love within which God is Father, the Holy Spirit proceeds from the Father, although in a way that is different from that by which the divine Begotten proceeds from the Father. Durrwell, distinguishing between the procession of the Son and that of the Holy Spirit, explains that whereas the Son "goes out" and differentiates himself in infinite otherness from the Father, the Holy Spirit proceeds from the Father without leaving him. The Holy Spirit remains in the Father. In this sense the Holy Spirit is the Spirit of God in God's fatherhood.

Nonetheless, the Spirit is also the Spirit of the Son.[64] This is manifest in the resurrection, the revelation of the mystery of sonship, which discloses that Jesus Christ lives in the power of the Holy Spirit. The resurrection thus reveals that the Holy Spirit belongs to the Son as much as to the Father although in a different way, a way that is appropriate to sonship and to the active receptivity that is constitutive of the mystery of the second person.

At this point Durrwell proceeds to an exploration of other ways in which we can understand that the Son participates in the procession of the Spirit. He first suggests that by reflecting on the obedience of the Son we may understand that the Son plays a part in his own resurrection in the sense that the Son assents, through his obedience, to the fatherhood of the Father. In other words the Son assents to the begetting power of the Father, which is the Holy Spirit; his obedience calls forth the effusion of the Spirit. In this way, Durrwell maintains, we can see that the Son clearly plays a filial role in the eternal procession of the Spirit. Reflecting on the divine mystery in terms of love also leads to the conclusion that the Son participates with the Father in the procession of the Spirit. Consider the Father as he begets the beloved Son. The Son then responds in love to the Father. The love of the Son, in his death and resurrection, then calls forth the love of the Father in response. The Holy Spirit, who is this love, thus flows from the Father not just in a primordial or originating sense but in loving response to the Son. In other words we can understand that the Son's love of the Father prompts the love of the Father for the Son. In this

---

[63]*SFS* 47–56; *HSG* 140–145.
[64]*SFS* 47–51.

sense, therefore, the Son plays a role in the outpouring of the Holy Spirit. The Spirit who is love flows from the Father, but also flows to the Son in response to the Son's love in what is an unceasing circulation of love: "The Father fills the Son with his Spirit of Love and the love that takes over the Son elicits from the Father the gift of the Spirit in a perpetual round."[65]

Thus from this perspective also Durrwell recognizes that the Son plays a role in the outpouring of the Holy Spirit. He concludes that the Son plays a vital role in the procession of the Holy Spirit.[66] Finally, sealing the argument, Durrwell proposes that the *perichoresis* of the Trinity, which he insists must be honored and accounted for in any study of trinitarian life, requires that the Holy Spirit proceed from the Father and from the Son.[67] He writes: "If one denied the Son all participation in the procession of the Spirit, one would not be honouring the holy perichoresis of the trinity."[68]

To deny the Son a role in the procession of the Spirit would be to fail to affirm the trinitarian *perichoresis*. Even more important than the *taxis* (the order of the divine persons) is the *perichoresis,* Durrwell insists.[69] He explains that if the Son did not participate in the procession of the Holy Spirit the monarchy of the Father would be that of a superiority and domination. The Son would receive in passivity, without response to the Father. He would not be equal but inferior to the Father, receiving the Holy Spirit without also being source of the Holy Spirit. The Spirit would then be reduced to the last person, after the Son, in whom the trinitarian movement comes to an impasse. Durrwell thus contends that the trinitarian *perichoresis* also demands that the Holy Spirit proceed from the Father and the Son *(filioque).* The Spirit is the Spirit of both.[70]

Nevertheless, while holding that the Spirit proceeds from the Father and from the Son as a single principle Durrwell insists that, contrary to classical Latin theology, the Holy Spirit does not come forth as from a single *undifferentiated* principle.[71] The Holy Spirit proceeds from the *differentiated*

---

[65]*SFS* 52.

[66]*SFS* 47.

[67]See above at n. 54 regarding *perichoresis* in the tradition.

[68]*SFS* 59.

[69]"Pour une Christologie selon l'Esprit Saint" 664.

[70]Durrwell comments that this solution to the procession of the Holy Spirit recognizes the legitimacy of the demands of both Greek and Latin Churches. In respect to the Greek Church the Father alone is font of the Spirit. The mystery of the Holy Spirit's procession is understood within the all-embracing mystery of the Father's begetting of the Son. In respect to the Latin Church the Son shares fully (and filially) in the spiration of the Holy Spirit (*SFS* 11). In fact Durrwell's "resolution" compares closely with the statements of the Council of Florence concerning the reconciliation of Greek and Latin theology in regard to the procession of the Holy Spirit. See *Decrees of the Ecumenical Councils* 1.525–527.

[71]*SFS* 60. The Second Council of Lyons (1274) and the Council of Florence (1438–1445) defined that the Holy Spirit proceeded from the Father and Son as from one principle, that is, by one single spiration (*DS* 850, 1300–1302, 1330–1331). The notion of common spiration of the Holy Spirit goes back to Augustine (see, for example, *DT* V.15) for whom it served to distinguish between the processions of the Son and the Holy Spirit.

communion of the Father and the Son, each acting as is proper to his person, one as Father, the other as Begotten. Again Durrwell stresses that the Holy Spirit is not consecutive to their unity in one same nature. It does not burst forth from the Father and from the Son after the begetting, for the Holy Spirit is in person this begetting that unites the Father and the Son.[72]

We note that in this discussion of the characteristics and procession of the Holy Spirit Durrwell appropriates the term "person" to each of the Three with little discussion of its application, yet as we see above in Durrwell's description of the hypostatic characteristics of the Holy Spirit, the nature of the Holy Spirit as person emerges in a quite different light from that of the persons of the Father and Son.[73] In *Holy Spirit of God* he argues that the term "person" is appropriately applied to the Holy Spirit:

> Although our thinking is incapable of imagining such a person, we can discern in the Spirit the two characteristics basic to every person: namely, an existence in his own right and the dynamism of the relationships in which that person exists. Scripture describes him [the Holy Spirit] as subject of his actions, existing therefore in his own right and as a mystery of communion. However, this second aspect is stressed with such evidence, the "relational" nature of the Spirit is so forceful that one might think that the other aspect (that of existence in his own right) is cancelled out. The Spirit is the unique operation of the other two Persons, their common will: he is *one* Person in two others, he exists in his own right but as absolute gift of himself, given to the other two Persons. We are confronted with a mystery that is certainly that of Love.[74]

Durrwell argues that if the aspect of relationship, of gift of self, is so vividly affirmed that the other aspect of personhood, that of an individual existence in its own right, is somewhat overshadowed "this means that a person is most fully a person in the gift of self, that *relationship is even primordial, that it constitutes the height and depths of a being*."[75] It ultimately means, he concludes, that salvation is to be found in relationships, in the communion between God and creation.

We see that in comparison with traditional trinitarian theology a rather different "model" of the Trinity emerges in Durrwell's trinitarian theology. His is effectively a "bi-polar" trinitarian model. There are only two poles, for the Father has only one Son, who, as the only-Begotten, is the unique term of the Father's paternal action. The third divine person, the Holy Spirit, is neither

[72]*SFS* 60–61; *HSG* 182 n. 17.

[73]Durrwell's treatment of the Three as persons is highly differentiated. In a discussion of the trinitarian indwelling, for example, he explains that the relations of the three divine persons with the human person are different, as are the relations of the human person with each of them. *Le Père: Dieu en son Mystère* 91.

[74]*HSG* 136. Note that—in comparison to Augustine and Aquinas—Durrwell is relatively uncritical in his use of the term "person."

[75]*HSG* 137.

the beginning nor the end, but envelops both poles of the paternity. Durrwell explains: "Although it [the Holy Spirit] may be neither the beginning (the Father), nor the conclusion (the Son), it is at the beginning and at the conclusion, since it is in it that the Father begets and the Son is begotten: far from being barren, it is the fertility of God."[76] Belonging to them both, the Holy Spirit encompasses them, as it were. It is in the Spirit that the Father begets, that the Father is the person of fatherhood, the one who begets. It is in the Spirit that the Son is begotten, the person of sonship, the one who receives his being as the begotten one. In this sense the Son is begetting in its reception. The eternal movement of begetting goes from one to the other. The Spirit is this movement that envelops and unites them while holding Father and Son in irreducible distinction.

In this way Durrwell, though maintaining that there are two processions, insists that both must be understood within the mystery of the Father's fatherhood, on the grounds that the Father only acts as Father.[77] The Father's person is thus constituted solely in and through his fatherhood. The Son's person is constituted in and through his sonship. However, without being the Son, the Holy Spirit also proceeds from the Father, and proceeds from the Father within the mystery of the Father's fatherhood. The paternal being of God is as much invested in the procession of the Spirit as in the generation of the Son. Indeed, this is why the Spirit is not inferior to the Father or to the Son and receives the same glory. Durrwell explains: "He [the Holy Spirit] proceeds in the begetting of the Son, he is the Spirit of the Father in his fatherhood. The entire activity of the Father is to beget the Son, and although God does not beget the Spirit, it is nonetheless in his fatherhood that he is the source of the Spirit."[78]

The Holy Spirit is thus constituted in the relationship of the Father and Son. It oscillates between them in a unique movement of unceasing ebb and flow through which the Father begets and the Son is begotten. The Holy Spirit is, in person, the begetting. Indeed, in his most recent article Durrwell writes: "If the Holy Spirit is the divine power of engendering and if all that theology says of the divine nature is personalized in him then God is essentially Father. The divine nature is there, in the infinite engendering of the infinite Son."[79] Again we find Durrwell identifying the Spirit with the divine nature. In Durrwell's theology God is one not by reason of an impersonal divine nature but because

---

[76]*SFS* 23; *HSG* 140–147.

[77]See *SFS* 23, 44; see also *SFS* 59–60, where Durrwell rejects the idea that the Father produces the Son on one hand and the Spirit on the other. In such a theology, he explains, the Father would not be acting as Father because the Spirit would proceed from him apart from the mystery of the begetting of the Son. Cf. also "Pour une Christologie selon l'Esprit Saint" 662–665.

[78]*HSG* 140.

[79]Durrwell presses farther and says that God is not simply to be defined as "that than which nothing greater can be thought" (*"id quo maius cogitari nequit,"* from Anselm's ontological proof of the existence of God, *Proslogion* III) but rather as the One than whose self-gift nothing greater can be thought: God is Father in the infinite engendering of the infinite Son: "Pour une Christologie selon l'Esprit Saint" 672.

God is Father and Son in the person of the Holy Spirit.[80] The Spirit is God's nature and unity in person. In the resurrection the mystery of the Father's begetting of the Son in the Holy Spirit is accomplished in creation.

We now turn briefly to appraise Durrwell's interconnection of trinitarian theology with the paschal mystery. Our concern is not to evaluate Durrwell's theology as such but to examine the interconnection he makes between the mystery of the Trinity and the paschal mystery.

The role of the paschal mystery in Durrwell's trinitarian theology

In Durrwell's theology everything fundamentally turns on the role of the resurrection. Though the death is of undeniable importance as the necessary passover it is the resurrection that is the center point in his reflections. There the Father raises the Son in the Spirit. This corresponds to the Father's eternal generation of the Son. The relationality of Father, Son, and Spirit is thus revealed and realized in creation, disclosing what is eternally true in God. In this way Durrwell arrives at the profoundly theological meaning of the resurrection.

Although Durrwell is not interested in a systematic statement of trinitarian theology as such he clearly rejects the psychological analogy of classical trinitarian theology. He insists that no psychological analogy is capable of plumbing the depths of the mystery of the One who is love itself. For him the mystery is given paradigmatically, indeed iconically, in the resurrection: the resurrection is the locus for an understanding of the mystery of the Trinity. It reveals the divine persons in relation to each other, their hypostatic characteristics, proper roles, and distinctive missions. As each of the divine persons emerges in distinction from the others there is no call for appropriation of roles or properties in Durrwell's theology.

In this way his understanding of the resurrection serves as prime analogue and shapes his trinitarian theology. Hence, unlike Augustine and Aquinas or even Richard of Saint Victor, Durrwell does not look to the human person for an analogy for triune being. He looks to the Trinity itself, revealed in its glory in the resurrection. However, he does on occasion invoke interpersonal analogies from the sphere of human experience. The analogy of human love, for example, allows him to elaborate on receptivity as characteristic of love.[81] This serves to support and augment the understanding of the Trinity as mystery of love that he seeks to convey. Nevertheless, the resurrection serves as primary analogue in his understanding of the Trinity. Indeed, rather than taking notions of personhood drawn from human experience and applying them to the Trinity, Durrwell effectively reverses the procedure. The Trinity reveals what it is to be personal: in God's consciousness and in ours relationship is pri-

---

[80]*HSG* 149.
[81]See, for example, *SFS* 49.

mordial. Salvation is thus described in relational and trinitarian categories. In the resurrection the Father's eternal generation of the Son is accomplished in creation. Creation itself is thus taken up into the inner-trinitarian communion. Incorporated into Christ in his paschal mystery, it enters into that divine relationality between the three divine persons that is constitutive of God's inner mystery. Thus Durrwell implicitly reverses a Greek philosophically fashioned ontology in which being logically precedes relationality. Pointing to an ontology in which relationality is no less important than substance, Durrwell insists that the Trinity is to be understood in terms of love: the self-giving love in which the Father generates his Son, the receptive love with which the Son responds to the Father, the love of the Holy Spirit, their mutual love, and their outreaching redeeming love by which creation is taken up into their trinitarian perichoretic communion. Death is the culmination of the self-yielding and self-giving of love. Through it, in communion with Jesus' death, creation enters into the trinitarian communion. So we see that at every turn in Durrwell's theology images of relationality abound.

The relationship between economic and immanent Trinity

Though Durrwell does not use the language of immanent and economic Trinity we note that he does in effect distinguish between these two aspects of the Trinity so as not to collapse the immanent into the economic Trinity. A subtle distinction between the two is evident in his work. At the same time they are inextricably related; indeed, Durrwell's dissatisfaction with traditional trinitarian theology is based on a concern that the two not be separated, that reflection on the immanent Trinity be grounded in revelation and our experience of the economic Trinity that takes place in Jesus' paschal mystery. As Durrwell explains, the difference between "economy" and "theology," between the economic and the immanent trinity, lies in a radical "for us":

> The distinction between the mystery of the Trinity in its eternity and the Spirit given to men and women, between "theology" and "economy", does not involve any discontinuity: in the passover of Jesus "theology" becomes "economy" and the eternal mystery is accomplished for us. The difference resides in that last phrase, "for us". While theology considers the mystery of the Trinity in itself, the latter becomes ours through Jesus Christ: in the mystery of salvation, the Father begets his Son for us, Christ is the Son of God for us, the Spirit is the divine begetting for us so that in the Son we may become children of God."[82]

There is therefore no discontinuity, for "theology" and "economy" find their point of connection in the paschal mystery of Jesus Christ, where the Father

[82]*SFS* 56.

begets the Son in the Holy Spirit "for us." In effect Durrwell makes an epistemological, as distinct from an ontological, distinction between the immanent and economic Trinity. The economic Trinity is the Trinity we encounter
in the paschal mystery: "Apart from this place and this 'Hour', apart from
Christ and his passover, the Father is not known in his fatherhood, nor the Son
as he truly is, nor the Spirit in whom the Father begets, in whom the Son is
begotten."[83] While the economic Trinity is the Trinity we know and experience
as the mystery of our salvation, it corresponds to the immanent Trinity.

Assessment of gains for trinitarian theology

In my assessment the significant thematic gains achieved in Durrwell's
trinitarian theology in relation to classical trinitarian theology can be summarized as follows:

1. A return to the biblical data

Durrwell's most significant advance of all is, I suggest, his insistence that
theology return to its biblical sources. In effect he reconnects theology with
the biblical data. Throughout his exploration his constant challenge to traditional trinitarian theology is that it is not sufficiently biblical in its emphasis
on Jesus' death in terms of satisfaction, in its failure to recognize the properly
theological significance of the resurrection, in its expression of the immanent
processions by means of the classical psychological analogy, in its distinction
between essentialist and personalist categories, and in its explication of the divine nature.

2. A wealth of interconnections

This fundamental regrounding of theology in the biblical data leads
Durrwell to other significant connections. Indeed, I suggest that Durrwell's
advance in trinitarian theology lies as much in the connections he makes as in
the conclusions he draws. The death is connected with the resurrection in the
one saving paschal mystery, and the paschal mystery is connected with the
Trinity, such that the paschal mystery becomes an analogy for the Trinity.

Durrwell's retrieval of the death and resurrection as essentially interconnected aspects of the one mystery, the paschal mystery, is a most important
step. With it the theological significance of each dimension, death and resurrection, and of the mystery as a whole, emerges with new clarity. The
very possibility of the interconnection of paschal mystery and Trinity is
thus established.

---

[83]*HSG* vii.

Undoubtedly Durrwell's rediscovery and reclamation of the properly theological significance of the resurrection mark a very significant development.
The resurrection is no longer relegated to the domain of apologetics as "empirical residue" in relation to a theology of redemption and to trinitarian theology.[84] But his insight into its centrality not only restores meaning to the
resurrection as such; it also effectively opens up a vast new realm for exploration in trinitarian theology. An expanded horizon emerges for theological reflection on the mystery of God; a new vista for the religious imagination
dawns, one in which data previously unintegrated and indeed disconnected are
taken up and integrated in a broader vision, a "higher viewpoint."[85] From this
higher viewpoint the death and resurrection are reconnected in the one paschal
mystery. The paschal mystery is then connected with the very person of Jesus
and his mission. Christ's redeeming action is no longer understood in the
categories of satisfaction theories but rather in terms of the all-encompassing
mystery of God as love. The paschal mystery is thus connected to the mystery of the Trinity. As we have seen, in the resultant trinitarian theology the
person and role of the Holy Spirit emerge with signal vividness. We see too
that the work of redemption is no longer relegated to the realm of creation,
an act essentially exterior to God, *ad extra*. In the redemptive act God *ad
intra* is realized *ad extra*. Soteriology is connected with the Trinity as all
creation is incorporated in Christ and with him enters into the glory of filial
being, and so into communion with God. Theology is thus connected to
economy, and economy to creation. These are the consequences of
Durrwell's ground-breaking rediscovery of the theological significance of
the resurrection.

However, from a systematic perspective numerous problems arise, although
we must keep in mind that Durrwell's biblical theology is expressly not intended as a dogmatic treatise or a systematic treatment of the Trinity in the traditional sense.[86] Durrwell is not primarily concerned to address questions
pertinent to systematic theology. His reference to speculative questions in the
tradition of trinitarian theology is episodic and only arises when he disagrees
with the traditional treatment, for example with regard to the processions of
the Son and Holy Spirit. Otherwise his theology stays resolutely within the
biblical frame of reference. This is both its strength and its limitation. It is its
strength because it insists that theology be grounded in the data and so

[84]See Introduction, n. 2.
[85]In Lonergan's terms a "higher viewpoint" is "a set of later insights which show the short-
comings and limitations of an earlier set." See Lonergan, *Understanding and Being*. Collected
Works of Bernard Lonergan 5, Elizabeth A. Morelli and Mark D. Morelli, eds. (2d rev. and augmented ed. Toronto: University of Toronto Press for Lonergan Research Institute of Regis
College, 1990) 54–56, 204–206. See also Hugo E. Meynell, *An Introduction to the Philosophy of
Bernard Lonergan* 207.
[86]See Durrwell's Foreword to the first edition of *The Resurrection* where he clearly states this
at xxiii–xxvi.

prompts a rediscovery of the biblical data in theology generally. It is also its limitation because it lacks and, indeed, eschews technical terminology and conceptuality with which to address systematic and ontological questions that inevitably arise from the actual data.

Consider, for example, the question of change in God. Durrwell does not address this issue; he neither affirms or denies immutability as a divine perfection. However, his theology begs the question: Does God change?[87] The question is particularly acute at the point where Durrwell speaks of the resurrection in terms of the raising of Jesus' humanity into the Trinity. He writes: "Henceforth, a man is wholly raised to the level of God, to the interior of the trinitarian mystery."[88] The question of immutability remains unresolved and indeed unaddressed. Moreover, were Durrwell to attempt to address it his biblical theology would not provide him with the conceptual apparatus to resolve it. A second example relates to the question of the unity of the Three, which inevitably arises in so vitally differentiated a three-personed theology as Durrwell's. Here Durrwell's theology begs the question: How does this trinitarian theology avoid tritheistic implications? In what does the divine unity consist? Again Durrwell is not concerned or equipped to address such speculative and ultimately ontological questions. He maintains that the Holy Spirit in person unites the divine persons. The trinitarian *perichoresis* in effect functions in his theology as the notion by which the unity of the Three is upheld. But the questions remain, speculative though they are. They draw attention to the fact that Durrwell's biblical theology eventually needs some sort of systematic metaphysical support. It is no substitute for a rigorous and properly systematic explication of the mystery.

All in all, although Durrwell's biblical theology is not concerned to address questions properly pertinent to systematic theology and that indeed demand a properly systematic treatment his essential and welcome point is that the biblical data are a vital source in addressing such questions. His exploration of the procession of Spirit, for example, where his express aim is to return to the biblical data in order to clarify the *filioque* debate, clearly exemplifies this.

Methodological observations

If we turn now to questions of theological method we find that a number of methodological shifts are evident in Durrwell's work. His method contrasts with the traditional approach to trinitarian theology in the following ways:

---

[87]For a study of this question see, for example, Thomas G. Weinandy, *Does God Change? The Word's Becoming in the Incarnation* (Still River, Mass.: St. Bede's Publications, 1985).
[88]"Mystère pascal et Parousie" 268.

1. Shift from philosophical system to biblical data

In what is effectively a critique of philosophically fashioned theology Durrwell insists that theology be grounded in the biblical data and rejects any explication in traditional trinitarian theology that appears to stand in tension with the biblical witness. His biblical trinitarian theology, while not without its problems, represents a new method of scriptural inquiry and prompts a return to the biblical data in theology generally. The result of this methodological shift is a more historical and experiential theology that is firmly grounded in a refined scriptural inquiry. As such it marks a search for a distinctive Christian realism in a more empirically-oriented culture that is neither competent nor confident in the realm of classical metaphysics and is clearly not persuaded by a theology shaped by substance-based metaphysical categories.

2. Shift from incarnation to paschal mystery

In his return to the biblical data Durrwell effects a shift from the incarnation to the paschal mystery as source for reflection on the Trinity. His focus is clearly not the incarnation and all the metaphysical-ontological questions it raises, but the paschal mystery to which the scriptural sources give such vivid witness and that he understands as the enactment of the trinitarian mystery of God in creation. Of course no rift between incarnation and paschal mystery is intended or implied. Durrwell does not set up a counter-theology to that of the tradition. Rather he attempts a fuller and more biblically-focused expression of it. In fact the paschal mystery emerges as the fullness of the incarnation. Durrwell writes: "in the passover of Jesus it is the mystery of the incarnation, that of sonship, that is firmly established."[89] The paschal mystery is the culmination of the incarnation and indeed the climax of all creation. The question is, therefore, not whether the incarnation *or* the paschal mystery achieves our salvation, but how in the Easter passover of Christ the eternal begetting of the Word is fully accomplished within creation, to be its consummation and final form.

3. Shift from immanent to economic starting point

In consequence of the shift from system to data Durrwell's exploration begins by way of reflection on the biblical narrative, not with doctrine or metaphysics, thus reversing the *ordo doctrinae* of traditional trinitarian theology. In this respect Durrwell effects a methodological shift from an immanent to an economic starting point, beginning not with the immanent processions but with the missions in the economy of salvation. The consequences are most significant. Not only is the resultant theology grounded in the biblical data but

[89]*HSG* 36.

it operates in a totally different context. Situated firmly in the setting of the paschal mystery as the mystery of our salvation, the trinitarian theology that results is recast and reconstituted in a distinctly soteriological context. The mystery of the Trinity is explicated as the mystery of our salvation.

4. Shift from a juridical understanding of redemption to one of love

Durrwell's return to the biblical data and his recognition of the paschal mystery as first and foremost an act of divine love, revealing and realizing the inner-trinitarian love between Father and Son in the unity of the Holy Spirit in creation, as "for us," leads Durrwell to refashion the prevailing theology of redemption. Redemption is not the satisfaction of a debt but trinitarian love accomplished in the economy for our salvation. In this methodological shift an explication of our redemption in terms of the exigencies of divine justice, expressed in terms of theories of satisfaction, is replaced by one of redemption as the revelation and realization of divine love and the entry of creation into communion with Christ in his filial glory in the trinitarian *perichoresis*. Here Durrwell effects another significant shift, expressing the mystery of redemption not in terms of justice, but love. The mystery of our salvation is a mystery of love. Again recall Durrwell's rejection of the psychological analogy and his insistence that both processions are processions of love. What is also significant at this point is that in making this shift Durrwell's theology points, implicitly at least, to the development of a trinitarian ontology in terms not simply of Being, but Being-in-Love. We shall later return to this issue.

5. Shift from classical ontology to biblical phenomenology of relationships

With the transposition into the key of love an ontological notion of the divine substance yields to a plumbing of the divine relations. This is accompanied by a shift from traditional metaphysically-fashioned categories to more affectively-laden categories of interpersonal relations. Metaphysical categories of classical theology thus give way to a more basic experiential symbolism expressed in personalist and relational categories. As we have noted, this shift is manifest at every turn in Durrwell's theology. Consider for example the prominence he accords to the images of fatherhood and sonship: the Father is not the font of the divinity by virtue of being unbegotten (that is, unrelated), but is rather the Begetter. His mystery is that of paternity. The mystery of sonship is one of filial obedience and receptivity. The trinitarian *perichoresis* is one of communion in love. The Holy Spirit emerges as the begetting in person, the one in whom one is the Father and the other is the Son, the one who holds them in communion while in utter distinction from each other. We note that the hypostatic traits of the Holy Spirit that Durrwell articulates—begetting, love, bond of unity, and communion—are essentially relational categories. Indeed Durrwell describes the Holy Spirit as the divine nature hypostasized—holy, spirit, love—that is, the divine attributes in person and thus in relation. This biblical phenomenology of relationships is complemented by numerous references, by way of analogy, to the human experience of love.

What is significant here is that in this shift Durrwell's theology implicitly adumbrates a new Christian metaphysics in which the relational aspect of personhood has primacy. Note too that in situating the unity of the three divine persons in terms of the trinitarian *perichoresis* Durrwell also points the way to move beyond the opposition of substantialist and personalist categories. We will later return to this issue.

In Durrwell's biblical theology we have found a radical shift, in both content and method, in trinitarian theology when approached from this perspective. The Thomistic *ordo doctrinae* is reversed, the psychological analogy rejected, and metaphysical conceptuality set aside in favor of a return to the biblical data and biblical conceptuality, and at the very heart of Durrwell's theology there is a rediscovery of the profound significance of the resurrection as a divine generation, the enactment of trinitarian love.

CHAPTER TWO

Ghislain Lafont:
Death and Being, Human and Divine

French theologian Ghislain Lafont, O.S.B., explores the interconnection of the paschal mystery and the Trinity in *Peut-on Connaître Dieu en Jésus Christ?*[1] and further in *Dieu, le Temps et l'Etre*,[2] published some fifteen years later. Lafont adopts a very different perspective from that of Durrwell and a different method of approach. Where Durrwell constructs a biblical theology Lafont approaches the interconnection as a systematic theologian well schooled in Thomistic theology and the traditional treatment of the Trinity[3] although also sensitive to the concerns of contemporary culture and theology.[4] Unlike Durrwell, Lafont has an essentially systematic interest in the interconnection. His primary concern is for the tools and rules of theological discourse in speaking about God.

Lafont proposes an exploration of the interconnection in order to find a solution to a problem of the post-Nicene separation of "theology" (that is, the doctrine of God, trinitarian theology) and "economy" (that is, soteriology), a separation of the mystery of God and the mystery of our salvation.[5] He locates the root of this problem in the Council of Nicea's proclamation of *homoousios*. Although a necessary counter to prevailing subordinationist tendencies and

---

[1]Ghislain Lafont, *Peut-on Connaître Dieu en Jésus Christ?* Cogitatio Fidei 44 (Paris: Les Éditions du Cerf, 1969). This work will subsequently be referred to in the notes as *PCDJ*.

[2]*Dieu, le Temps et l'Etre,* translated into English by Leonard Maluf as *God, Time and Being* (Petersham, Mass.: St Bede's Publications, 1992). All references will be taken from the English edition. This work will hereafter be referred to in the notes as *GTB*.

[3]See Lafont, *Structures et méthodes dans la Somme Théologique de Saint Thomas d'Aquin* (Paris: Desclée de Brouwer, 1961).

[4]See, for example, his Introduction to *PCDJ* and his Foreword to *GTB*.

[5]*PCDJ* 17–20.

the Arian heresy this proclamation effectively resulted in a separation of the doctrine of the Trinity, on the one hand, from salvation, on the other. Consequently theological speculation was oriented toward the inner-trinitarian mystery and disconnected from soteriology.

Lafont's historical survey and assessment of the causes of this separation of "theology" and "economy"[6] was one that not all were to find convincing.[7] What is of interest to us, however, is that he calls for a vast rearticulation and interconnection of "theology" and "economy." He identifies the problem as essentially a christological one and recognizes that the challenge is to develop a christology that links theology and economy together, with the paschal mystery as the key to this rearticulation.[8] He therefore proposes that the task of speculative reflection on the paschal mystery is to comprehend the nature of the unique link in Jesus Christ of humanity to the Word, the Son of God. *By that very fact* one *then* proceeds to the property of one of the divine persons, the Son, and the nature of his unique link to the two other divine persons, Father and Spirit.

Lafont thus suggests a theological exploration proceeding from salvation in Jesus Christ to the personal mystery of Jesus Christ and thence to the trinitarian mystery, that is, from "economy" to "theology." In other words he too recognizes that Christ's paschal mystery is not only redemptive but revelatory and that reflection on Christ in his paschal mystery leads to an understanding of the immanent trinitarian relations and processions. As we shall see, his exploration also leads him to challenge the adequacy of metaphysical conceptuality for theological reflection.

The anthropological and theological meanings of the paschal mystery

Lafont's express project is to articulate the mystery of the Trinity in light of the paschal mystery while paying due respect to the transcendence of the immanent Trinity.[9] It is founded on the conviction that the paschal mystery is the fundamental locus where both the meaning of the history of salvation and the reality of God who saves are simultaneously revealed. The connection between the Trinity and the paschal mystery lies in the very person of Jesus, the incarnate Son. Lafont justifies his focus on the paschal mystery on scriptural grounds, recalling that in his letters Paul clearly establishes the link between the proclamation of Jesus crucified and the epiphany of the Son of God.[10]

---

[6]*PCDJ* 31–167. Lafont selects the works of Gregory of Nyssa, Augustine of Hippo, and Thomas Aquinas for detailed consideration.

[7]See Bernard Sesboüé's review of Lafont's book, *Recherches de Science Religieuse* 59 (1971) 97.

[8]*PCDJ* 12.

[9]*PCDJ* 287.

[10]*PCDJ* 233, 235.

Underlying Lafont's rearticulation of the mystery of the Trinity is his understanding that a plurality of trinitarian languages is necessary in our discourse about God *in se* and God in relation to creation. Some plurality is inevitable, he argues, because the problem for post-Nicene theology is that we are not able to combine the unity of God and God's tri-unity in a single affirmation; the same is true for statements about the transcendence of God who is sufficient *in se* and the personal self-involvement of this same God in creation. Lafont thus maintains that what we might call a multiplication of languages, what he describes as *"la loi de redoublement du langage"*[11] is necessary.[12] In other words, plurality or multiplicity of languages is indispensable and irreducible in theological discourse. Nevertheless Lafont argues that since the paschal mystery is the modality of the Word of God spoken to humanity in view of giving itself to it,[13] we should privilege that language and discourse that rests on the elements of intelligibility that result from an analysis of the paschal mystery.[14]

Turning to an analysis of the meaning of the paschal mystery Lafont recognizes, in the death of Jesus, "a moment which corresponds and responds to the gift of God to humanity."[15] On this basis he identifies two levels of meaning in the paschal mystery. One we might describe as "anthropological," concerning the destiny and vocation of the human person. The other we can describe as "theological," concerning the trinitarian mystery itself. From this theological perspective the paschal mystery is the paradigmatic image of trinitarian life in creation. It is the created projection of the eternal trinitarian circumincession that allows us to discern the interior modality of trinitarian life.[16]

From the "anthropological" perspective the paschal mystery of Jesus Christ shows that entry into communion with God necessarily passes through a stage of death.[17] Because it is transfiguring, the gift of God is in a sense mortifying.[18] The paschal mystery shows that this transfiguration of existence paradoxically requires a renunciation of existence, that human response to the Word necessarily involves *"un dépassement,"* a surrender and transcendence of the self. Physical death is the sign of *"ce dépassement"* in the economy of sin and redemption.

[11]*PCDJ* 160, 234, 261, 275.
[12]In his strong critique of Rahner's theology of the Trinity Lafont argues that it does not recognize explicitly the necessary duality of language in trinitarian theology. Rahner, Lafont argues, has in effect reissued the pre-Nicene theology with all its ambiguities. Here too, however, Lafont falls under criticism in Bernard Sesboüé's review, *RSR* 59 (1971) 97.
[13]*PCDJ* 236, 326.
[14]*PCDJ* 234.
[15]*PCDJ* 248.
[16]*PCDJ* 254–262, 325.
[17]See, e. g., *PCDJ* 241 and 243.
[18]*PCDJ* 248.

However, this radical dying to self is proposed, not imposed.[19] The human person is invited to this radical self-transcendence, to freely accepted loss of self *(perte absolue de soi librement consentie)*[20] in response to God's self-communication and offer of communion. Although death is a real wrenching, a rupture from our immediate existence, the human person is not annihilated. Indeed the paschal mystery reveals that the possibility of this total "ecstasis" of self—an "excentration" or "decentering" of self in a radical other-regarding relationality—is our ultimate meaning and vocation: through it we enter into the life of the trinitarian communion. The paschal mystery thus discloses that humanity, the world, indeed all creation, find their meaning and salvation in this transfiguration and entry into the trinitarian exchange.[21]

From a theological perspective the paschal mystery offers a vital key to trinitarian being. Because it manifests the Son of God in the paschal mystery of death and resurrection it implies that this renunciation and this accomplishment of glory, expressed in precisely this way, signify something that is eternally lived in God.[22] Since Jesus in his paschal mystery is the perfect image of trinitarian life[23] the paschal mystery is revelatory of the interior modality of trinitarian being. Thus Lafont suggests that the death and resurrection of Jesus are the expression, in the symbolic language of a human life, of the eternal trinitarian exchange; on this basis we are then led to contemplate the trinitarian processions.[24] In other words, in its essential structure the paschal mystery is the created projection of the eternal trinitarian exchange, the divine circumincession, an exchange that is anterior to the events of salvation history.[25] In this sense Jesus in his paschal mystery is *"le Paradygme de la vie trinitaire."*[26]

Jesus' death and the resources of negation in naming God

Lafont proceeds to an exploration of Jesus' death and there identifies two "moments" or levels of negativity. There is first that aspect of death that is true for us all, the "anthropological" aspect. The human creature, called forth by the Word of God, must freely and radically transcend its regime of autonomous and homogeneous existence in order to respond to God's offer of communion. This aspect of death is transitory *(transitoire),* essential to the necessary passage *(le "trépas" nécessaire)* to another human condition, from

[19]*PCDJ* 244.
[20]*PCDJ* 236, 326.
[21]*PCDJ* 254.
[22]*PCDJ* 236.
[23]*PCDJ* 261.
[24]*PCDJ* 260–261.
[25]*PCDJ* 260.
[26]*PCDJ* 234.

created existence to "divinized" existence.[27] From this perspective the paschal mystery of Jesus is clearly by no means a solution to the problem of death. On the contrary, death *as radical renunciation of autonomy for the sake of communion* is the first step of all resurrection.[28] It is the supreme expression of one's surrender of autonomy and one's self-transcendence through which we enter into communion with God.

However, because of Jesus' identity as the Son and thus his singular link to the Word of God there is clearly also something in his paschal mystery that is definitive and relates to his unique person. This is, at it were, the "theological" aspect of the mystery. At this point Lafont focuses on the utterly unreserved gift of self that Jesus makes.[29] In a total *ecstasis* of self in love Jesus gives himself without reserve to God and is thus raised to communion with God.[30] Lafont suggests that here the perfection of spiritual being—"the law of spiritual being" as he calls it[31]—is disclosed. In Jesus' *choice of divine communion in preference to any autonomy of existence* the paschal mystery reveals that at the interior of the life of God the perfection of being lies in communion, as distinct from any autonomy or independence in a substantialist sense. Moreover Lafont recognizes that this also has important consequences for theological discourse: it means that in the designation of the divine persons this aspect of communion should be privileged over any notion that connotes autonomy.

Lafont thus understands that the paschal mystery reveals theologically that an element of death appears as necessary, indeed essential, to the expression of God's self-communication, and anthropologically that a sort of death, and ultimately physical death, is required in order to respond. In this sense death mysteriously lies at the heart of being, both human and divine. Lafont presses further and suggests that the paschal mystery demands an exploration of the resources of negation by which we can speak about the inner life of God.[32] If the paschal mystery of Jesus' death and resurrection really signifies what is eternally lived in God, it follows that negation, symbolized and realized in the death of Jesus, is a necessary and vitally significant element in theological discourse at least as far as it involves our human language about God.

Lafont's reevaluation of the notion of person

Lafont turns his attention to the designation of the divine persons. Convinced that the paschal mystery demands an element of negation in our attempt to speak of God, he looks for conceptual tools that are "both negative

[27]*PCDJ* 249.
[28]*PCDJ* 248.
[29]*PCDJ* 249.
[30]*PCDJ* 250.
[31]*PCDJ* 262.
[32]*PCDJ* 262.

and expressive of the reality and the life of the divine persons."[33] He observes that in the paschal mystery the divine persons emerge in a dynamic of activity and exchange. The divine persons appear in the first place as gift, reciprocal movement, absolute surrender of self in the other, and only then as hypostases. On this basis he is critical of the use of the notion of hypostasis in traditional trinitarian theology. Indeed, he identifies the notion of hypostasis as the root cause of the post-Nicene separation of economy and theology.[34] The problem in traditional trinitarian theology as he sees it is the notion of hypostasis, understood first as entity and interpreted virtually exclusively in ontological terms. While hypostasis is understood in terms of subsistent relation, Lafont argues, the accent effectively remains on subsistence and not on the aspect of relation, which is eclipsed. As such the notion of hypostasis is more expressive of autonomy than communion. In Lafont's assessment the traditional designation of the divine persons as hypostases fails to render "the perfection of spiritual being," that continual exchange at the very heart of being itself of which Jesus' death and resurrection in their essential structure are the created projection and in their concrete reality the visible manifestation: God is love.[35] It simply does not convey the divine persons in their dynamic communion of activity and exchange.

Lafont's dissatisfaction with the traditional trinitarian notion of hypostasis leads him to reevaluate the notion of person and the manner of its application to the divine persons.[36] He seeks a notion of person that expresses the more dynamic, operative, and relational aspect of personhood. He is particularly critical of Aquinas's appropriation of Boethius's definition of person as "an individual substance of rational nature,"[37] for this understanding of person does not take into consideration the spiritual project, the principle of operation and of relations that constitutes the person *qua* person. It does not convey the dynamic and interpersonal aspect of personhood. A correction is necessary, or at least the introduction of a complementary approach so that what is specific to, indeed constitutive of the person is included. In fact, in questioning the appropriateness and value of Boethius's definition in Aquinas's theology Lafont proposes a notion of person that is more closely in accord with the treatment of the processions and relations that precedes Aquinas's treatment of the persons in the *Summa Theologiae*.[38]

---

[33]*PCDJ* 263.

[34]*PCDJ* 166–167.

[35]*PCDJ* 262.

[36]*PCDJ* 267–271.

[37]*De persona et duabus naturis* 3 (MPL 64.1343). We note that Aquinas does modify the definition to some extent in order to avert a tritheistic understanding of three individual separate substances in the godhead. Aquinas speaks of the divine person not as *substantia* but as *subsistentia*. See *ST* Ia. 29, 1.

[38]*PCDJ* 123–126.

Since it is at the level of spiritual activity that the person is manifested and realized Lafont suggests that the notion of person is more appropriately expressed on a register of spiritual activity or operation rather than in terms of subsistence. On this register of spiritual activity Lafont identifies three important characteristics of person: operation, reciprocity, and reflexivity.[39] The object of this spiritual activity is the other who is knowable and lovable (operation). Authentically personal life is then actualized by the unveiling of self through all the possible modalities of communication and correlatively by reception in oneself of what is offered by the other. A reciprocal communion is thus established (reciprocity). In this sense Lafont proposes that we can speak of the "reflexive construction of the personality," meaning that the person may be understood to "result" from this unceasing reciprocal operation (reflexivity). Lafont thus arrives at an understanding of spiritual personality as reflexively forged through its operation, indeed its *interpersonal* operation. We shall later see that he then introduces these characteristics—operation, reciprocity, reflexivity—into his reflections on the mystery of the Trinity.

Hence instead of applying the traditional notion of hypostasis to the divine persons Lafont proposes first to express the Father, Son, and Holy Spirit at the level of trinitarian operations with which in a real sense (because of the perfect actuality of God) they are identified. Priority, he insists, should be given to the designation of the divine persons starting from act and by means of verb over their designation at the level of substance and by means of nouns—not necessarily in the order of discovery, but in order of signification.[40] Thus he argues that one should speak first (that is, logically) at the level of *verbs* that signify the operations of the persons, for it is in effect at this verbal level that the person is grasped on a dynamic register of activity and exchange. From a designation of the Three by means of verbs one can then proceed to their distinction and identity at the level of nouns.[41] In other words, privilege the verbal designations and then situate the hypostatic and nominal designations in relation to them.[42] While Lafont reiterates that a plurality of theological language is necessary and irreducible he insists that the *order* of language is very important. Designation by means of verbs is to be privileged over designation by means of nouns. He thus proceeds to the task of articulating this expression of the divine persons that is in the first place verbal (designation by means of verbs) and thence of situating those designations that are hypostatic and nominal (designation by means of nouns) in relation to it. To this we now turn our attention.

[39]*PCDJ* 268–269.
[40]*PCDJ* 271.
[41]*PCDJ* 270.
[42]*PCDJ* 271. We encounter some difficulty with language at this point. Lafont refers to *désignations verbales* and *désignations nominales*. The problem with the English translation of these terms is that "nominal" and "verbal" sound somewhat alike and there is risk of losing the intended distinction. The reader needs to keep Lafont's clear distinction in mind.

1. Designation of the divine persons by means of verbs[43]

Designation by means of verbs emerges from a consideration of the divine persons in terms of their *trinitarian operations*. God is revealed as the One who communicates; the trinitarian operations are thus acts of communication. Hence Lafont arrives at a designation of God (the Father) as pure "to engender," or instead of this infinitive Lafont suggests using the corresponding abstract noun, "generation" or "communication."[44] Corresponding to the Father who is pure communication, the Son is designated as "to receive" or "nativity" or "receptivity." The Holy Spirit is "communion." At this point Lafont observes that when the divine persons are regarded first as *acts* that are identical in their divine reality but distinct in their dynamic modality—communication, nativity, communion—one avoids the isolation of the Holy Spirit that, as Durrwell also noted, has been a problem in the tradition. According to Lafont the problem is averted because with these verbal designations one chooses *three terms of the same logical value* whose interconnection is patent.[45]

Moreover when this dynamic equivalence of the divine persons is admitted and given priority by means of verbal designations the resultant image of the Trinity is one characterized by the dynamism of life and love. From the point of view of the divine essence this way of expressing the divine persons dynamically conveys the trinitarian circumincession, the flux and reflux, the unceasing gift and return in the divine being.[46] From the point of view of the divine persons each is expressed not in terms of substantialist or essentialist or even self-subsistent categories but rather in terms of its essential orientation toward the other. In this way verbal designations also serve to convey a certain negation, expressing the "non-priority" and indeed "non-property" of each person in itself, for the divine person is expressed *not* in terms of being-for-itself *(un en-soi),* but rather as being-in-and-for-another. Thus in designation by means of verbs Lafont finds the conceptual tool which is "both negative and expressive of the reality and life of the divine persons" that he had sought. It is not, he stresses, that this negativity connoted by verbal designations is an aspect of the divine person as such, but rather that designations by means of verbs better express the divine reality than positive nouns.[47] The negativity inherent in these verbal designations better conveys the positivity of inner-trinitarian love so manifest in the paschal mystery.

[43]*PCDJ* 272–277.

[44]The reader will note that we have shifted almost without comment to designation not by means of infinitive verbs but by means of abstract nouns. While his stated intention is to privilege verbal designations, in fact Lafont more often chooses to replace the infinitive form of the verb (for example, "to engender") with the corresponding abstract noun (for example, "generation"). When Lafont comes to the Holy Spirit no infinitive at all is mentioned. The Holy Spirit is "communion." In a passing comment Lafont simply explains that the abstract nouns perhaps better convey the dynamism and fullness of the mystery we wish to express: *PCDJ* 272.

[45]*PCDJ* 276.

[46]*PCDJ* 276. Note Lafont's stress on circumincession (with "c") here. He wants to stress the dynamic nature of the reciprocal indwelling of the divine persons.

[47]*PCDJ* 276.

2. Designation of the divine persons by means of nouns[48]

While privileging verbal designations Lafont does not exclude nominal designations (Father, Son, Spirit); their foundations, after all, are scriptural. Lafont's task at this point is to situate designations by means of nouns in relation to the designations by means of verbs. In order to make the transition from the language of dynamic equivalence (verbal designations) to hypostatic (nominal) designations he returns to the notions of reciprocity and reflexivity that he has previously identified as characteristic of personhood. He maintains that we can speak analogically of reflexivity as constitutive of the divine person.[49] Consider, for example, the Father. He can be considered as "the reflexive result" *(le résultat réflexe)*[50] of the infinite generation that terminates in the Son in the sense that the act of generation, which is the act or operation characteristic of the Father, constitutes the Father as subject. Thus Lafont arrives at the designation of the person as subsistence, as constituted by reflection on the act of communication that defines the person. Moreover Lafont takes the matter farther, maintaining that because of the perfection of the divine being we may shift from the register of *intentional reflexivity* to that of an *"ontological reflexivity."*[51] In other words the intersubjectivity he arrives at in this way has a real ontological ground. This designation of the divine person is therefore not just intentionally but ontologically grounded.

Privileging the notion of constituent reflexivity in the designation of the divine persons by means of nouns, Lafont proceeds to an at least partial appropriation of the language of personal self-consciousness. He considers the divine persons in terms of "three distinct reflexivities and consciousnesses of act" and so arrives at an understanding of the Three as "personal reflexive consciousnesses."[52] By way of illustration Lafont considers the "personal reflexive consciousness" of the Word. In the sense that the Son is pure "receptivity" he is not first conscious of himself but of the Father who begets him and of the Spirit as "milieu" that links him to the Father. Thus the act that first constitutes the Son as Son renders him first conscious of the Father and the Spirit. In the second place it renders the Son conscious of himself as proceeding from the Father and, through the Father, as source of the Spirit.[53] This personal consciousness in God is first consciousness of self in relation to the other.[54] In other words consciousness of self as a distinct person comes only in the second place.

Lafont is, however, alert to the tritheistic implication of independent and unrelated subsistences. He maintains that the result of this analogical attribution

[48]See *PCDJ* 277–287, especially 282–287.
[49]*PCDJ* 278.
[50]*PCDJ* 280.
[51]*PCDJ* 284.
[52]*PCDJ* 285.
[53]*PCDJ* 286.
[54]*PCDJ* 286.

of reflection on the intentionality of act to God is not three self-consciousnesses, which would be tritheism. There is no contradiction, he argues, in affirming the unity of the consciousness of self of God considered as pure act and the Trinity of the three "personal reflexive consciousnesses." Just as the three persons do not multiply the divine substance, the three "personal reflexive consciousnesses" do not multiply the divine self-consciousness. "Personal reflexive consciousness" bears only on the acts and relations between the persons and not on a modification of the unique consciousness of the Divinity. The essential point here is that Lafont concludes that the register of consciousness should not be excluded from theological attempts to express the divine persons. He records just one proviso: it is necessary that they not be considered as absolute, unrelated, autonomous consciousnesses.[55]

Thus Lafont's exploration of the interconnection of the paschal mystery and the Trinity leads him to introduce a language of self-consciousness and constituent subjectivity in order to designate the divine persons and to argue for the legitimacy of a "notional" usage of consciousness in trinitarian theology. He identifies two benefits in this approach. First, the divine person is explicated at the level of operation, not at the level of subsistence. Second, this explication of the person at the level of spiritual act effectively admits psychological categories into trinitarian theology, thus allowing a closer connection between the ontological register of hypostasis or of person and the psychological register (together with the psychological analogy) of word and love.[56]

Let us briefly summarize Lafont's exploration of trinitarian theology in the light of the paschal mystery in *Peut-on Connaître Dieu en Jésus Christ?* The interconnection of the Trinity and the paschal mystery leads Lafont to privilege an understanding of the divine persons in terms of acts. Primacy is therefore accorded to designation by means of verbs. The designation of the divine persons by means of nouns, based on reflection on the intentionality of act, follows and is situated in relation to the designation by means of verbs. The result is that Lafont admits the language of self-consciousness and constituent subjectivity into trinitarian theology and consequently also admits psychological categories. Again he reiterates the necessity of a plurality of theological languages. It is not a matter of replacing an anterior classical language of trinitarian theology but of supplementing it and indeed of privileging the intelligibility that the paschal mystery yields, in such a way that the other languages are situated in regard to it and not the reverse.

[55]*PCDJ* 286. While we cannot take up this issue it is interesting to note that in regard to this last point Lonergan and Lafont in fact hold very similar positions; however, we also note that Lafont stands in some tension with Lonergan's understanding of "consciousness." For Lonergan the consciousness of the subject is given in the act, not as a reflection, for that would make it an object. In other words it is the subject thinking about itself not as object but as a primal given.

[56]*PCDJ* 290. Note again that Lafont interprets his effort as a refinement of the Thomistic approach to the mystery of the Trinity.

The principle of heteronomy: narrativity and analogy

In this later work, *Dieu, le Temps et l'Etre,* the insights of the first book remain, assumed and briefly acknowledged but without further development.[57] Indeed, reference to the earlier work is scant. In this later work death and being again emerge as the central themes,[58] but a more methodologically attuned reflection on death and being here leads to the two principles of narrativity and analogy as together constituting what Lafont describes as "the principle of heteronomy."[59] Consideration of the paschal mystery is thus located in a broader context than in the previous volume, now more alert to questions of method. Lafont maintains that both narrativity and analogy are necessary in the theological task of naming God. He argues that the salvation narrative has some need of analogy simply in order to be told. Conversely analogy is not a process closed in on itself but one that renders possible the theological mediation between God and the history of salvation. Still, neither is sufficient. Each is necessary to the theological task. Narrativity and analogy thus constitute the two correlative and articulated principles, the two "valences"[60] of this principle of heteronomy.

The principle of narrativity places a strong emphasis on the narrative qua narrative. We are reminded that a narrative appears first of all as story, something to be heard. It is communication before it is information. Only after it is heard does it lend itself to repetition and to interpretation and construction of meaning. In this sense the principle of narrativity gives primacy to hearing as structurally and chronologically prior to any production of meaning.[61] Nevertheless narrative alone is not enough. As Lafont comments: "The passage to the historical realm does not suffice to avert the danger of missing (at the level of theological elaboration) the true God."[62] The divine "historical" names need to be supported by analogy, for only in this way can they remain truly divine names.

Analogy thus emerges in Lafont's study as an authentic and necessary procedure in our God-talk, a regulatory interpretative tool that spans without dissolving the necessary ontological distinction between God and creation, something narrative by itself is unable to do. Moreover the principle of analogy does not reduce the unsayable to what can be said but links up all discourse to the analogue that founds it. Thus requiring a surrender of self-sufficiency and an openness to what does not come from the self, the principle of analogy

---

[57]See *GTB* Foreword, x–xi.

[58]Lafont comments in the Foreword that he could well have entitled this volume "God at the Juncture of Death and Being": *GTB* ix.

[59]*GTB* 95–109. Note that Lafont does not actually define the term "heteronomy." He uses it in the sense of not self-governing, not self-determining, that is, heteronomy as opposed to autonomy.

[60]We shall hold to the term "valence" as the one used by the translator in *GTB* rather than the term "valencies." See *GTB* 106.

[61]*GTB* 134.

[62]*GTB* 277.

evokes an act of consent to a certain non-presence to oneself and an anterior-ity that one does not found. In this sense Lafont recognizes that the principle of analogy, in effect, implies a "form of death" to any temptation to autonomy or absolute self-affirmation.

Although the principle of heteronomy is necessarily twofold—narrativity and analogy—Lafont insists that their order is by no means inconsequential. The narrative always has primacy.[63] It must first be heard and only then yielded to interpretation and construction of meaning at which point analogy is introduced to serve and protect the meaning of the narrative. The anterior-ity and primacy of the founding narrative and the distinction between hearing and the production of meaning are thus essential to Lafont's consideration of the paschal mystery in this second book. Moreover, as Lafont explains, the narrative stands to inspire and control the production of meaning. Indeed, the truth of any reinterpretation is determined in terms of the way the founding narrative continues to make itself heard. If authentic the resultant productions of meaning will have the same effects of conversion to God and of human lib-eration as the founding narrative itself.[64]

In the context of this principle of heteronomy Lafont then considers the paschal mystery as narrative. He attends to what he describes as its two phases, death and resurrection. However, as in the earlier volume, Lafont is more concerned with systematic questions of theological language in naming God and his examination of the content of this paschal-mystery narrative is relatively brief. Sonship and fatherhood emerge as principal themes.

The paschal mystery as founding narrative

In Lafont's analysis the biblical narrative of the paschal events strongly suggests the close link between death and sonship.[65] In Mark's account the centurion looks at the cross of Christ, at the dead Christ, and perceives that he is the Son. It is not Jesus' ability to come down from the cross that shows that Jesus is Son of God: it is his death. For Mark the very manner in which Jesus died witnessed to the fact that he was the Son. It is in his failure, in his death, that the very identity of Jesus as Son is disclosed. In Luke's account Jesus gives himself over totally to the one he does not cease to call Father, as if death was precisely the moment par excellence for saying "Father." For Luke this totally stripped and pure invocation is disclosive of who the Son really is, as though the Son appears in the purity of his relationship to the Father only in this moment when all else is lost. It is this perseverance in the invocation of the name of the Father that bears witness to Jesus as Son of God, disclos-ing that Jesus' sonship moves toward a pure invocation whose symbol is death

[63]*GTB* 275.
[64]*GTB* 143–146.
[65]*GTB* 156–170.

to absolutely any other reality. Thus Lafont observes that both synoptic writers clearly underline the link between the death of Jesus and his divine sonship. The two accounts point in the same direction: Jesus was Son, and all the more so in his death.

As for the Father, in the course of the trial he withdraws without seeming to make the slightest saving gesture on Jesus' behalf, offering no assistance. Right up to the last moment on the cross God does not intervene to come to the aid of the one who finally has revealed himself as Christ and Son. Through his perseverance Jesus is led to reveal the ultimate and primary character of his identity as Son while the Father withdraws and is silent. In Jesus' death we thus have the rather disconcerting revelation that the Father is "the one who abandons." Through his abandonment, however, the Son is led to the perfection of filial relationship. Abandonment by God becomes abandonment to God, the Son's realization of his divine sonship. The Father's withdrawal is thus revealed as "the mysterious face of Fatherhood."[66]

Lafont recognizes that the link between Jesus' death and his identity as Son is also revelatory for our existence and destiny. The paschal mystery reveals that our human history is a pedagogy of Sonship[67] and that our destiny is to participate in the Sonship of God. Sonship is however not a static quality, but an endless and dynamic process, the bringing together of one's entire existence into the invocation of the "Father." The paschal mystery shows that this total and pure filial invocation is uttered only at the end of a long process whereby all images and all names, even the authentic names of God, are challenged. Lafont describes the pain that is involved here as the reverse side of a positive pedagogical process by which God draws the human person to Godself and the human person yields in an ever more filial attitude. Thus indicating that our knowledge of God undergoes a number of transformations in this pedagogical process, the paschal mystery introduces the "form of death" into our understanding of theology itself. The process through which we come to a knowledge of God will be marked by a series of ruptures and transfigurations and a transcendence of every equilibrium until the moment when the human person is dynamically one with the Son in a genuine hearing of the word of begetting by God.

The resurrection discloses the modality of this pedagogical process in full light,[68] showing that these mysterious withdrawals of God were really the revelation of the name of Father and the invitation to a new relationship of communion. It reveals that God withdraws in order that the human person by persevering in invocation and obedience enters freely into the ever-expanding depths of this filial relationship with God. It is here that Lafont finds the place to reflect on the Holy Spirit as the love through which the process appears not

[66]*GTB* 169.
[67]*GTB* 216.
[68]*GTB* 242–247.

only as possible but also as desirable, the love that makes us enter with faithful endurance into God's very withdrawal.[69]

Finally, in the resurrection, the Father's response of affirmation to the Son's invocation on the cross, we have the fundamental name of God: "[the one] who has raised Jesus from the dead." The risen Christ passes totally and forever into an imperishable dynamic in which he invokes the Father. In that eternal dynamic, Lafont writes, the Father raises him by a permanent act because it too is invocation. Lafont explains:

> To invoke Jesus as Son is to give him, in this process of begetting, the transformed riches of creation, the glorious plenitude of the human essence finally arrived at its true stature. It is to "exalt" Christ, to "raise" him, not by a single and soon forgotten action, but by a permanent act, because it too is invocation. God no longer holds back anything of what his goodness as creator and his fidelity as covenant partner had given and withheld, in order to open the field of filial relationship: the transformation amounts to the manifestation, in the body and in the earth, of that relationship offered from the beginning, henceforth permanently established and forever alive. On the basis of the reciprocal invocation and from within it Jesus can be constituted Lord, can now be the New Temple and the first fruits of a transfigured cosmos. . . . This is why one can say that just as the cross appeared as the space of sonship, so the resurrection reveals itself as the field of fatherhood, or to put it another way, if the cross is the place where the name of "Father" is revealed, the resurrection gives access to an understanding of the name "Son", for Jesus first of all, but after him and in him, for every human being.[70]

Here, then, is the meaning of our salvation in Lafont's theology: it is existence in the Son. It is to enter, in Christ, into the trinitarian communion of life and love, the trinitarian circumincession. Death is the supreme expression of the self-surrender that is necessary in order to enter into this filial communion. Anthropologically the paschal mystery discloses that this total *ecstasis,* gift of self to God, is our vocation. Theologically it is the revelation of the interior dynamic of God, "icon of the proper reality of God,"[71] manifesting the Trinity as "that 'Admirable Exchange' where the fullness of God is ceaselessly and entirely communicated between Father, Son and Spirit in that dynamic movement of communion that has traditionally been called 'circumincession.'"[72]

---

[69]*GTB* 243.

[70]*GTB*, 243–244. It is interesting to see a close correspondence here between Lafont's understanding of the resurrection as a *permanent* act and Durrwell's understanding of the act of resurrection as proceeding from the eternal generation. However this remains essentially an aside in Lafont's reflections.

[71]*GTB* 310.

[72]*GTB* 310.

The role of the paschal mystery in Lafont's trinitarian theology

Certainly, as we have seen, the paschal mystery and the dynamic interpersonal exchange it discloses serve in Lafont's theological reflections to challenge the way traditional trinitarian theology designates the divine persons. However, more deeply still Lafont is acutely conscious that this interpersonal exchange unfolds precisely in an interplay of life and death, in a distinctly paschal dynamic. While he attends to both the death and the resurrection as crucial aspects of the paschal mystery it is his treatment of Jesus' death and his understanding of its ramifications for theological language that is most striking. Here is the cutting edge in Lafont's theology, for he recognizes that this paschal dynamism that is expressed in terms of passion, death, and resurrection is somehow paradigmatically expressive of trinitarian life and love, "icon" of divine being. Paradoxically the *negativity* of death is the signal vehicle for the expression of the *positivity* of love. Lafont thus insists that this element of negativity must somehow feature in our language about God. This is a very novel development. The theological tradition certainly admitted an aspect of negativity in apophatic theology via an understanding of the unknowability and utter transcendence of God grounded in mystical theology. However here the element of negativity is taken up for a very different reason: death is recognized as intrinsic to being, human *and* divine.

Consequently Lafont substantially refashions the notion of person as subject of interpersonal operations, communications, and relations, and in his second book, in an apparent challenge to the traditional scheme in which ontological categories dominate, he insists on the primacy of the biblical narrative. Indeed the element of negativity that emerged in the earlier work and was there given expression by means of verbal designations, effectively translates in the second volume into the methodological principle of analogy, for analogy in its own way demands and expresses a "form of death," a self-transcendence, a renunciation of autonomy.

However, although the paschal mystery affects his theology in these significant ways, in the final assessment it is *not* the paschal mystery that fundamentally determines or shapes Lafont's trinitarian theology. Lafont clearly works within the traditional Thomistic framework and at one precise point in that framework. It is Aquinas's introduction of the Boethian definition of person that he considers unnecessary and unhelpful. Lafont himself describes his effort to insert a more adequate designation of the divine persons within the traditional scheme.[73] The treatment of the divine essence and the psychological analogy that precedes the treatment of the divine persons in the Thomistic *ordo doctrinae* is assumed in Lafont's work. (Note, too, that in this second volume the paschal mystery is treated under the rubric of narrative and not as analogy per se.) Indeed in summarizing the benefits of his approach

[73]*PCDJ* 290.

Lafont comments that his reworking of the notion of person in terms of reflection on the act of communication that constitutes the person as such effects a better connection with the traditional treatment of the trinitarian
processions and relations and so achieves a more systematic treatment of the
hypostases.[74] In the final analysis then Lafont effectively brings his reflections
on the paschal mystery *into* the traditional treatment of trinitarian theology
rather than constructing an alternative trinitarian theology.

Nonetheless we cannot fail to note the theological significance of death that
emerges so strongly in Lafont's theology. He recognizes that death lies at the
heart of being, both God's and ours (though of course in different ways).
Although he brings this remarkable insight to bear only on his exploration of
the designation of the persons he perceives that precisely, indeed paradigmatically, in that particular paschal modality the character of trinitarian circumincession is disclosed and enacted. Lafont's exploration of the paschal
mystery thus leads him to recognize not only that there is a paschal character
in human life in terms of the form of one's response to God's offer of communion in trinitarian life but that there is a certain paschal character in the
eternal triune being of God. Here is the crux of the matter for us. Despite my
overall assessment that Lafont incorporates reflections based on the paschal
mystery *into* the traditional Thomistic treatment of trinitarian theology there
is this distinctive paschal character in Lafont's trinitarian theology that derives
directly from his reflection on the paschal mystery and is not to be found in
the traditional treatment. Lafont thus takes a highly significant step forward in
understanding that something analogous to death is attributable to triune relationality and being as an expression of the positivity of divine love.

The relationship between economic and immanent Trinity

It is interesting to note that Lafont himself does not use the term "economic" Trinity and only very rarely the term "immanent" Trinity even though
he engages in an extended discussion of Rahner's *Grundaxiom*.[75] Lafont himself consistently situates the discussion in terms of economy and theology
(*l'"Economie" et la "Théologie"*).[76] Even in direct reference to Rahner's
axiom Lafont conspicuously avoids the use of "economic Trinity" and instead
refers to "the Trinity revealed in the economy of salvation."

Lafont is critical of Rahner's axiom if it means that the immanent Trinity is
purely and simply the Trinity of the economy of salvation. He admits without
hesitation that the economy of salvation manifests the Trinity and communicates filial adoption in the Spirit. Hence the significance, I suggest, of his

[74]*PCDJ* 291.
[75]Karl Rahner, *The Trinity* 21–24.
[76]*PCDJ* 171–228.

avoidance of the terms immanent and economic Trinity, as if use of the terms would mean admitting two trinities. On the other hand he insists that it is not possible to affirm purely and simply the second part of Rahner's axiom, "and inversely" (the immanent Trinity is the ecomonic Trinity), on the ground that one cannot deduce the economy of salvation from the immanent Trinity. The mystery of the divine being *in se* must be respected, Lafont insists, and not be reduced to its self-communication in the economy. The liberty of God must be maintained in regard both to creation *and* to salvation. This is not assured if the divine liberty is effectively reduced to the decision to create. A transcendent, properly divine freedom must also bear on the divine decision to communicate itself.

Lafont thus clearly maintains a distinction between the immanent and economic Trinity. The former remains as the utterly transcendent reality in his theology; in fact, he warns against collapsing the two.[77] Still the immanent Trinity and the Trinity revealed in the economy of salvation are inseparably related, the latter manifesting the immanent Trinity. The paschal mystery in its essential structure is the created projection of the eternal trinitarian exchange. The dynamics of the trinitarian exchange in the economy, played out in the paschal mystery, correspond to and are a modality of God's eternal triune being. Recall that Lafont identifies the central systematic task as a christological one.[78] Ultimately it is the Chalcedonian understanding of the human and divine natures of the one person of Christ that grounds Lafont's interconnection of the paschal mystery with the mystery of God's triune being and his connection, without confusion, of the immanent and economic Trinity.

Assessment of gains for trinitarian theology

Lafont's exploration of the interconnection of the paschal mystery and the Trinity results in a theology with a very strong emphasis on the divine persons. The divine unity, together with the traditional treatment of trinitarian theology, is presupposed. As we have noted, Lafont's specific concern relates to a particular aspect of the Thomistic treatment of trinitarian theology: how best to designate the divine persons. A critique of ontologically-fashioned notions of the divine *persons* guides his work, but as I have explained, the critique is cast and the solution proposed within the traditional Thomistic framework.

On the other hand, as I have commented, the notion of person is substantially refashioned. Here Lafont steps beyond the traditional categories in his reflection on the person as center of interpersonal operation and exchange. The consideration of each divine person as subject per se is posterior to that of the divine person's operation constituting the other, consideration of the "ecstatic" aspect of personhood preceding the "enstatic."[79] Personhood is thus

---

[77]See *PCDJ* 167.
[78]See above, n. 8.
[79]*PCDJ* 281.

firmly situated in the realm of relationality rather than in terms of substantiality or mere rationality (as in Boethius's definition). Thus Lafont expresses the divine persons at the psychological level of interpersonal trinitarian relations rather than the ontological level of subsistent relations of origin. The shift points to the development of a new Christian metaphysics of personhood expressed in interpersonal and relational terms. What is interesting is that in this respect Lafont's theology also indicates the development of a trinitarian ontology expressed in personalist categories. However, as we have noted Lafont sees his own contribution as an *insertion* into the traditional Thomistic framework and does not propose a revision of the Thomistic divine ontology or *ordo doctrinae*.

All in all Lafont remains in the realm of theoretical mediation of meaning, in the terms and categories of scholastic treatment albeit with some modification. The traditional Augustinian-Thomistic understanding of the divine unity in terms of substance categories is assumed. He considers that the problem of explicating both the divine unity and tri-unity is solved by accounting for the unity on the level of substance and the tri-unity on the psychological level of interpersonal relations and communications.[80] Lafont assumes the traditional conceptual framework whereby the distinction between the unity and tri-unity is expressed in terms of substantial and relative categories respectively. Apparently locked into the traditional framework, he is unable to recognize or admit the possibility of transcending the opposition between substantial-essentialist and relational-personalist categories to which Durrwell adverted, and to countenance the possibility of the use of personalist categories to designate the divine nature or essence.

A question remains. Certainly Lafont clearly recasts the notion of person in more dynamic and relational terms. His treatment of the divine persons is rendered far more richly than the traditional explication in terms of pure relations. We can also agree that it does in fact achieve a more systematic progression in the Thomistic treatment of trinitarian theology. However, while Lafont's treatment is elegant systematically the question remains as to whether it achieves a significant advance in terms of its affective charge. For all its elegance Lafont's treatment of the divine persons ultimately succumbs to the same kind of abstraction that is problematic in Thomistic theology and in much the same way becomes detached rather quickly from its economic roots. Oddly enough this is reflected in his actual treatment of the persons where, as he himself admits, the person of Holy Spirit is rather obscure.[81] Although he claims to have solved the "problem" of the "isolation" of the

---

[80]*PCDJ* 290.

[81]Lafont comments: "It is more difficult to pass from the role of the Holy Spirit in the paschal mystery to its intradivine reality because revelation is not very explicit on the concrete relation of the Spirit and the Son in the mystery of Jesus Christ" (*PCDJ* 274). Here Lafont's theology stands in stark contrast with Durrwell's biblical theology in which, as we have seen, the Holy Spirit emerges with special vitality.

Holy Spirit in traditional trinitarian theology by means of verbal designations, the person of the Holy Spirit in fact remains relatively undeveloped in his theology. It seems, I suggest, that his treatment fails to meet the principle he himself enunciates in the earlier volume where he proposes that the intelligibility the paschal mystery offers should be privileged. It also fails to meet the criteria set out in the second volume, where he proposes first that primacy be accorded to the narrative and second that subsequent productions of meaning be judged according to whether or not they have the same effects of conversion to God and of human liberation as the founding narrative itself.

Nonetheless the distinctly paschal element Lafont brings into an understanding of the trinitarian relationality and divine being is, I suggest, a most significant and commendable feature. Although he himself does not develop this central insight at great length or effect a complete recasting of trinitarian theology in the light of the paschal mystery Lafont's achievement is to point to the *paschal* character not just of the Son but of the inner-trinitarian being *in se*. Indeed, recognizing that this paschal character is *anterior* to the paschal mystery that unfolds in the events of salvation history, Lafont verges on an understanding that it is indeed a *paschal* mystery *because* it is a trinitarian mystery. Although Lafont's own exploration of trinitarian theology addresses but one particular aspect of the traditional treatment of the mystery, even there the consequences are considerable. A full treatment of trinitarian theology from such a perspective, however, clearly remains to be constructed.

The traditional Thomistic framework within which Lafont situates his exploration is both the strength and the limitation of his approach. Because he is unable or unwilling to set aside the traditional framework he does not allow the paschal mystery itself to shape a fully reconstituted trinitarian theology, even though he perceives something quite profound in the paschal character of the events of our salvation. Here too I think that it is fair to suggest that he does not meet his own methodological criteria. Ultimately primacy is not fully accorded to the paschal mystery. Reflection on the biblical narrative at every turn yields to considerations of essentially systematic questions. In the final assessment Lafont's trinitarian theology shares the weaknesses of the traditional Thomistic explication of the mystery.

Methodological observations

We can identify two noteworthy methodological developments in Lafont's theology:

1. The beginnings of a reversal of the traditional ordo doctrinae

Assuming the traditional Thomistic *ordo doctrinae* in general, Lafont addresses one precise point in the Thomistic scheme and at that point he sets out by reflection on the divine persons as revealed in the paschal mystery and moves from a consideration of their operations and relations and to the person *qua* person or hypostasis. Here, in an approach that proceeds from the economic to the immanent, we see the beginnings of a reversal of the traditional *ordo doctrinae*. We recall that Lafont's overriding concern is to effect a reconnection of economy and theology by resituating trinitarian reflections in the context of Jesus' paschal mystery, which suggests a more radical reversal of the traditional approach. However, as we have noted, Lafont remains within the traditional systematic method of trinitarian theology. Although at that precise point he is apparently more historical than systematic in his approach, with a much stronger economic perspective than is found in the Thomistic treatment, his reflections on the paschal mystery are effectively incorporated into the traditional approach rather than the reverse.

2. *The principle of heteronomy*

The methodological gains are greater in Lafont's second study. "The principle of heteronomy" that he proposes expresses the necessarily bi-modal form of our discourse about God. Here, I suggest, is a valuable contribution to theological method. The principle of narrativity represents a reclamation of narrative in theological method and indeed accords a place of primacy to it. At the same time, however, Lafont offers a sobering reminder to any who would propose a simple, naïve return to narrative theology. The return to the data of history of itself is no assurance of the authenticity of our efforts to name God. The data beg interpretation and interpretation demands analogy. In other words the "historical" names have to be supported by analogy, for only in this way can they truly name the transcendent God. Lafont, however, stresses that analogy is introduced to *serve* the narrative. This is an insight that challenges us throughout our study. The point is that while an understanding of the dynamic and, indeed, paschal character of the inner-trinitarian communion that is revealed in the narrative of the paschal mystery demands an ontological grounding, nonetheless the question remains as to the nature of that ontological foundation. Lafont assumes the traditional ontology that is expressed in terms of being and act, but his recasting of the notion of person in fact points to the development of a divine ontology that is expressed in more personalist and relational characteristics.

Having considered the work of Durrwell and Lafont we already discern considerable differences in method and in focus. In Durrwell's interconnection of the mysteries by way of a biblical theology we find a rediscovery of the theological significance of the *resurrection*. In contrast Lafont situates an exploration of the interconnection within the terms of the traditional systematic Thomistic framework. In his reflections the profound theological significance of the *death* of Jesus emerges.

CHAPTER THREE

Hans Urs von Balthasar:
Love Alone Is Credible

Hans Urs von Balthasar's theological vision is deeply informed by the drama of Jesus' paschal mystery. His theology, like that of Lafont, presupposes and builds on the orthodox christological and trinitarian statements. Unlike Lafont he is not constrained by the traditional approach and treatment and indeed a subtle and sophisticated critique of Augustinian-Thomistic trinitarian theology pervades his work. For von Balthasar an essentialist ontology that is then complemented by an understanding of the Three as subsistent relations simply and utterly fails to convey adequately the sheer glory of the divine being that is revealed in the paschal mystery. His theology is strongly revelation-centered. Faith as he understands it is first of all an act of perception. It is beholding before it is believing. Von Balthasar therefore insists that we attend to what is in fact revealed and given, as gift, in the "form" *(Gestalt)* of Jesus.[1] He turns to the sheer givenness of revelation of the Trinity in the paschal mystery and attempts to express the "incarnationally concrete character" of the mystery: "What is necessary today, after long experience of the history of theology, is an effort at an authentic *theological* deepening of the

---

[1]For discussions of Jesus as "form" *(Gestalt)*, a vital element of von Balthasar's theological aesthetics, see Michael Waldstein, "An Introduction to von Balthasar's *The Glory of the Lord*," *Communio* 14 (1987) 12–33; Peter Henrici, "The Philosophy of Hans Urs von Balthasar" in David L. Schindler, ed., *Hans Urs von Balthasar: His Life and Work* (San Francisco: Ignatius Press, Communio Books, 1991), especially 154–155; Louis Dupré, *"The Glory of the Lord:* Hans Urs von Balthasar's Theological Aesthetic," *Communio* 16 (1989) 384–412; John O'Donnell, *Hans Urs von Balthasar* 18–32; Louis Roberts, *The Theological Aesthetics of Hans Urs von Balthasar* (Washington, D.C.: Catholic University of America Press, 1987); Angela Scola, *Hans Urs von Balthasar: A Theological Style* (Grand Rapids: Eerdmans, 1991).

particular mysteries of salvation in their incarnationally concrete character
. . . without losing to view the Trinitarian background and so the functional
aspect of the work of Jesus, which means no less than the relations within the
Trinity that define his Person."[2]

For von Balthasar the doctrine of Trinity (and indeed christology and soteriology) has its center and origin in the events of the three days of the *Sacrum
Triduum*, the midpoint of which is the descent into hell on Holy Saturday.
"For it is precisely in the Kenosis of Christ (and nowhere else) that the *inner*
majesty of God's love appears, of God who 'is love' (1 John 4:8) and therefore a trinity."[3] There in Jesus' paschal mystery he recognizes that God has not
just redeemed the world but disclosed God's own being.[4] We see in "the
Lord's actions . . . not only a sublime *metaphor* of eternal love, but Eternal
Love itself."[5] In the mystery of the Son's death, descent into hell, and resurrection, love alone is credible. He writes: "God's message to man in Christ
. . . is credible only as love—and here we mean God's own love, the manifestation of which is the manifestation of the glory of God."[6] Only love makes
sense of it. Here is von Balthasar's *leitmotif*.[7] Love alone is credible, he explains, because it is the only thing that is truly intelligible, the only thing that
is truly "rational." Love is "that than which nothing greater can be thought."[8]
It is the primacy of love and the sheer glory of God's love, which von
Balthasar sees as having been overlooked by much of the Latin theological
tradition, that lies at the heart of his theology.

A man of great learning whom Henri de Lubac described as "perhaps the
most cultivated of his time,"[9] von Balthasar is undoubtedly one of the giants
of twentieth century theology. One cannot but be overawed by the magnitude
and magnificence of his theological achievement, so deeply steeped in theology, culture, literature, and aesthetics, and in its own way almost defying
anything but an aesthetic response. His is an extraordinary corpus, a rich ta-
pestry of Christian and non-Christian thought. His writing, however, is dense
and difficult in its style, content, and complexity. MacKinnon speaks of the

---

[2]Hans Urs von Balthasar, *Mysterium Paschale: The Mystery of Easter*, translated with an
Introduction by Aidan Nichols (Edinburgh: T & T Clark, 1990) 41. This work will hereafter be
referred to in the notes as *MP*.

[3]Hans Urs von Balthasar, *Love Alone: The Way of Revelation: A Theological Perspective*,
edited by Alexander Dru (London: Burns & Oates, 1968) 71.

[4]*MP* 29.

[5]Hans Urs von Balthasar, *Prayer*, translated by Graham Harrison (San Francisco: Ignatius
Press, 1986) 184.

[6]*Love Alone: the Way of Revelation* 7–8.

[7]Henrici comments that "love alone is credible" is probably the densest summary of von
Balthasar's thought. "The Philosophy of Hans Urs von Balthasar" 153.

[8]Recall Durrwell's critique of this Anselmian understanding too. (See ch. 1 n. 79 above.)

[9]Henri de Lubac, "A Witness of Christ in the Church: Hans Urs von Balthasar" in *The
Church: Paradox and Mystery*, translated by James R. Dunne (Shannon: Ecclesia Press, 1969)
105.

"daunting complexity" of von Balthasar's method.[10] As we noted in the introduction to our study, O'Hanlon refers to "its circular repetition and apparent
glorious disorder"[11] while O'Donnell observes "a certain capriciousness in
Balthasar's method."[12] Yet despite the apparent disorder and labyrinthine style
of his work it is in fact not without a logic and system of its own, albeit in its
admittedly untraditional way.

In our account of von Balthasar's theology we shall refer principally to
Mysterium Paschale, first published in *Mysterium Salutis* in 1969[13] as a contributing chapter in a larger dogmatics, where we find a theology of the
paschal mystery and a vital interconnection with the mystery of the Trinity.
However von Balthasar's sense of the paschal mystery resonates throughout
his entire corpus and a number of the associated systematic questions are addressed in his great trilogy. Therefore in addressing this particular theme we
shall also refer to *The Glory of the Lord,*[14] *Theo-Drama,*[15] and *Theo-Logic,*[16]
in which he explores revelation from the perspectives of the three transcendental attributes of a scholastic metaphysics of being: the beautiful, the good,
and the true. As von Balthasar explains, the beautiful *(pulchrum)* is "the manner in which God's goodness *(bonum)* gives itself and is expressed by God
and understood by man as the truth *(verum).*"[17] These references to the trilogy
will be particularly valuable in assisting us to situate his exploration of the interconnection of the paschal mystery and the mystery of the Trinity in
Mysterium Paschale in terms of his larger theological vision. We shall also
make reference to other works where he makes the connection between the
two mysteries explicitly.

[10]Donald MacKinnon, "Some Reflections on Hans Urs von Balthasar's Christology with
Special Reference to *Theodramatik* II/2 and III" in *The Analogy of Beauty: The Theology of Hans
Urs von Balthasar,* edited by John Riches (Edinburgh: T & T Clark, 1986) 169.
[11]O'Hanlon, *The Immutability of God* 175.
[12]O'Donnell, "Truth as Love" 210.
[13]Later published as *Pâques: Le Mystère,* translated by R. Givord (Paris: Éditions du Cerf,
1981) and in English as *Mysterium Paschale: The Mystery of Easter.* All references will be taken
from the English edition *(MP).*
[14]German title *Herrlichkeit: Eine theologische Ästhetik,* vols. I, II/1, II/2, III/1/1, III/1/2,
III/2/1, III/2/2 (Einsiedeln: Johannes Verlag, 1961–1969). English translation *The Glory of the
Lord: A Theological Aesthetics,* vols. I–VII, edited by Joseph Fessio, s.j., and John Riches (San
Francisco: Ignatius Press, 1982–1989). References will be taken from the English edition except
where translations are not yet published.
[15]German title *Theodramatik,* vols. I, II/1, II/2, III, IV (Einsiedeln: Johannes Verlag,
1973–1983). English translation *Theo-Drama: Theological Dramatic Theory,* vols. I, II, III (San
Francisco: Ignatius Press, 1988–1992). The remaining two volumes have yet to be published in
English.
[16]German title *Theologik,* vols. I, II, III (Einsiedeln: Johannes Verlag, 1985–1987). English
translation, entitled *Theo-Logic,* is still in process.
[17]Hans Urs von Balthasar, *The Glory of the Lord* 1.11 (Foreword).

The inner-trinitarian "event"

Underpinning von Balthasar's theology of the paschal mystery and its interconnection with the Trinity is the insight that the trinitarian processions as traditionally understood already imply movement in God. Von Balthasar recognizes that this eternal movement in God, which he describes in terms of "the eternal 'event' of the divine processions,"[18] is what grounds the possibility of the incarnation and the paschal mystery in the economy. As von Balthasar explains: "That God (as Father) can so give away his divinity that God (as Son) does not merely receive it as something borrowed, but possesses it in the equality of essence, expresses such an unimaginable and unsurpassable 'separation' of God from Godself that every other separation (made possible by it!), even the most dark and bitter, can only occur within this first separation."[19]

The separation and union of the paschal event is thus grounded in the separation and union within the inner-trinitarian divine life where the Father, in generating the Son, does not cling to his divinity but "in an eternal 'super-Kenosis' makes himself 'destitute' of all that he is and can be so as to bring forth a consubstantial divinity, the Son."[20] (Von Balthasar's language at this point is admittedly somewhat extreme, but as he explains: God, as God, "has" nothing apart from what God "is").[21] In this primordial "separation" of God from God lies from all eternity the "space" for all the contingencies of human freedom. Every possible drama between God and the world is thus already contained in, allowed for, and indeed infinitely surpassed and transcended in that eternal, supra-temporal "event" of inner-trinitarian love. "It is a case of the play within the play: our play 'plays' in his play."[22] The drama between God and the world lies within this primordial inner-trinitarian "drama" between God and God: "We are saying that the 'emptying' of the Father's heart in the begetting of the Son includes and surpasses every possible drama between God and the world, because a world can only have its place within the difference between the Father and the Son which is held open and bridged over by the Spirit."[23]

The whole salvation event is in this way understood in this theology to occur within the eternal divine intersubjectivity. In other words von Balthasar

---

[18]*MP* viii.

[19]*Theodramatik III. Die Handlung* (Einsiedeln: Johannes Verlag, 1980) 302.

[20]*MP* viii. In the French edition, *Pâques: Le Mystère*, the word is translated as *"supra-kénose"* (p. 10). Given the significance of the addition of "supra" here and in its other applications I suggest that "supra-kenosis" would be a better translation in the English text than "super-kenosis".

[21]*Theo-Drama: Theological Dramatic Theory III. Dramatis Personae: Persons in Christ,* translated by Graham Harrison (San Francisco: Ignatius Press, 1988) 518.

[22]*Theo-Drama: Theological Dramatic Theory I. Prologomena,* translated by Graham Harrison (San Francisco: Ignatius Press, 1988) 20.

[23]*Theodramatik III* 304.

perceives that the immanent trinitarian personal distinctions, based on the opposition of relations, are sufficiently real and infinite to embrace without loss of unity the kind of opposition between Father and Son that is involved in their common salvific plan. He recognizes that divine love has the power freely to unfold in such different modalities that the Son's experience of opposition in the God-forsakenness of the death and descent remains a function, a modality, of his loving relationship to the Father in the Holy Spirit. Thus the inner-trinitarian "event" of God's love is understood always and already to contain within it that infinite distinction and distance within unity that grounds "all the modalities of love, of compassion, and even of a 'separation' motivated by love"[24] and all the risks inherent in the creation of genuinely free human beings. Divine inner-trinitarian love, which unites the infinite distances between the divine persons, already contains within it all innerworldly events, distance, sin, and pain.

Hence in von Balthasar's theology the inner-trinitarian "event" of self-giving and self-emptying love is the condition of the possibility of divine activity in kenotic events *ad extra*, containing within itself all the modalities of love—such as *kenosis*, abandonment, suffering, death, and descent—that appear in creation in the course of salvation history. This means that the kenotic form of Jesus Christ in the paschal mystery is not new or foreign to God but is, in fact, thoroughly consistent with this eternal supra-temporal "event" of triune love. It is, indeed, the created form of what is always already in God. We meet this affirmation repeatedly in von Balthasar's work: all forms of *kenosis ad extra* are contained within the primal *kenosis ad intra*. The Father's generation of the Son represents the first *kenosis* and underpins all other forms of *kenosis*. It manifests the utter self-giving *(Selbsthingabe)* of the Father to the Son, a self-yielding surrender of divine being. The Son's self-giving to the Father in his death on a cross is already contained within this eternal procession: it is a modality of the Son's procession. The trinitarian processions are thus understood already to involve an interpersonal dynamic interaction within the godhead, the different modalities of which are then expressed in the economy—particularly in the paschal mystery when the separation of Father and Son is most extreme.

This understanding of the inner-trinitarian "event" of love prompts a decisive about-turn in von Balthasar's understanding of God and the divine perfections. Divine omnipotence, for example, is manifested not as "absolute power" but as the selfless self-emptying that is characteristic of love. Divine sovereignty is shown primarily not in holding on to what is proper to Godself but in self-surrender.[25] Divine freedom is the freedom of self-dispossession:

> God is not only by nature free in his self-possession, in his ability to do what he will with himself; for that very reason, he is also free to do what he will

[24]*MP* viii–ix.
[25]*MP* 28.

with his own nature. That is, he can surrender himself; as Father, he can share his Godhead with the Son, and as Father and Son, he can share the same Godhead with the Spirit. . . . In generating the Son the Father does not "lose" himself to someone else in order thereby to "regain" himself; for he is *always* himself by giving himself. The Son too is always himself by allowing himself to be generated and by allowing the Father to do with him as he pleases. The Spirit is always himself by understanding his "I" as the "We" of Father and Son, by being "expropriated" for the sake of what is most proper to them.[26]

Fatherhood in God is the total giving of all that the Father is and has to the Son. In this eternal act of generation the Son receives his being from the Father and returns it to him in love that is equally without reserve. The third divine person, the Holy Spirit, is the fruit and personification of their mutual love:

Only in his holding-onto-nothing-for-himself is God the Father at all; he pours forth his substance and generates the Son; and only in the holding-onto-nothing-for-himself of what has been received does the Son show himself to be of the same essence of the Father, and in this shared holding-onto-nothing-for-themselves are they one in the Spirit, who is, after all, the expression and personification of this holding-onto-nothing-for-himself of God and the eternal new beginning and eternal product of this ceaselessly flowing movement.[27]

Indeed the power of divine love is shown by the way in which the Other in God is able to be infinitely Other without detriment to the divine unity. The richness, vitality, and freedom of divine love are manifest in the variety of modalities that love can assume.

Thus von Balthasar uses the term "event," qualified by the use of "supra-temporal," to convey a liveliness and vitality within God that is inherent in that difference-in-unity at the heart of the classical trinitarian theology but that traditional notions of immutability and impassibility fail to communicate.[28] The "event" expresses the divine essence as constituted by this eternal relational process of reciprocal self-surrendering, this unceasing giving and receiving, offer and response between the divine persons. "One must allow

---

[26]*Theo-Drama: Theological Dramatic Theory II. Dramatis Personae: Man in God*, translated by Graham Harrison (San Francisco: Ignatius Press, 1990) 256.

[27]Medard Kehl and Werner Löser, eds., *The Von Balthasar Reader*, translated by Robert J. Daly and Fred Lawrence (Edinburgh: T & T Clark, 1985) 27.

[28]*Mysterium Paschale* is expressly situated in terms of prevailing notions of a suffering God and the various polemics against the traditional understanding of the impassibility and immutability of God. See von Balthasar's preface in *MP*, vii–ix. Von Balthasar is concerned that the traditional account of divine immutability does not adequately convey the dynamism and liveliness of trinitarian love that is revealed. We shall return to this issue.

an 'event' into God who is beyond the world and beyond change,"[29] as he explains:

> The real, which is theology's object, is not simply something that has taken place historically (a fact) or a string of data that can be enumerated; nor is it merely something supratemporal to be abstracted from such facts, an idea that is somehow of importance for today, an "essence" or some "being" at rest in itself. It is utterly and completely an event, breaking vertically into the chain of facts which make up the world as seen from the inside and as such revealing both the living God's mode of being and his mode of acting.[30]

Nevertheless with the qualification "supra-temporal" von Balthasar deliberately distances himself from any univocal attribution of change to God. When he speaks of "event" he uses the term analogously. It expresses a liveliness in the triune God that is actual, not (as in us) as imperfection, deficiency, or need, but as the perfection of the divine love that is unchanging and eternal. At no stage is there any question of attributing any created event to God, who is eternal. Process notions are explicitly rejected: God does not need the world and its processes in order to become Godself.[31] Hence "event" is always used by von Balthasar to describe a liveliness in God that is "supra-temporal." In a similar way he speaks of "supra-kenosis" to describe the renunciatory character of inner-trinitarian divine love.

However, while carefully maintaining an ontological distinction between creature and Creator and assiduously avoiding any univocal attribution of mutability to God von Balthasar does indeed mean that strict philosophical immutability, as traditionally understood, is no longer theologically tenable. He posits a real *kenosis* in God that has ontological status and is not merely functional or soteriological. His notion of the inner-trinitarian "event" of triune love thus leads him to modify substantially the traditional understanding of the divine attributes and to attribute receptivity, "supra-kenosis," "supra-mutability," increase, and even "suffering" to God as divine perfections. We shall return at a later point to this issue. We first turn to von Balthasar's enthralling treatment of the paschal mystery as it unfolds over the *Sacrum Triduum*.

The death on the cross[32]

Von Balthasar begins his reflections on the interconnection of the paschal mystery and the Trinity with an exploration of Jesus' death on the cross. Four key elements are central to his interpretation:

[29]*MP* 24.

[30]*Theo-Drama I* 26.

[31]See for example John Riches, ed., *The Glory of the Lord: A Theological Aesthetics VII. Theology: The New Covenant,* translated by Brian McNeil (San Francisco: Ignatius Press, 1989) 17; *Theo-Drama II* 261; *Theo-Drama III* 529.

[32]*MP* 89–140.

1. Jesus' death is the turning point where divine love and justice coincide.
2. The cross is an event of trinitarian surrender.
3. Jesus' obedience is a key to his hypostatic identity.
4. Jesus' mission is *identical* to his person.

1. Death as turning point

The soteriological dimension of the paschal mystery is fundamental to von Balthasar's interpretation. From this perspective the cross is the accomplishment of divine judgment on sin because, von Balthasar explains, a God who is love must hate sin; this is why God does not remit sin without expiation.[33] In the paschal mystery God's love confronts sin, but here indeed is "the turning point" in salvation history where God's justice, which rejects sin, and God's love coincide. In this sense, von Balthasar explains, the cross is "the turning, the transition, the Pasch. And in the turning point, in the crucified, these coincide: God's wrath which will not come to terms with sin but can only reject it and burn it out, and God's love which begins to disclose itself precisely at the point of this inexorability."[34]

Again love alone is credible. On the cross God (the Father, who in this regard assumes the role of loving judge) hands over his Son to bear our sin. The Son, sent by the Father into the God-forsakenness of the cross, out of love freely takes on himself the sin of the world. In the agony of the cross and in the cry of abandonment he enters into the abyss of sin and separation from God that is divine judgment on sin. His is a vicarious, expiatory substitution *(Stellvertretung)* for sinners without, however, any cooperation in sin.[35]

2. The cross as event of trinitarian surrender

Another key element in von Balthasar's interpretation of the cross of Good Friday is that of surrender or delivering up *(Hingabe,* in reference to the New Testament use of *paradidōmi).*[36] For von Balthasar the cross, and indeed the whole paschal mystery, is an event of triune surrender, of mutual self-giving and self-yielding love. In this way he understands that the "delivering up" of the Son by the Father is perfectly complemented by the self-surrender of the Son.[37]

---

[33]*MP* 119, 138.

[34]*The Von Balthasar Reader* 149.

[35]For a discussion of Jesus' substitution see Ellero Babini, "Jesus Christ, Form and Norm of Man according to Hans Urs von Balthasar," *Communio* 16 (1989) 451–454.

[36]*MP* 107–112.

[37]In contrast, for Jürgen Moltmann the cross is an event of double God-forsakenness. The Father and Son are held apart in death and divine being is rent asunder. *The Crucified God,* translated by R. A. Wilson and John Bowden (London: SCM, 1974) 235–249. I shall consider Moltmann's theology in relation to von Balthasar's in the concluding chapter of this book.

Nonetheless von Balthasar also stresses Jesus' experience of abandonment on the cross, to which the biblical data attest: "the concentration of everything contrary to God in the Son is experienced as being abandoned by the Father."[38] Indeed he argues that of all the words from the cross primacy must go to the cry of abandonment.[39] The Father does not intervene to save the Son from suffering and death. The Son dies and is buried and descends to the depths of hell, cut off from God and at least to this degree God-forsaken. In von Balthasar's theology, however, this separation to the point of the Father's abandonment of the Son to death is a modality of the inner-trinitarian "event." Indeed it is "the highest worldly revelation" of that "event" of difference *(diastasis)* between the Father and the Son in the Spirit: "This 'infinite distancing' which brings into itself the mode of the estrangement from God of the sinner will still however always be the highest worldly revelation of the *diastasis* (difference) between Father and Son in the Holy Spirit within the eternal nature of God."[40] The abandonment on the cross is thus understood as the economic form, a modality, of the difference-in-unity constitutive of the triune God. As such it reveals what God is in God's eternal triune self.

3. The obedience of Jesus

In von Balthasar's theology the surrender on the cross is a sublime expression of Jesus' kenotic obedience. Here von Balthasar finds a vital key to Jesus' hypostatic identity. He recognizes that this obedience is not some additional feature of the hypostatic identity of the Son but is precisely the expression in creation of Jesus' identity as the Incarnate Son and his relationship to the Father. The cross reveals that it is of the Son's very being to keep nothing for himself but to yield everything to the Father. His obedience is constitutive of his identity as the Son, expressive of his divine sonship and freedom. Furthermore this obedience is by no means a form of subservience or subordination of the Son in relation to the Father. It is instead an expression of his sovereign liberty as the divine Son. Von Balthasar explains: "The obedience with which the Son performs the Father's will is not the obedience of a 'serf' . . . it quite evidently comes from God himself; it is the freedom which reigns between Father and Son."[41] No one takes his life from him. His death is the supreme act of his liberty.[42] Jesus' obedience expresses his love for the Father and the unity of love between them: "But this obedience is so thoroughly love for the Father and by that very fact so altogether one (John 10, 30) with the

[38] *The Von Balthasar Reader* 148.
[39] *MP* 125.
[40] *The Von Balthasar Reader* 135.
[41] *Prayer* 188.
[42] Von Balthasar, "Death is Swallowed Up by Life," *Communio* 14 (1987) 49–54.

Father's own love that he who sends and he who obeys act by virtue of the same divine liberty of love."[43]

Jesus' obedience is therefore grounded in his divine personhood and in his eternal relation to Father and Spirit. Admittedly in so far as Jesus, as human being, stands before the Father the will of the divine Father is bestowed on him through the Spirit; it is always in the Holy Spirit that the Son takes up the mission that comes from the Father.[44] However the Father's will, which the Holy Spirit brings to the Son, is not only the will of the Father. The decision that creation be saved by the incarnation and paschal mystery is the decision of the Trinity as much the Son's, the Father's, and the Spirit's. As the Son's own trinitarian will it is therefore "the opposite of something that comes over him from outside and above—whether as duty imposed on him or as an extraneous Dionysian transport. Rather, even in the distance of the economy of salvation, it is something eternally at home."[45]

Here, then, is the role and significance of Jesus' obedience in von Balthasar's theology: "his obedience presents the kenotic translation of the eternal love of the Son for the 'ever greater' Father."[46] It is the translation or expression, in the economy, of the Son's inner-trinitarian love for the Father. Its archetype is the filial love of the Son in the Trinity, his receptivity and responsiveness to the Father and all that the Father has to give him.

4. The identity of Jesus' mission and his person[47]

Following Aquinas, von Balthasar understands that the Son's *missio* is the economic form of his eternal *processio*.[48] However, von Balthasar takes the matter farther than Aquinas, who maintained that any of the Three could have become incarnate,[49] and recognizes that Jesus' mission in the economy is "most profoundly appropriate to his divine person":

---

[43]*MP* 208–209.

[44]In this regard von Balthasar observes what he describes as "a trinitarian and soteriological inversion of roles" in the trinitarian drama in the economy whereby, in the economy of salvation, the relationship between Son and Spirit is reversed. "While the Spirit proceeds within the divinity from the Father and the (or through the) Son, the Son becomes man through the Spirit and is guided in his mission by the same Spirit" (*The Von Balthasar Reader* 180). See also *Theo-Drama III* 189–191; 521–523; *The Von Balthasar Reader* 180–181. For further comment on this rather contentious notion see O'Donnell's comments in his article "The Holy Spirit in the Life of Jesus," 28 (especially n. 5) and 38. In von Balthasar's theology the "inversion" is another instance of the economic form of the triune "event" of love, another modality of the infinite number of possible modalities of infinite love already and eternally allowed for in the divine inner-trinitarian "event" whereby the Father begets his beloved Son in the love of the Holy Spirit.

[45]*The Von Balthasar Reader* 179.

[46]*MP* 91.

[47]Von Balthasar's exploration of Christ's mission and person is extensive. See *Theo-Drama III* 149–259.

[48]*ST* Ia. 43, 2 ad 3.

[49]*ST* 3a. 3, 5.

And if it is true that one in God took suffering upon himself to the point of abandonment by God and acknowledged it as his own, then obviously it was not as something alien to God that does not touch him inwardly, but as something most profoundly appropriate to his divine person, to the extent that . . . his *missio* by the Father is a modality of his *processio* from the Father.[50]

The mission of Jesus, which he fulfills by his obedience, is properly his own. It is not given to the Son accidentally but as a modality of his eternal personal being.[51] It is therefore an expression of his person as the Son. In this way von Balthasar maintains that in Jesus there is perfect identity between his person as Son and his redemptive mission. Von Balthasar concludes that the person is identical with the mission: "The point of identity is his mission from God *(missio)*, which is identical with the Person *in* God and *as* God *(processio)*."[52]

Thus von Balthasar assumes Aquinas's understanding of the missions as the processions with a temporal effect but presses to an understanding that in Christ mission and person are identical.[53] Jesus is the Son who is sent. His mission is uniquely and properly the Son's. To know his mission in this ontological trinitarian sense is to know who he is, whence he comes, his role, his person, and through him the other two persons, their relations and roles.

Indeed von Balthasar's concept of person, whether human or divine, is rooted in the concept of mission *(Sendung)*.[54] In what is effectively a correction to the classical treatment of the processions he distinguishes between a *Geistessubjekt*, a conscious subject, and a person: "It is when God addresses a conscious subject, tells him who he is and what he means to the eternal God of truth and shows him the purpose of his existence—that is, imparts a distinctive and divinely authorized mission—that we can say of a conscious subject that he is a 'person.'"[55]

A *Geistessubjekt* has intellect and will but becomes a person in the mission that he or she receives from God. Hence although von Balthasar's understanding of the missions owes much to Aquinas's exposition the category of mission holds a much more prominent place in his work than in Thomistic

[50]*The Von Balthasar Reader* 134.
[51]*Theodrama III* 201.
[52]*Theodrama III* 533. Indeed, von Balthasar adds: "this is the main conclusion of the present volume."
[53]On this identity of person and mission MacKinnon comments that von Balthasar "in his handling of the difficulties involved in that identification shows his relative weakness as a philosopher. How can anyone *be* his Mission? What of the difficulties of analogy involved in such predication?" MacKinnon suggests that "a greater philosophical expertise would have helped his exposition" ("Some Reflections on Hans Urs von Balthasar's Christology" 171–172).
[54]O'Donnell discusses this aspect of von Balthasar's work in "The Form of His Theology" 460–462.
[55]*Theo-Drama III* 207. See also "On the Concept of Person," *Communio* 13 (1986) 18–26.

trinitarian theology. There mission (invisible and visible) pertains to the re-demptive work of the divine persons in the economy. For von Balthasar the person as person is revealed in the mission. As he presses from mission to procession to the person, mission emerges as a vital trinitarian category in his theology.

The descent into hell[56]

In von Balthasar's treatment of the descent into hell he is arguably at his most imaginative and perhaps also at his most controversial. Profoundly in-spired by the mystical experiences and visionary theology of Adrienne von Speyr,[57] for whom Christ's experience of hell was a central insight, von Balthasar describes Holy Saturday as standing in "the mysterious middle be-tween cross and resurrection, and consequently properly in the centre of all revelation and theology."[58] A trinitarian as well as a soteriological event, the descent "forms the necessary conclusion to the cross as well as the necessary presupposition of the resurrection."[59] It is in the descent into hell on Holy Saturday that Jesus' *kenosis* reaches its utmost limit and his mission reaches its fullness.

Five key elements emerge in his treatment of the descent:

1. Far from being active, the descent is instead an utterly passive "sinking down." It first of all reveals Jesus' solidarity in human death.

2. The descent also represents Jesus' solidarity with humanity in its sinfulness. In the descent his solidarity extends to those who are dead in a theological sense. In the utter defenselessness of love he enters into the loneliness and desolation of the sinner.

3. In accompanying the sinner in hell God freely and lovingly shares in the exercise of human freedom. The reality of human free-dom is thus affirmed, including the dramatic possibility of rejecting God. Here von Balthasar addresses the relationship between divine and created freedom.

[56]*MP* 148–181; also *The Glory of the Lord VII* 228–235; idem, "The Descent into Hell," *Chicago Studies* 23 (1984) 223–236; idem, *Dare We Hope "That All Men Be Saved"?, with a Short Discourse on Hell,* translated by David Kipp and Lothar Krauth (San Francisco: Ignatius Press, 1987); *The Von Balthasar Reader* 420–422.

[57]Of the relationship of his work to that of von Speyr, von Balthasar writes: "It was Adrienne von Speyr who showed the way in which Ignatius is fulfilled by John, and therewith laid the basis for most of what I have published since 1940. Her work and mine are neither psychologically nor philologically to be separated: two halves of a single whole which has as its center a unique foun-dation." *My Work: In Retrospect* (San Francisco: Ignatius Press, Communio Books, 1993) 89; see also 19, 30, 105–107. See also von Balthasar's *First Glance at Adrienne von Speyr,* translated by Antje Lawry and Sergia Englund (San Francisco: Ignatius Press, 1981).

[58]*The Von Balthasar Reader,* 404; and standing, von Balthasar adds, "like an unexplored, in-explicable blank spot on the map!"

[59]Ibid. 404.

4. In the descent Jesus suffers what von Balthasar refers to as a "second death" in which Jesus sees "sin in itself." The reality of sin is acknowledged, but in the context of the ever greater love of God.

5. The descent is a trinitarian event. At this point von Balthasar strains to the ultimate paradox: that in the descent, in this loss of glory, the glory of the Lord is revealed.

1. Jesus' solidarity with humanity in death

Descending into hell, Jesus is dead with the dead: he is in solidarity with humanity in the experience of death. The descent, according to von Balthasar, is in no sense a glorious or victorious entry;[60] it is rather a "sinking down" into the abyss of death. It is an utterly passive "being removed,"[61] as in the burial of a corpse. This extreme passivity that characterizes the Son's descent stands in stark contrast with the active self-surrender of Jesus on Good Friday.[62] There on the cross his death is the act of his liberty, but on Holy Saturday, in this passive "being removed," Jesus' surrender is marked by the utter passivity of the dead. Now his is the obedience of the dead Christ.

2. Jesus' solidarity with the sinner

Von Balthasar recognizes, however, that the descent is more than solidarity in physical death. It represents Jesus' solidarity with those who have definitively isolated themselves from the love of God. In the descent Jesus identifies with the sinner's radical separation and estrangement from God. His descent in freedom is a descent into the hell of those who in their freedom have rejected God. He is in solidarity with humanity in its sinfulness without, however, implying any cooperation by Jesus in sin itself, for he himself is not bound by any of the bonds of sin.[63] What meaning and logic does this have in von Balthasar's theology? He explains:

> If the Father must be considered as the Creator of human freedom—with all its foreseeable consequences—then judgement belongs primordially to him, and thereby Hell also; and when he sends the Son into the world to save it instead of judging it, and, to equip him for this function, gives "all judgement to the Son" (John 5, 22), then he must also introduce the Son *made man*

[60]Here von Balthasar clearly stands aside from understandings in patristic theology that Jesus' descent to the underworld, *sheol*, was to preach to or, according to another interpretation, triumphantly liberate the spirits of the prophets of pre-Christian times. See, for example, Pol. *Phil.* 1; Ign. *Magn.* 9; Irenaeus, *Adv. haer.* 3.20.4; 4.22.1; 4.27.2; 5.31.1; 5.33.1; Justin, *Dial.* 72; Clement of Alexandria, *Stromata* 6.6; Origen, *Contra Cels.* 2.43; Tertullian, *De anima* 55; Athanasius, *Epictetus* 5–6.
[61]*The Glory of the Lord VII* 230.
[62]*MP* 172. See also O'Donnell, *The Mystery of the Triune God* 66–69.
[63]*MP* 176.

into "Hell" (as the supreme entailment of human liberty). But the Son cannot really be introduced into Hell save as a dead man, on Holy Saturday.[64]

It is because the Son comes not only for the elect but for sinners, not only for the living but for the dead, not to judge but to save us that he descends into hell. For this reason, indeed for our sake the Father, Creator of human freedom, introduces the incarnate Son into hell. However the descent, the solidarity with the dead, and the remitting of all judgment to him can only take place on the Holy Saturday when the Son himself is dead, a cadaver, obedient in corpse-like passivity. Thus in the weakness of love God comes to the sinner in hell, as von Balthasar explains in the following key passage:

> Into this finality (of death) the dead Son descends, no longer acting in any way, but stripped by the cross of every power and initiative of his own, as one purely to be used, debased to mere matter, with a fully indifferent (corpse) obedience, incapable of any active solidarity. Only thus is he right for any "sermon" to the dead. He is (out of ultimate love however) dead together with them. And exactly in that way he disturbs the absolute loneliness striven for by the sinner: the sinner, who wants to be "damned" apart from God, finds God again in his loneliness, but God in the absolute weakness of love who unfathomably in the period of nontime enters into solidarity with those damning themselves.[65]

In the absolute weakness of love God comes to the sinner in hell and enters into the utter loneliness and hellish desolation of the sinner ("a being-only-for-oneself"[66]). Exactly in this way, to use von Balthasar's expression, Jesus "disturbs" the absolute loneliness striven for by the sinner. By no means is the human person's freedom to make that choice denied, overridden, or undermined. Hell remains as the ultimate entailment of human liberty.

3. The reality of human freedom

The divine persons are thus revealed in the paschal mystery precisely in their engagement with the reality of human freedom. The very drama of the relationship between God and the world that culminates in the descent is ultimately the encounter, indeed, the confrontation of two freedoms, the created finite human and the infinite divine freedom of the Creator and Judge. Von Balthasar's concern at this point is the relationship between God's comprehension of human freedom and indeed God's permission of evil on the one hand, and on the other hand finite freedom's capacity to choose against God.[67]

---

[64]*MP* 175.

[65]*The Von Balthasar Reader* 153.

[66]Ibid. 422.

[67]For von Balthasar's discussion of the descent into hell and its relationship to human freedom see *Theo-Drama II* 173–316. See also "Trinity and Future" in *Elucidations*, translated by John Riches (London: SPCK, 1975) 50–56.

God's creation of a genuine human freedom necessarily implies the risk of the human person choosing to reject God and so becoming lost. However, such a risk can be assumed responsibly if in some way God is able to gather such possible or actual lostness into Godself: and here precisely lies the burden of von Balthasar's argument. In his dramatic depiction of the descent into hell he shows that this gathering up of our lostness into God is in fact achieved. Moreover God achieves it, but not by overwhelming or overriding human freedom by pressure or coercion, by a power from outside, as it were. That would be to violate and ultimately to deny genuine human freedom. Rather our lostness is gathered into God by God, in the utter powerlessness of love, sharing in the exercise of human freedom and freely entering into our lostness and our hellish desolation. In this way human freedom is respected, not overridden, as God chooses to accompany the sinner in the sinner's choice. Thus in von Balthasar's understanding of the descent God, out of love, enters into hell and gathers the abyss of our lostness into "the abyss of absolute love."[68]

Hence in the descent we see that God, even as Redeemer, respects the genuine freedom bestowed in creation on the human person and that is capable of resisting and rejecting God's love. Human freedom and all its possibilities are not in any way undermined. However, in von Balthasar's profoundly incarnational theology of the descent God chooses to *share* in the exercise of human freedom and accompanies sinners in their choice. Their choice is definitive. Hell remains as the ultimate entailment of human freedom. But the sinner is no longer alone: God enters into the sinner's loneliness as someone who is even more lonely. The sinner thus finds himself or herself in the company of the God-forsaken Son of God who is so for the sinner's sake. The sinner's is a co-solitude *(Miteinsamkeit).*[69]

Human freedom is respected. Only in the absolute weakness of love does God descend into hell to accompany the sinner in his or her choice. In love God enters into this solidarity with those who reject all solidarity.[70] But neither is God's freedom thwarted by created human freedom, as von Balthasar explains:

> One would still be able to say that God gives human beings the capacity to perform what seems for human beings to be a definitive (negative) choice against God, but that does not need to be judged/evaluated/assessed by God as definitive. And not in such a way that the human person's choice is called into question from outside—which would amount to a disregard of the freedom bestowed on it—but rather in such a way that God with his own divine choice accompanies the human person into the most extreme situation of his (negative) choice. This is what happens in the passion of Jesus.[71]

---

[68]See *Elucidations* 52.
[69]*The Von Balthasar Reader* 153. See also O'Donnell, "The Form of His Theology" 465.
[70]*The Von Balthasar Reader* 153.
[71]Ibid. 152–153.

Thus neither the freedom to sin nor the deadly consequence of sin is denied. The human person may reject God. The human person may choose hell. But divine love is not obstructed by human folly. On the contrary, God accompanies the sinner in his or her choice, shares in the sinner's experience of hellish isolation, loves even when rejected. Henceforth hell belongs to Christ. While still a place of desolation it is "a christological place."[72] It too exists in that "space" that is the Trinity: "In rising from the dead, Christ leaves behind him Hades, that is, the state in which humanity is cut off from access to God. But, by virtue of his deepest Trinitarian experience, he takes 'Hell' with him, as the expression of his power to dispose, as judge, the everlasting salvation or everlasting loss of man."[73]

In von Balthasar's theology of the descent, hell—a real possibility for genuine human freedom—is gathered up into the Trinity to exist in the boundless creativity and compassion of the Trinity's all-embracing love. Hence even hell is understood as a "sphere" in God:

> Creaturely freedom and its future can only be gathered up into the sphere of God without loss and prejudice if they are allowed their full range of open possibilities within the sphere of the world and if this sphere is nevertheless understood as a sphere *in God*, which God can enter, can determine, in which he can work his purposes. He does enter it, determine it, achieve his purposes in it in the death, descent into hell, and resurrection of the Son of God; that is . . . the all-embracing event which establishes the possibility of human freedom and history. But it is all-embracing not as a boundary imposed upon it from without but as an opening up from within, as God shares in the exercise of human freedom, of new horizons which outstrip the possibilities of such freedom.[74]

Again this gathering up of our lostness that occurs in the descent can be achieved because the full range of possibilities of human freedom is eternally "within" God in that primordial supra-temporal "event" of inner-trinitarian love. In that "event" of the Trinity all the contingencies and consequences of a genuine created freedom were, from all eternity, ever allowed for and infinitely transcended.

4. The reality of sin

Von Balthasar presses farther still and recognizes that in the experience of utter forsakenness that is integral to the Son's mission[75] Jesus' experience goes beyond our human experience of death. So great is Jesus' solidarity with the sinner that von Balthasar says that Jesus experienced hell itself. Identifying

[72]Ibid. 422.
[73]*MP* 177.
[74]*Elucidations* 53.
[75]*Theo-Drama III* 450.

himself with all that is opposed to God, that is brought about by humanity in the exercise of its freedom, Jesus experiences what von Balthasar (following Nicholas of Cusa), calls "a vision of death," a *visio mortis*, or a "second death."[76] In this "second death" Jesus sees "sin in itself,"[77] "sheer sin as such, no longer sin as attaching to a particular human being, sin incarnate in living existences, but abstracted from that individuation, contemplated in its bare reality as such (for sin is a reality!)."[78]

Von Balthasar explains that "this contemplative and objective (passive) moment is what distinguishes Holy Saturday from the subjective and active experience of suffering in the Passion."[79] In this "purely passive 'vision' of sin in all its separateness"[80] sin is contemplated in "its bare reality." The sheer reality and enormity of the sin of the world is thus powerfully depicted by von Balthasar as real proof and real consequence of the reality of genuine finite freedom.

We note, however, that in depicting sin in this graphic way von Balthasar, though well acquainted with the tradition, stands in considerable tension with the traditional understanding of sin as an absence of being, a defect of intention, *privatio boni*, but not having "bare reality" or "being" as such.[81] Metaphysically speaking sin is not an event or substance; it is not being but its privation. Yet von Balthasar in effect dramatically reifies sin. We pause for a moment to draw out the meaning of this arresting imagery in his theology.

This reification of sin first allows von Balthasar clearly to distinguish between the sinner and the sin. It thus enables him to express both God's abhorrence of sin and the depths of the divine compassion and love for the sinner. Indeed this image of Jesus seeing "sin in itself," quite separate from its individuation, permits von Balthasar to express the divine compassion for the sinner in an extraordinarily powerful way. The sin is judged while the sinner is loved beyond imagining, lovingly accompanied in his or her choice. Admittedly von Balthasar at this point comes within a hair's breadth of the notion of universal salvation, *apokatastasis*, but, as Saward comments, this "is no mechanical Origenist universalism."[82]

However, while von Balthasar's theology powerfully expresses the divine love there is, on the other hand, no evading the dreadful reality of sin and no denying God's condemnation of sin in this theology. Instead we have a remarkably concrete portrayal of the enormity of evil. Sin is graphically portrayed as a

---

[76]*MP* 168–174. See also *The Glory of the Lord VII* 232–233.

[77]*MP* 173.

[78]*MP* 173.

[79]*MP* 172.

[80]*MP* 179.

[81]See William E. May, "Sin," in Joseph A. Komonchak, Mary Collins, and Dermot Lane, eds., *The New Dictionary of Theology* (Wilmington, Del.: Michael Glazier, 1987) 954–967; also Stephen J. Duffy, "Sin," in Michael Downey, ed., *The New Dictionary of Catholic Spirituality* (Collegeville: The Liturgical Press, 1993) 889–901.

[82]Saward, *The Mysteries of March* 130.

formidable reality, a violent and even seemingly overwhelming presence, a monstrous affliction. By no means dismissed, sin is recognized and judged for what it is: alien to God and alien to life. Though von Balthasar does not develop the symbolism any farther his powerful image of sin in itself, separate from the sinner, also adumbrates, I suggest, a modern understanding of corporate or institutionalized sin in which the human person appears not only as agent but as victim of sin. It thus allows a larger consideration of the social and structural dimension of sin, of the sin that is much more than any personal defect of intention or individual transgression.

Finally and perhaps most importantly, this "reification" of sin also allows von Balthasar in effect to contrast the *infinity* of God's love, the unimaginable excess of this love, with the *finitude* of sin. While the horror and reality of sin is powerfully acknowledged, in reifying it von Balthasar effectively diminishes it in contrast to the infinity of God's love. Here is the nub, the crux of the matter that von Balthasar would have us understand: that all creation is incorporated into God's trinitarian love, that love alone is credible, that the mystery we behold here is a mystery of inexhaustible love.

5. Trinitarian character of the descent[83]

Clearly the trinitarian character of the descent is crucial to von Balthasar's theology. First, the descent is only possible because God is triune. The Father sends the Son into hell. The Son, *while remaining God,* descends into God-forsakenness, assumes the condition of sinful humanity, and embraces all that is opposed to God. As the God-forsaken Son of God and in this sense as one who is even more lonely[84] Jesus accompanies the sinner in the sinner's choice to damn himself or herself and to reject God.[85] Throughout it all he remains God. The Spirit accompanies him and is the bond between Father and Son, uniting them in their separation. Indeed the abandonment of the Son by the Father is possible only because at this point of extreme separation they are united in love by the Holy Spirit: "This opposition between God, the creative origin (the 'Father'), and the man who, faithful to the mission of the origin, ventures on into the ultimate perdition (the 'Son'), this bond stretched to breaking point does not break because the same Spirit of absolute love (the 'Spirit') informs both the one who sends and the one sent. God causes God to go into abandonment by God, while accompanying him on the way with his Spirit."[86]

Von Balthasar describes the Son's being, his whole existence, as always accompanied by the Father, something that is "expressed precisely in the pres-

---

[83]See in particular *MP* 174–176.
[84]*The Von Balthasar Reader* 422.
[85]Note how in n. 65 above von Balthasar speaks of sinners as "those damning themselves."
[86]*Elucidations* 51.

ence of the Holy Spirit."[87] In other words because God is triune, with both difference and unity guaranteed by the Holy Spirit, the inner-trinitarian difference between Father and Son in the unity of the Holy Spirit can accommodate all created differences including the death and descent.

Second, the descent into hell is the final consequence of the unanimous trinitarian will to salvation and therefore of the Son's redemptive mission. Von Balthasar writes:

> That the Redeemer is solidary with the dead, or better, with this death which makes of the dead, for the first time, dead human beings in all reality—this is the final consequence of the redemptive mission he has received from the Father. His being with the dead is an existence at the utmost pitch of obedience, and because the One thus obedient is the dead Christ, it constitutes the "obedience of a corpse" (the phrase is St Francis of Assisi's) of a theologically unique kind. By it Christ takes the existential measure of everything that is sheerly contrary to God, of the entire object of the divine eschatological judgement, which here is grasped in that event in which it is "cast down". . . . But at the same time, this happening gives the measure of the Father's mission in all its amplitude: the "exploration" of Hell is an event of the (economic) Trinity.[88]

Third, the incarnation and the paschal mystery are only possible because the Son's being is constituted by this kenotic obedience. In the descent the Son's *kenosis* reaches its most extreme limit—his is, in a theological sense, "the obedience of a corpse." Again von Balthasar recognizes that this kenotic obedience is a modality of the Son's love for the Father: "The Son can go into the estrangement from God of hell, because he understands his way as an expression of his love for the Father and he can give to his love the character of obedience to such a degree that in it he experiences the complete godlessness of lost man."[89]

The event of the descent reveals that it is the Son's will to obedience that grounds the event of the incarnation and paschal mystery. With the death and descent of Jesus in corpse-like obedience and the utter passivity of being dead von Balthasar understands that it is as if the "superstructure" of the incarnation is removed and the critical elements of the drama of salvation thus disclosed. The eternal Son's trinitarian will is the "substructure" on which his kenotic obedience is based. In obedience to his mission he enters into the depths of sinful existence and separation from God, confronting the "substructure" of our existence. Von Balthasar writes: "Thereby, with the removal of the whole superstructure of the Incarnation, the eternal will of the Son within the Trinity

[87]*The Von Balthasar Reader* 176.

[88]*MP* 174–175. Notice the reference to "the Father's mission" (in the French translation *"la mission paternelle"*: see *Pâques: Le Mystère* 168). Von Balthasar means the Father's salvific plan, not that the Father is sent as such.

[89]*Elucidations* 51.

to obedience is exposed, as the substructure that is the basis of the entire event of the Incarnation: and this is set face-to-face with the hidden substructure of sinful existence, exposed in Sheol, as the state of separation from God, the 'loss of glory.'"[90]

Von Balthasar reiterates that the very possibility of incarnation and the paschal mystery, and even of creation itself is grounded in the eternal inner-trinitarian event of the divine processions. Finally he strains to the ultimate paradox: that in hell, in the supreme obedience of the Son, in the ugliness and formlessness of a corpse, the glory of the Lord is revealed: "It is 'glory' in the uttermost opposite of 'glory', because it is at the same time blind obedience, that must obey the Father at the point where the last trace of God seems lost (in pure sin), together with every other communication (in pure solitariness)."[91]

It is absolute glory because it is absolute love. Love alone resolves the extraordinary contradiction. This for von Balthasar is the essential meaning of the descent. Love alone is credible. Love enters into the realm of death and desolation and gathers our lostness into God's triune self. In the descent God, who is love, freely takes responsibility for the success of creation in the context of human freedom and sin. In the midst of those dark realities so radically affirmed in von Balthasar's theology is the revelation of the sheer graciousness and utter glory of the love that is God. Though so radically affirmed, the realities of death and hell are also radically transformed into an expression of divine love and compassion.

The resurrection: revelation of the Trinity[92]

Nevertheless it is in the resurrection that the revelation of the Trinity appears in full light: the Father to whom is attributed the initiative in raising the Son, the Son who appears as the Living One, and the Spirit who is sent forth into the world.[93] Although the events of the cross and the descent into hell prepare for it, it is only with the resurrection that we perceive fully the trinitarian character of the paschal events: "The decisive revelation of the mystery of the Trinity is not, therefore, something which precedes the *Mysterium Paschale* itself. As has been shown above in discussing the Passion, that revelation is prepared in the counter-position of the wills on the Mount of Olives and by the divine abandonment on the Cross, yet only with the Resurrection does it come forth openly into the light."[94]

The resurrection reveals that even in the moment of their extreme separation Father and Son were united by virtue of the same divine liberty of love in

[90]*The Glory of the Lord VII* 231.
[91]Ibid. 233.
[92]*MP* 189–266.
[93]*MP* 191.
[94]*MP* 212–213.

the Trinity's eternal plan of salvation: "On the one hand, in the opposition of the two wills of the Father and Son on the Mount of Olives and in the abandonment of the Son by God on the cross, the drastic counterposing of the divine Persons in the economy became visible. On the other hand, . . . this very opposition appears as the supreme manifestation of the whole, integrated saving action of God whose internal logic . . . is once again disclosed in the inseparable unity of the death of the Cross and the Resurrection."[95]

This "inseparable unity" of death and resurrection is also expressed in the very body of the Risen Lord. In this life out of death the wounds of his self-surrendering love remain. He is forever the Slain Lamb: "This new life that has definitively put death behind itself (Rom 6:10) remains nevertheless life out of death, life characterized by its passage through death. It is life which on the one hand has power over death . . . but on the other hand remains profoundly marked by the event and experience of death insofar as this highest achievement of life was—and remains—the same as total self-surrender."[96]

The self-surrender and obedience of the Son, strong elements of von Balthasar's treatment of the death and descent, remain as key themes in his interpretation of the resurrection. Jesus is also obedient in the resurrection: he allows the Father to raise him from the dead. The Father raises him and indeed raises him to the visibility proper to the paschal mystery, not to the preincarnate condition of the invisible Word. As von Balthasar says: "In raising from the dead, that is, in raising bodily his Word made man, God takes no backward step in relation to the Incarnation of his Word."[97] The Father then *shows* to the world his risen and glorified Son, now *become* what as God he already and always was, for this is no extrinsic or alien freedom that is bestowed on the Son, as von Balthasar explains: "When, accordingly, the Father grants to the Son, now raised into eternal life, the absolute freedom to show himself to his disciples in his identity with the dead Jesus of Nazareth, bearing the marks of his wounds, he gives him no new, different or alien freedom but that freedom which is most deeply the Son's very own. It is precisely in this freedom that the Son reveals, ultimately, the freedom of the Father."[98] Thus when the Father shows to the world his risen and glorified *Son,* he himself is also, albeit implicitly, disclosed, and precisely through the *person* of Christ.[99] In the sovereign spontaneity and freedom with which the Son shows himself in the post-resurrection appearances the Father's freedom is also manifested.

The resurrection is also the revelation of the Spirit.[100] It was the Spirit who "held open and bridged over" the separation of the Father and the Son in the

[95]*MP* 203.
[96]*Life Out of Death: Meditations on the Easter Mystery,* translated by Davis Perkins (Philadelphia: Fortress Press, 1985) 39. The image of the Slain Lamb is a powerful and pervasive one in von Balthasar's theology.
[97]*MP* 206.
[98]*MP* 209.
[99]*MP* 207.
[100]*MP* 210.

cross and descent into hell. The Holy Spirit is also the "instrument" and "milieu" of the resurrection.[101] While it is the Father who takes the initiative in raising the Son and, as Creator, brings his salvific plan for creation to its completion in the resurrection, the resurrection of Jesus is accomplished in the powerful transfiguring action of the Spirit of God.[102]

The gift to the world of the Holy Spirit, the Paraclete, is made possible through the paschal mystery: the Spirit is sent, following the return of the Son to the Father. The "re-union" of the Father and the Son (in his human nature, von Balthasar adds) appears as the condition of the breathing forth of the Spirit into the world as from a single principle.[103] The resurrection thus shows that the Spirit proceeds from the Father and the Son. Their common spiration of the Spirit is also attested in the free and unanimous consent of Jesus and the Father to the salvific plan. This unanimity of consent, von Balthasar says, "is the economic form of their common spiration of the Spirit."[104] He explains: "What hovers between Jesus and the Father as the mediation of mission is the economic form of the eternal unanimity between Father and Son, which becomes a distinct witness to both of them and with which both of them seal their Yes. It is, as it were, their 'We', which is more than the sum of their 'I' and 'Thou'."[105]

Von Balthasar describes the Spirit as having a twofold face from all eternity that, to use his expression, has both an objective and a subjective aspect. The Holy Spirit "is breathed forth from the one love of Father and Son as the expression of their united freedom—he is, as it were, the objective form of their subjectivity; but, at the same time, he is the objective witness to their difference-in-unity or unity-in-difference."[106] The Holy Spirit thus personifies the subjectivity of Father and Son in their one love and in this sense exists in person as the objectification of their love, the manifestation of their innermost subjectivity. However, the Holy Spirit is also objective witness and guarantor that this love involves a unity-in-difference or difference-in-unity. With the gift of their common Spirit into the world following Jesus' death and resurrection God is disclosed in the depths of the divine triune mystery.[107]

The role of the paschal mystery in von Balthasar's trinitarian theology

The dramatic events of the paschal mystery, as revelatory of trinitarian relationality and the inherently and intensely dramatic character of divine life,

[101]*MP* 211.
[102]*MP* 204.
[103]*MP* 210.
[104]*Theo-Drama III* 188.
[105]Ibid. 511.
[106]*Theo-Drama III* 187; see also *The Von Balthasar Reader* 181.
[107]*MP* 214.

clearly occupy center stage in von Balthasar's theology. The paschal mystery itself thus serves as analogy properly speaking, not as mere metaphor for his understanding of the Trinity. We find no recourse to the traditional psychological analogies. Indeed von Balthasar, like Durrwell, resists the traditional explication of the processions in terms of the acts of intellect and will and maintains that both processions should be understood as processions of love.[108] Admittedly, again like Durrwell, von Balthasar looks to the analogy of the human experience of love to develop an understanding of the perfections of love. However, his considerations are always in the larger context of the love that is manifested in the paschal mystery. Human interpersonal or intra-subjective experience is never employed as primary analogue in his trinitarian thinking for that is to be found in the paschal mystery as it manifests, in different ways, the love of the Three.

As for Durrwell, the focal trinitarian image is that of the Father's generation of the Son but von Balthasar takes the matter farther and recognizes that all possible modalities of love are forever allowed for in this primordial act of love that is constitutive of the Trinity itself. The events in the economy—the suffering, abandonment, separation, and descent—are thus able to be situated in terms of the eternal event of self-giving, self-emptying love. By no means alien or foreign to God, the paschal mystery reveals what God is eternally and manifests the nature of God's inner-trinitarian love. In this way von Balthasar clearly avoids attributing mutability to God since this is God's eternal nature, and yet he also is able to attribute to God something that is analogous to movement and change. Technically he does not step outside of traditional notions of God since this "event" is implicit in the divine processions themselves, inherent in that primordial difference-in-unity as traditionally understood, although not previously elaborated in this way.

The distinctly *kenotic* character of divine love emerges in von Balthasar's theology. The triune God is constituted by a kenotic self-giving and receiving between the persons: this, indeed, is the glory of God. This then profoundly affects von Balthasar's understanding of the divine perfections. The God revealed in the *kenosis* of the cross and descent is not to be understood in terms of Greek philosophical notions of immutability and impassibility. The divine perfections are instead refashioned in terms of the perfections of self-giving, self-yielding, kenotic love. O'Hanlon describes this feature of von Balthasar's work as perhaps his greatest legacy to theology.[109] However we also note that there is no pan-kenoticism here.[110] This kenotic aspect of the divine being, although highly significant, is only one aspect of the glory of God's love, which also manifests itself in such aspects as joy, increase, and wonderment.[111]

---

[108]See O'Donnell's comments in this regard in "Truth as Love" 200–203; and "The Form of His Theology" 465–468.

[109]O'Hanlon, "The Legacy of Hans Urs von Balthasar" 406.

[110]*MP* 29.

[111]See O'Hanlon, *The Immutability of God* 120.

Salvation is then understood in the context of this vision of the Trinity as mystery of kenotic love. The paschal mystery means that God, in love, has entered into the hiatus of death—physical and spiritual—and has taken the full measure of our situation not from the outside, as it were, but from the inside, sharing our desolation, bearing our sin, as Son experiencing God-forsakenness. Through the Son's death and descent we are saved from isolation, loneliness, and alienation, and saved for entry into the trinitarian communion. In the utter defenselessness of love God has entered into creation, into its very depths, and incorporated it into Godself. This is salvation.

Again a strong sense of the participation of all creation in the trinitarian communion emerges. Even the darkest and most bitter realities are situated in terms of the primordial event of trinitarian love. No place is cut off or excluded from the love of God: even hell belongs to Christ and is taken up and into the trinitarian communion of love. Even the chaos of sin is allowed for and mysteriously accommodated in the trinitarian communion of life and love. Despite the reality of sin no one is God-forsaken, not even the one who chooses to reject God's love. It is love that ultimately prevails. Once again love alone is credible.

The relationship between the economic and immanent Trinity

Von Balthasar maintains a clear distinction between the immanent and economic Trinity.[112] Although he recognizes that it is only on the basis of the economic Trinity that we can have knowledge of the immanent Trinity and dare to speak about it he does not infer that the economic constitutes the immanent Trinity. He seeks a much more subtle and nuanced understanding of the relationship. On the one hand God loves us and saves us in this way because God is really like this. It is truly as God that God is involved in the world: there is therefore not only an ethical but an ontological connection between the economic and immanent Trinity. On the other hand suffering and death *ad extra* are not to be attributed univocally to God *ad intra;* rather the grounds for the possibility of what takes place *ad extra* are to be found in God *ad intra.*

Indeed, von Balthasar is critical of the modern tendency to confuse the immanent with the economic Trinity and rejects the tendency to dismiss the notion of the immanent Trinity as dangerously ambiguous. The two must be distinguished in order not to reduce God to one who seeks self-fulfillment in creation by a kind of mechanical necessity. Such a reduction misses the mystery of God as love, for the God who shows such unreserved love toward creation is already love itself, absolutely and eternally, as the Trinity. God does not become love: God is love. As von Balthasar explains:

---

[112]*Theo-Drama III* 157, 190–191, 506–509; also *Theodramatik III* 297–305.

We need to find a way of seeing the immanent Trinity as the ground of the cosmic process (including the cross), yet in such a way that it does not look like just a formal process of self-mediation (as for Rahner), nor as mixed up in the cosmic process (as for Moltmann). Instead, we have to think of the immanent Trinity as that eternal and absolute self-giving, so that God in Godself is seen as being absolute love. This is the only thing that will explain God's free self-giving to the world as love, without God needing the cosmic process and the cross to become (and "mediate") Godself.[113]

Von Balthasar thus argues that it will not do to identify the two too closely, as he believes Rahner does, or like Moltmann to propose a Hegelian-type identification in which the cross becomes the fulfillment of the Trinity in the manner of process theology.[114] There can be no identification of world process with the eternal processions of the divine hypostases. Nevertheless, while distancing himself from Moltmann's notion of suffering in God von Balthasar vindicates Moltmann's fundamental thrust in taking serious account of the biblically-attested pathos of God, a feature that is so lacking in the traditional notions of God's *apatheia*.

The immanent Trinity remains as the transcendent theological reality in von Balthasar's theology, not swallowed up in the economic Trinity as though the two were identical. Thus when he speaks of *kenosis*, for example, the *kenosis* of the Son in the incarnation and paschal mystery is not identical with the inner-trinitarian "*kenosis*" of the processions. Rather the *kenosis* of the Son in the paschal mystery is the economic form or modality of the divine love of Father and Son and so provides an analogy for the inner-trinitarian relations. When *kenosis* is attributed to the immanent Trinity it is predicated analogically, not univocally. Thus the incarnational *kenosis* is the assumption of a passible human body and human nature by the Son right to the point of death and descent. The trinitarian *kenosis*, on the other hand, is the immanent giving and receiving of the impassible and immutable divine nature of the three divine persons. It refers to the eternal self-giving and self-emptying communion of the divine persons *ad intra*. In this subtly nuanced way von Balthasar carefully maintains the distinction between the immanent and economic Trinity.

At the same time von Balthasar avoids a rift between the immanent and economic Trinity, stressing that the economic is rooted in the immanent Trinity. We know no other economic Trinity than the one that entered history: the Trinity of the Son who is eternally subject to the Father and of the Spirit over him who mediates the Father's will to the Son. That any one of the Three could have become incarnate, as Aquinas argues, is not, as we have noted, a question countenanced by von Balthasar. Such speculative questions about the divine persons do not arise in his determinedly revelation-centered theology.

---

[113]*Theodramatik III* 300.
[114]See also *Theo-Drama III* 529.

Assessment of gains for trinitarian theology

In a corpus as vast and comprehensive as that of von Balthasar there are many areas on which we could focus our attention in an attempt to assess the possible gains he achieves. We highlight the two aspects of his theology that are particularly significant advances in relation to traditional trinitarian theology.

1. A trinitarian ontology of love

Von Balthasar's theology undoubtedly points the way to a new expression of divine ontology. As MacKinnon comments: "It is Balthasar's achievement to insist that any valid Christology must press from drama to ontology at that point and place [the cross]: and this is not by eliding the dramatic, but allowing the ultimate to open itself to our awareness as love there, and not elsewhere."[115] We have seen that he moves from the paschal mystery, as the economic form of the supra-temporal "event" of trinitarian love, to a trinitarian ontology of love. An understanding of the being of God that goes beyond traditional boundaries of Augustinian-Thomistic theology ensues as von Balthasar argues for the convertibility of being and interpersonal love and indeed for a certain primacy for the latter.[116] Thus although he does not deny the validity of the traditional substance-based metaphysics von Balthasar avoids an essentialist ontology without, however, adopting process notions.

With two analogies foremost in view—the paschal mystery and the phenomenon of love—he considers God's being and the trinitarian processions not in terms of metaphysically-conceived absolute being, *Actus Purus Ipsum Esse,* but rather in terms of the intrinsically dynamic *Actus Purus Ipsum Amare.*[117] The result is a scripturally inspired ontology of interpersonal love in which the traditionally dominant notion of God as undifferentiated being is much more clearly contextualized and personalized in the concrete mystery of triune love given "for us" in Jesus' paschal mystery. A distinct shift in emphasis from "being" to "love" is thus evident in his trinitarian ontology, grounded in the insight that God is revealed not as the fullness of being but as love.

A more developed use of personalist and relational categories and a refashioning of the traditional categories in more relational terms results. Consider for example his refashioning of the notion of person whereby mission is incorporated into his understanding of personhood. Again the traditional metaphysical categories of being and substance are not rejected but rather

[115]MacKinnon, "Some Reflections on Hans Urs von Balthasar's Christology" 172.

[116]See Werner Löser, "Being Interpreted as Love: Reflections on the Theology of Hans Urs von Balthasar," *Communio* 16 (1989) 475–490.

[117]O'Donnell comments that von Balthasar "has performed a great service for the Church in trying to *think* as radically as possible the New Testament affirmation that God is love" ("Truth as Love" 202).

subsumed by personalist categories of love and the relationality that is constitutive of love. In this shift from the traditional emphasis on God as *Actus Purus* being yields to love, *Ipsum Esse Subsistens* to *Ipsum Amare Subsistens*. A "higher theological viewpoint" of considerable integrative power thus emerges. In our assessment von Balthasar's development of a trinitarian ontology of love with its more personalist and relational categories is a highly significant advance. Admittedly this new ontology remains, I suggest, to be developed in a more systematic and, indeed, more generally accessible fashion. But von Balthasar's great contribution is to open the way ahead.

2. The divine attributes

In von Balthasar's treatment of the divine attributes we see another most significant advance. First, in contrast to the Augustinian-Thomistic approach that considers the mystery of the divine essence and attributes before treating the Trinity of persons von Balthasar takes the eternal and supra-temporal "event" as his starting point for a consideration of the divine perfections. Second, von Balthasar's daring way of speaking of the trinitarian love, together with a very untraditional stress on the receptivity of love and the boundless variety of modalities love can assume, leads to a very new understanding of the divine attributes. With regard to immutability and impassibility he does not repudiate the patristic and scholastic tradition.[118] Nevertheless he does consider that a fuller understanding is possible, one that more adequately expresses the trinitarian dynamism the paschal mystery reveals. He writes:

> If we look back from the mature Christology of Ephesus and Chalcedon to the hymn of Philippians 2, and do so with the intention of not exaggerating its capacity for "dogmatic" assertiveness, we can hardly help registering a "plus factor" in its archaic language—stammering out the mystery as this does—to which the established formulae of the unchangeability of God do not really do justice. One senses a further residue of meaning, with which the German, English and Russian kenoticists of the nineteenth and twentieth centuries sought to come to terms.[119]

The paschal mystery reveals that God is manifestly more glorious than philosophically fashioned notions of immutability and impassibility could convey or admit. On the other hand God is clearly not mutable in the way that creatures are: von Balthasar emphatically rejects any attribution of mutability to God.[120] Although distancing himself from Aquinas on a number of issues he

---

[118]See *MP* vii–ix, 23–41. For further discussions of von Balthasar in relation to the immutability of God see O'Hanlon's article, "Does God Change?—H. U. von Balthasar on the Immutability of God," 161–183; and O'Hanlon's fine study, *The Immutability of God.*

[119]*MP* 26.

[120]See, for example, von Balthasar's comments against the use of mutability and immutability in *Theo-Drama II* 9, 280, 293; *Theo-Drama III* 523. Introducing *Theo-Drama II* he writes: "The

agrees with him in recognizing that both mutability and immutability must be denied of God if any imperfection is implied by either.[121] As von Balthasar explains: "There is a theological truth which mediates between the two irreconcilable extremes: those of, on the one hand, a 'divine immutability' for which the Incarnation appears only as an external 'addition', and on the other a 'divine mutability' of such a sort that, for the duration of the Incarnation, the divine self-consciousness of the Son is 'alienated' in human awareness."[122]

Since God is neither imperfectly mutable nor imperfectly immutable von Balthasar attempts a more subtle and nuanced approach and proposes that a combination of the two terms, mutability and immutability, is appropriate. Thus he suggests that the dynamism of the inner-trinitarian event involves a "supra-mutability," a notion that modifies the traditional philosophical notion of divine immutability but without entailing a univocal attribution of mutability. When pressed he settles for immutability, never mutability, but in doing so he seeks to invest the traditional understanding of God's immutability with a considerably modified meaning.[123]

It is important to reiterate that von Balthasar makes no univocal attribution of change, temporality, or suffering to God. God does not become what God was not: God is in the paschal mystery what God is eternally. That is the vital significance and role of the notion of the inner-trinitarian supra-temporal "event" in von Balthasar's theology. It allows him to speak, within the framework of analogical discourse, of immanent modalities of trinitarian love such as receptivity, mutability, and even suffering as divine attributes. In this way his trinitarian theology allows and facilitates a radical reshaping of the understanding of the traditional perfections such that something analogous (but *only* analogous) to such notions as these can be understood as divine perfections.

Let us take receptivity as an example.[124] Traditionally it was always possible to ascribe something analogous to an active potency to God but not anything analogous to a passive potency that in us is grounded in our nature as finite creatures. Receptivity, as a passive potency proper to the imperfection of a creature, was thus not attributable to God, who is perfect.[125] Von Balthasar, however, takes a different tack and recognizes that receptivity is intrinsic to the perfection of the interpersonal relations within God. First, receptivity is implied in the trinitarian processions themselves: the Son and the

---

God of theo-dramatic action is neither 'mutable' (as in the mythological view) nor 'immutable' (in the terms of philosophy). We shall have to see, as the drama unfolds, how it is impossible for him to be either the one or the other" (*Theo-Drama II* 9).

[121]For Aquinas's treatment of the perfections see *ST* Ia. 4; for his treatment of divine immutability *ST* Ia. 9.

[122]*MP* 34.

[123]The question remains, however, as O'Hanlon comments, whether his solution is ultimately an obfuscation rather than a clarification. See O'Hanlon, *The Immutability of God* 135–136.

[124]I am indebted for this example to O'Hanlon, "Does God Change?" 170.

[125]See *ST* Ia. 3, 1; Ia. 4, 1 and 2; Ia. 20; Ia. 25, 1.

Holy Spirit receive their divine being. From this perspective to receive is clearly just as divine as to give. Even from the Father's perspective there is a sense in which the Father receives his being from the Son. Receptivity is also revealed as a divine perfection in Jesus' paschal mystery: he accomplishes his mission in obedience, in this way manifesting a passivity that is integral to and a modality of inner-trinitarian being. On the basis of these kinds of considerations it follows that we may attribute something analogous to receptivity as a perfection in God although it cannot be a passive potency as in us, for in God, there is no lack or deficiency of being. Hence by stressing the *positive* aspect of receptivity as an aspect of interpersonal love von Balthasar posits an *active* receptivity in God, who is love. He thus argues for a notion of God as *Actus Purus* in which, because of the revelation that God is love, God remains pure being, *Esse,* but the form of the divine activity is such that it may integrate passivity positively. In this way von Balthasar moves beyond traditional categories of potency and act within which receptivity, as a passive potency, is rejected as a divine attribute. As O'Hanlon notes, however, the question remains whether von Balthasar is finally coherent.[126] I will not undertake an evaluation of this aspect of von Balthasar's work. What is clear in any event is that such an understanding of the divine attributes needs to be inserted into a strong ontological framework if the problems inherent in such a strategy are to be averted. We shall later return to this issue.

In a similar way suffering, surprise, and increase, as perfections of love, can to be attributed to God in the carefully qualified manner of analogical discourse, which allows for similarity within an ever greater dissimilarity,[127] but grounded in the revelation that God is love. Von Balthasar also attributes "supra-kenosis" to God based on the revelation of God in the paschal mystery. Here too there is never any question of attributing any ontological negativity to God. Rather the *kenosis* revealed in paschal mystery and implied in the divine processions as aspects of inner-trinitarian love is attributed to God in a non-univocal way (and again this is the significance of the qualification "supra-").

Methodological observations

Von Balthasar's contribution to theological method is as remarkable as his contribution to trinitarian theology. His construction of a theological aesthetics and dramatic theory itself constitutes a significant and innovative contribution. A detailed consideration of these aspects of his work must, however, be set aside for another study. The following features emerge with significance for us at this stage.

---

[126]O'Hanlon, *The Immutability of God* 124.

[127]The Fourth Lateran Council expresses the necessary but limited nature of our language about God in terms of there being a greater dissimilarity than similarity between Creator and creature. (*DS* 806).

1. A reversal of the ordo doctrinae

In his insistence that theological reflection begin with perception, a be-holding of the "form" of God as revealed in the person of Jesus Christ, von Balthasar reverses the *ordo doctrinae* of Thomistic trinitarian theology and proceeds from a consideration of Jesus Christ in his paschal mystery to the inner-trinitarian relations and thence to the processions. Thus he moves from the paschal mystery to the mystery of the Trinity, from the economic to the immanent. The paschal mystery is recognized as the supreme revelation of the divine trinitarian life, actualizing trinitarian relationality in the economy.

2. A refashioning of trinitarian categories

One of the characteristic features of von Balthasar's work is what MacKinnon describes as "conceptual interpenetration." With this phrase he refers to the way von Balthasar "enables his readers to grasp an order in which they [Gospel concepts] are found so inseparable that indeed they interpene-trate one another."[128] Consider, for example, the Son's mission, his death and descent into hell, which is explored for the light it sheds on the person of the Son. Here we find a "conceptual interpenetration" of mission and person such that the meaning of each concept is profoundly affected by the other and in-deed cannot properly be considered without regard to the other. This "con-ceptual interpenetration" in von Balthasar's theology is further evidence of the depth and extent of the interconnection he makes between the paschal mys-tery and the mystery of the Trinity.

A thorough recasting and reprioritizing of the traditional trinitarian catego-ries results. Consider, for example, the category of mission that, as we have noted, emerges as a vital trinitarian category in von Balthasar's theology. Here it is the missions rather than the relations of origin in the immanent Trinity that play the predominant role in distinguishing the divine persons. The under-standing of mission is not, as it were, restricted to the economic realm. Although the notion of the mission as a projection of the divine reality into creation is certainly implicit in Aquinas's treatment von Balthasar takes the notion considerably farther, recognizing that the person *qua* person is revealed in the mission. In contrast to traditional trinitarian theology where relations of origin serve to express trinitarian relationality, in von Balthasar's theology the missions concretely express the persons and the relations. An understanding of the relations is thus subtly transposed into more dynamic terms. They are not merely relations of origin or subsistent relations in the immanent Trinity. They are relations of self-emptying kenotic love revealed and effected in the economy. The traditional understanding of the divine persons and their rela-tions is thus refashioned and rendered in a more dynamic fashion.

---

[128]MacKinnon, "Some Reflections on Hans Urs von Balthasar's Christology" 168.

Consider too von Balthasar's treatment of the trinitarian processions; he is very critical of the Latin tradition that accords primacy to the psychological analogy of the human mind and its acts of intellect and will. If there is to be a correspondence between the immanent and the economic Trinity, von Balthasar argues, and if the missions of the divine persons are the extension of their processions, then we must see both processions as processions of love. The Son is not only perfect image of the Father but perfect surrender and response in love. In this way von Balthasar breaks away from the Augustinian-Thomistic model and adopts something more akin to that of Richard of Saint Victor, although he does not uncritically adopt the Victorine model. Ultimately he finds both analogical approaches inadequate. He considers the intrasubjective psychological analogy of Augustinian-Thomistic theology so concentrated on the individual as to be guilty of a certain "I-centeredness" *(Ichgeschlossenheit)*[129] while the intersubjective model of love of Richard Saint Victor "fails to take into account the crude anthropomorphism involved in a plurality of beings."[130]

Throughout von Balthasar's theology we see a reworking of the traditional trinitarian categories into more dynamic, personalist, relational terms. The traditional theological categories of nature, essence, and substance are not rejected but transformed as they are resituated in the context of the paschal mystery and von Balthasar's ontology of love.

3. From metaphor to analogy: use of the full continuum of language in theology

What is particularly remarkable in von Balthasar's theology is that he operates within the full continuum of human speech about God ranging from the metaphorical and highly imaginative (controlled, he argues, within the ontological framework he establishes) to the more purely abstract and strictly analogical.[131] Admittedly the metaphorical approach alone is not sufficient because it risks ambiguity and misunderstanding. At the same time, though the use of analogy must be grounded in ontological foundations, theology must not be reduced to ontology alone. Otherwise theology loses its power to convey the personal and unique dimension of the mystery. Thus insisting that metaphor and not only analogy properly speaking is necessary for speech about God, von Balthasar *combines* abstract conceptual language with more metaphorical and image-laden terms in a complementary approach. Acknowledging the difference and the tension between the two modes of discourse, he

---

[129]*Theologik II. Die Wahrheit Gottes* (Einsiedeln: Johannes Verlag, 1985) 56. See O'Donnell, "The Form of His Theology" 466; also "The Trinity as Divine Community" 7.

[130]*Theo-Drama III* 527.

[131]See *MP* 246–249. For a discussion of this aspect of von Balthasar's work see O'Hanlon's *The Immutability of God* 137–144, and also O'Hanlon's "The Legacy of Hans Urs von Balthasar" 404–405.

attempts to achieve a mutually corrective differentiated combination of conceptual and metaphorical language. Indeed, he argues that his theological lin-
guistic approach involves a controlled use of imagery and metaphor that is
more faithful to the biblical data. His use of the terms "immutability" and
"supra-mutability" is an example of his combined conceptual and metaphorical approach. While immutability belongs to the more abstract, traditionally
ontological level of discourse, "supra-mutability" belongs to the metaphorical
level.

Von Balthasar's achievement here is to recognize the two levels of discourse and use both in a complementary and combined fashion. Admitting
their systematic irreconcilability and unavoidable imprecision, he argues that
this indeed serves a positive function in pointing to the transcendent mystery.
In other words he maintains that this intrinsic imprecision in his method is appropriate to the inherently partial nature of human knowledge in respect of the
abiding mystery and transcendence of God. However, as O'Hanlon comments
in regard to the term "supra-mutable," although the term does convey the mystery in a positive way it is nevertheless "linguistically artificial and of imprecise meaning."[132]

Imprecision and ambiguity are certainly problems, and more so as one approaches the metaphorical end of the speech continuum. Von Balthasar's metaphors are particularly at risk when transposed out of the context in which
they are used and in which they take their meaning, and outside of the ontology that supports and controls them. However, while prone to ambiguity,
von Balthasar's use of metaphor is richly evocative and, indeed, most apt to
the sheer beauty and glory of the mystery he wishes to convey. As McDade
comments: "In von Balthasar's hands, Catholic theology feels again the power
of symbol, metaphor and dramatic categories within a theology caught in the
tension between what *can* be said and what *must* be brought to expression."[133]
As we have seen in his captivating treatment of the descent von Balthasar's
metaphors are strong and resound with an extraordinary psychic resonance
that cannot be ignored. In their own powerful way they probe the very fron-
tiers of orthodoxy.

In each of the three authors whose work we have now examined we have
found a profound sense of the significance of the paschal mystery for trinitarian theology. Where Lafont effectively calls for a conversion to *hearing* the
founding narrative of the paschal mystery, von Balthasar calls for a conversion
to *seeing* Jesus as the "form," the *Gestalt* of God's triune love. However, unlike Lafont and in this respect more akin to Durrwell, von Balthasar sets the
traditional Thomistic approach aside and proposes a radical reversal of the traditional *ordo doctrinae* and a complete reconstitution of trinitarian theology.

[132]O'Hanlon, *The Immutability of God* 140.
[133]McDade, "Catholic Theology in the Post-Conciliar Period" 429.

Despite these authors' very different methods of approach considerable areas of convergence clearly emerge in their apprehension of trinitarian being. We turn now to Sebastian Moore. Where our three preceding authors have been concerned with an explication of divine subjectivity, Moore adopts an entirely different perspective and method: his concern is the human subject and the process of religious conversion.

CHAPTER FOUR

Sebastian Moore:
The Grass Roots Derivation of the Trinity

As we noted in our introduction, the inclusion of Sebastian Moore in our study may strike some readers as rather odd because his works would appear, at least at first glance, to have a somewhat flimsy character about them. Given the short volumes and sketchy chapters with little reference to other authors and no documentation, the lapidary sentences and the breaks into poetry, one is left with the impression of workbooks rather than fully developed theological investigations. Of interest to us here, however, is that he does treat the interconnection of these mysteries and moreover, in contrast to our previous authors, he adopts a very novel approach, addressing *human* subjectivity as distinct from *divine* intersubjectivity.

Moore is fundamentally concerned that traditional trinitarian theology fails to address the psychological dimensions of conversion and so does not mediate the transcendent to contemporary consciousness. He is convinced of the need for a *psychological* (as distinct from a metaphysical) mediation of the mystery. As he explains:

> It seems to me that a primary theological need in our time is for the psychological to mediate the transcendent. Until this comes about, the psychological dimension remains subjective, the transcendent dimension extrinsic. The perennial vigor of Christianity stems from a dangerous memory, of the experience of a group of people being brought to a crisis whose issue was such a freedom in face of our mortality as can only come from the transcendent ground of being. The psychological mediation of the transcendent is *remembered*.

. . . To be awakened at this level is to have one's answer to the common view that the Christian myth has lost its power.[1]

Hence Moore sets out to interpret the paschal mystery in distinctly psychological categories, thus to conduct what he himself describes as "a full psychological appropriation of the story of Jesus."[2] He approaches the interconnection with questions concerning the transformation of consciousness that Jesus' paschal mystery prompts: What psychological transformation occurs when a person affirms Jesus as God? Of what inner change is that belief the expression? How does it liberate and what does it liberate? How did the first believers know? What was the first knowing? In a programmatic passage he explains:

> The need for this psychological "adapter" for the story of Jesus becoming Christ, of a charismatic individual passing from addictive object to the self of humanity, is urgent at this time when the only really significant question concerns the motivation of people for those radical changes without which the human race and this planet will hardly survive. How is the necessary change of consciousness to come about? There are signs of it in many of today's movements. It is urgently necessary that psychological change be shown to the world as the self-disclosing of the ground of being, that the Paschal Mystery have restored to it, beyond all the strategies of a rhetoric now threadbare, its intellectual and psychological power.[3]

The nature and process of psychological change is Moore's interest, something quite unlike the concerns of our other authors in their more explicative analyses of the mystery of the Trinity, implicitly assuming as they do that one can in effect "see" directly the paschal mystery the scriptural narratives describe as an event in the realm of the divine. However, Moore's goal is clear. It is not to write a systematic statement on trinitarian theology but rather to mediate faith to contemporary culture in psychological terms. He seeks to identify at the level of "felt meaning" in human self-awareness and subjectivity what psychological transformation of the individual occurs in the event of religious conversion. He argues that "classical salvation doctrine has seen the drama of Jesus as played out in the sight of God. We have to see it as played out in the experience of the men and women it transformed and transforms in the presence of God."[4] The task is therefore to describe the process by which Jesus' story transforms our personal story, for theology, Moore explains, "is the making-contemporary of the drama of Jesus as the transforming of my

[1]*Jesus the Liberator of Desire* (New York: Crossroad, 1989) x.
[2]*The Fire and the Rose are One* (London: Darton, Longman & Todd, 1980) xiii.
[3]Moore, "Author's Response" in "Review Symposium: Sebastian Moore's *Jesus the Liberator of Desire*. Three perspectives by Stephen J. Duffy, Elisabeth Koenig and William P. Loewe," *Horizons* 18 (1991) 127–128.
[4]*The Inner Loneliness* (London: Darton, Longman & Todd, 1982) 116.

story, and being able to speak coherently about this transformation. For the great story is essentially the smaller-story transformer. That is how it is great."[5]

Concerned, therefore, to facilitate a change of consciousness, a religious conversion, in contemporary culture, Moore attempts a post-critical constructive return to the biblical narrative. The emphasis is on the experience and process of conversion itself that is actually taking place in the believer's consciousness, and that *precedes* the stage of explication of the mystery of the Trinity. Moore perceives that some extraordinary irruption of new meaning takes place in the believer's consciousness in the process of conversion, just as must have occurred for the very first Christians. He turns his attention to the disciples and their experience of Jesus' death and resurrection. Clearly they experienced some dramatic change of consciousness that led them, strict monotheists that they were, to proclaim that Jesus was Lord. Moore then sets out to give an account in psychological terms of the disciples' experience of salvation in Jesus Christ in his paschal mystery, in this way to identify and describe the "grass roots" experience of conversion from which issues the proclamation "Jesus is Lord."

Moore's theology does not make for easy reading. It is itself the fruit of an exercise in self-appropriation on Moore's part, an appropriation of his own conversion within the paschal mystery of Christ. It calls for a similar exercise in the reader. As Stephen Duffy comments:

> Reading Moore involves far more than gathering information or even arriving at a bloodless theoretical understanding. It is an exercise in self-appropriation. That is why reading him is a workout. It involves more than keenness. It demands self-awareness, and a level of it that is not for some easy to sustain. One not only has to read Moore but to discover oneself in oneself. His work has an Augustinian-Lutheran ring in that he too writes in the blood of his experience. Moore's workbooks challenge the reader to taste and see, for only by sounding one's own experience can one grasp the liberating, transforming power of the crucified.[6]

However this is precisely Moore's point. His approach is grounded in the fundamental insight that events occur for us in an existential sense when they are enacted in our consciousness. He rejects as a myth the notion that understanding is like taking a look, "seeing," and is instead convinced, on the basis of an appropriation of the dynamic of consciousness, that understanding emerges from consideration of all appropriate data, including the subjective data of consciousness in all their concreteness. Moore's task is thus to identify the psychological transformation that takes place in the process of religious conversion in order to facilitate that process in his readers.

---

[5] "Four Steps Towards Making Sense of Theology," *Downside Review* 111 (1993) 88.
[6] "Author's Response" 102.

Moore's resources:
narrative, psychology, and intentionality analysis

In his attempt to describe the psychological process of religious conversion and thus to identify the "grass roots" derivation of the Trinity Moore turns to the resources of narrative and psychology. However, his originality lies not in the appropriation of narrative or of psychology as such but rather in his application of Bernard Lonergan's method of intentionality analysis to both narrative and psychology. Moore thus situates his exploration of the experience of conversion within the framework of intentionality analysis and engages the categories of human interiority[7] together with those of psychology, particularly in relation to the affective dimension of subjectivity.

Bringing these resources to bear, Moore attempts a reconstruction of the disciples' original psychological experience of Jesus' death and resurrection, on which foundation the New Testament was built. Despite the controversial nature of such a construction Moore is surely correct at least in recognizing that some remarkable psychological experience freed the disciples to proclaim defiantly that Jesus is Lord. It is this extraordinary transformation of consciousness at the very beginning of Christian faith that Moore attempts to reclaim in order to find a meeting point between Christian faith and contemporary self-understanding. As he explains:

> We talk about the Trinity as though it were from the start a highly recondite doctrine for which we have to seek analogies at the human level. Actually, it is given to us from the start at the human level, in a form that already contains the clue for thinking about it in itself. . . . The Passion, Death and Resurrection of Jesus is the estuary in which this river branches out into the Trinitarian mystery of Jesus "at the right hand" of the Father, the Father dependent for his manifest meaning on Jesus, the Spirit the abundance of this to-each-other-ness of Father and Son "poured out in our hearts". The pedagogy of the Trinitarian mystery is perfect. Jesus in person carries us over from its human articulation . . . into the fullness of the economy of Father, Son and Spirit.[8]

Equipped with the resources of intentionality analysis and psychology, Moore thus returns to the Easter event and reconstructs the narrative of the disciples' experience. Given that he has scant explicit biblical evidence on which to base his reconstruction it is, in this sense, a highly speculative enterprise. Moore, aware of his boldness, comments on his work: "I have dared

---

[7]In Bernard Lonergan's terms interiority is that realm in which, in a heightening of intentional consciousness, one attends not merely to objects but also to the intending subject and his or her acts. In this realm as distinct from the realms of common sense and theory one appropriates "one's own interiority, one's subjectivity, one's operations, their structure, their norms, their potentialities" (*Method in Theology* [New York: Seabury, 1972] 83).

[8]"Four Steps Towards Making Sense of Theology" 79.

to surmise how the human psyche, at the beginning of our era, was shocked into a bliss of which God alone could be the author and from which, thank God, it will never recover."[9] Needless to say, such a project is highly prone to misunderstanding. A sound grasp of its meaning and significance requires that it be correctly located methodologically. We move now to situate his project in relation to the tradition of theology and the development in theological method, in order to highlight its methodological import.

Theology in "the third stage of meaning"

Moore himself situates his theological project in its historical context, demonstrating an acute methodological consciousness.[10] We summarize his brief description of the stages of theological development as understood from the perspective of intentionality analysis:[11]

In the first stage of consciousness the mediated immediacy of the transcendent mystery in religious experience finds expression in symbols, images, and the narrative extension of symbol in myth. This is because the transcendent mystery is related to human consciousness as the ultimate value that grounds all other values and the presence of value generally first registers in the realm of affectivity. The apostolic and patristic eras correspond to this stage of mediation of religious meaning. But a problem inevitably arises with this symbolic discourse and prompts a shift into a second stage of meaning. Because it is bound to the dynamics of affectivity, symbolic mediation of meaning is inherently ambiguous and calls for clarification and definition. Medieval theology developed precisely in response to this challenge. It arose in reply to questions that demanded a coherent and systematic mediation of the intelligibility of the Christian story. Its mediation of religious meaning is theoretic, not symbolic, in character. However another problem subsequently arises, prompting a further shift into a third stage of meaning. The world of theory stands in stark contrast with the ordinary world of religious experience and the undifferentiated mind finds such theoretic mediation of the transcendent abstract and even unintelligible. An existential concern inevitably surfaces, calling for a further transposition in the mediation of meaning: What does the Christian story mean "for me"? or, in Moore's words, what does it mean for human self-awareness? Traditional Latin theology in a theoretic mode offers no obvious answer to these sorts of questions. Its metaphysical mode is non-psychological. Yet in fact these are the kinds of questions being asked today. They concern the human subject, human experience, and the manner in which things come to be known. A further transposition

---

[9]*The Fire and the Rose are One* 108.

[10]Ibid. 3–4. See also William P. Loewe, "Encountering the Crucified God: The Soteriology of Sebastian Moore," *Horizons* 9 (1982) 221–225.

[11]Note that Moore follows Lonergan's methodology. See Lonergan, *Method in Theology*.

of mediation into a third stage of meaning is required in order to answer them and thus to meet the contemporary concern for existential and personal meaning.

Moore is thus well aware of where he stands in the theological tradition and its attempt to mediate the transcendent. His is not a repetition of or pre-critical return to the symbolic discourse of the first stage of consciousness, nor does he seek to employ metaphysics in an objective theory to express and control the intelligibility of Christian faith, as occurs in the second stage of meaning. In other words, he is not merely supplementing traditional dogmatic theology or replacing systematics. His concern is the fundamental derivation of Christian doctrines in order to refresh their meanings in an experiential way, so to reorient modern consciousness toward religious conversion. In terms of Lonergan's analysis of the stages of meaning that define the tasks of theology[12] Moore's work is an example of theology in "the third stage of meaning." This new stage corresponds to the specific exigencies of contemporary culture in which the shift from classical to historical consciousness, the turn to the subject, demands an axial shift beyond the metaphysical mediation of classical theology and calls for a critical grounding of theology in the world of human interiority. The question is no longer what is the story *per se,* nor is it a question of what the story means in terms of the rational mind. The question at this point is what does the story mean in terms of human subjectivity. Hence Moore turns to the realm of human interiority for the meaning of Christian revelation for human self-awareness and sketches a structure of Christian conversion that is more apt to appeal to modern consciousness. As his work amply demonstrates, the shift from theory to interiority occasions a very new appreciation of the data of revelation and indeed of what constitutes and qualifies as data.

In this third stage of meaning a renewed Christian systematics is grounded not in theory, as in medieval theology, but in interiority. Interiority is therefore not just a supplement (as for example it effectively was in Augustine's elaboration of various psychological analogies): it is the very foundation of theology.[13] The theological task in this stage is to describe the transformation that occurs in the realm of consciousness. Moore's project, addressing what conversion means in terms of the transformation of existential self-awareness, exemplifies theology in this new stage of meaning.

The disciples' pre-paschal experience

Moore's understanding of the psychological process of religious conversion hinges on a reconstruction of the disciples' experience of Jesus' paschal mys-

---

[12]Lonergan, *Method in Theology* 81–90.
[13]Ibid. 83, 85.

tery, which he explores in *The Fire and the Rose are One*[14] and to which we now turn our attention. In an imaginative reconstruction of their experience he claims to shape a theological construct in which to retell the original story of Jesus "no longer in terms of myths, no longer in terms of its rational implications, no longer in terms of different human experiences, but as the story of the real self in all people."[15] He discerns that a massive psychological displacement accompanied the disciples' encounter with Jesus crucified and risen that opened them to the revelation of the triune God. Recognizing that their experience is foundational for the theological search for christological and soteriological meaning, Moore traces the psychological stages through which the trinitarian differentiation of God's being is revealed in the disciples' consciousness. What has been forgotten and must be reclaimed, he insists, is that the formulation that God is Trinity is the intellectual recognition of the original psychologically and spiritually revolutionary experience of the disciples it radically transformed. It is that original experience that Moore seeks to recover: this is the remarkable originality of his project.

Before proceeding to consider Moore's reconstruction of the disciples' *paschal* experience we must, however, first refer to Moore's understanding of the disciples' *pre-paschal* experience, for only on that basis can Moore give full weight to what happened later in Jesus' death and resurrection and its trinitarian implications. Moore describes their pre-paschal experience in terms of desire. Indeed the religious significance and dynamic finality of desire are central in Moore's anthropology and theology.[16] He proposes that the human person may be defined through desire, a desire to be oneself for another. In its deepest form this desire is religious: it is at base a desire for God. The true human self, Moore therefore maintains, is relationship to and natural desire for the incomprehensible mystery.[17] Thus Moore understands the pre-paschal experience of the disciples in terms of a pre-religious desire for God, that was then awakened in them by Jesus. However, at the same time he recognizes that their pre-paschal understanding of God is also shaped by guilt, which conceives the infinite in terms of infinite power over and against human weakness.

---

[14]The exploration by means of reflection on the experience of the persecutors of Jesus that guided Moore's earlier book, *The Crucified is No Stranger* (London: Darton, Longman & Todd, 1977), is retracted. See "Retraction 3" in *The Fire and the Rose are One* 140–147. For this reason we have chosen not to bring *The Crucified is No Stranger* into our present study. It is interesting to note that the more generalized notions of God and the self in the earlier work are replaced by far more differentiated trinitarian and paschal categories in *The Fire and the Rose are One*.

[15]*The Fire and the Rose are One* 4.

[16]Janice Daurio suggests that "the work of Sebastian Moore might be called a theology of desire" ("Toward a Theology of Desire: The Existential Hermeneutic in the Soteriology of Sebastian Moore," *Downside Review* 106 [1988] 195).

[17]This in itself is not a new insight: it corresponds to the natural desire to see God in classic Thomistic anthropology: *ST* Ia 2ae. 1–5. What is innovative in this first step is that Moore offers a description of this consciousness in phenomenological terms.

Guilt sees God in terms of power, jealous and dominating. Moreover it is resentful of this inequality between Creator and creature. It is from this guilt that the disciples need to be liberated in order to arrive at an understanding that God's power is not the power of domination but rather the all-powerful weakness of self-giving love.

The three-stage dialectic of the disciples' paschal experience[18]

In his reconstruction of the disciples' paschal experience Moore describes the process of psychological displacement that occasions the event in their consciousness of the revelation of the Trinity in terms of three stages of awakening, desolation, and transformation of desire.

1. First stage: awakening of desire

In their encounter with Jesus the disciples initially experience ecstasy, unspeakable joy in the company of this man who himself lived totally from a radical desire unburdened by sin and guilt. In this stage of lyric joy their hearts are stirred, their hopes aroused, their desire awakened as Jesus releases their boundless desire undistorted by guilt. In him they catch the contagion of a person free from sin, free from the guilt that put a debilitating brake on their desire for God. From him they catch a sense of God not as remote and enigmatic, to be invoked in a distant and formal way, but as loving presence.

A new sense of self is implied in this experience. It is a self at ease with God, a self liberated from guilt projections and shadows. However at the same time this self finds in Jesus an addictive object. As such, it is a self that is exposed and vulnerable to death. This self will die when Jesus dies. This self will be inconsolable if Jesus fails. In this sense this new experience of self is essentially ambiguous. The corollary of their experience of Jesus at this stage of lyric joy is that if Jesus were to fail, if this God were to prove powerless, then God too would effectively "die." Should Jesus be buried, God too would be "buried." There would certainly be no returning to the traditional God should this new, life-giving God present in Jesus prove in the end to be ineffectual. Should the Jesus movement fail and Jesus die the disciples would experience a despair that only God could dispel. In that event if God were to be "real" then God would have to give Jesus back in the form of new life and existence.

---

[18]*The Fire and the Rose are One* 80–87. See also "For a Soteriology of the Existential Subject" in Matthew Lamb, ed., *Creativity and Method: Essays in Honor of Bernard Lonergan, S.J.* (Milwaukee: Marquette University Press, 1981) 229–247.

2. Second stage: desolation

Jesus was in fact crucified. This initial period of ecstasy came to a hideous conclusion with the failure of his mission and his death on the cross. The disciples were left in confusion and shame. With his death the desire that had been brought to life by him itself experienced a mortal crisis. The disciples were plunged into despair and desolation, their hopes dashed and their hearts numbed in deathly silence. Because of the unique person Jesus was, his interaction with his disciples during his time with them before his death produced a unique effect in them and correspondingly his death produced a unique crisis. Having awakened their desire in them he perforce became the focus of their desire. With his death they suffered a crisis of desire. In this sense his death was their death. Their desire was plunged into emptiness.

So great was their desolation that the experience was psychologically registered as more like the death of God than God's mere absence—and Moore emphasizes that it was the death of "the real God, the God that Jesus lived by and lived for."[19] However it was also the death of the shadow-God, that all-powerful and demanding God of their guilt-ridden projections. However, the death of this God brought their resentment of God and of God's all-powerful life to an end. With that obstacle thus overcome a radically new possibility of hearing the word of God as love arises.

3. Third stage: transformation of desire

In the experience of total desolation and of a despair that only God could dispel they were made ready for this new breakthrough. Indeed only such an experience in which utterly everything is lost could have readied them for it. In the resurrection the disciples were then revived from their spiritual collapse by their encounter with the risen Jesus. It was the moment of conversion, dissolution of guilt, and a sense of superabundance of new life. They felt alive again, alive as never before. In that encounter they experienced a radical transformation of desire. The risen Jesus, reawakening and reaffirming their desire, became present to them as the liberator of their desire. Having awakened their desire during his life, then become its focus, now in his death and resurrection he transformed it and liberated it for its properly infinite object. Moore summarizes the process:

> Still this desire, while feeling its infinity, was necessarily channelled into the finite Jesus, its awakener. At the climax of the story, the channel is destroyed, to produce a death of ego in which *everything* is lost. With the risen Jesus, desire infinite in its essence becomes infinite in its exercise. Desire is liberated, becomes itself. This is why the Risen One is invisible, partakes of

[19]"For a Soteriology of the Existential Subject" 246.

the invisibility of God known in the Spirit. Resurrection is the liberation of desire.[20]

The resurrection is thus the explosive *dénouement* that pulls the disciples beyond the limits of their pre-paschal existence. Their desiring selves are liberated for the infinite ground and object of their desire.[21] Through Jesus' death and resurrection their desire is brought beyond death, into the mystery of God. Just as Jesus "buried" God for them he now makes God alive for them. He himself becomes the center of a new God-consciousness for them, as Moore explains: "In other words, the first believers experienced a re-centring of their God-consciousness. Psychologically there was a displacement of divinity from the old God whom guilt kept remote and overpowering, into Jesus. I am convinced that the root of Christianity's subsequently *formulated* belief in the Godhead of Jesus is here, in this first experience of him as 'what it felt like for their God to be alive again, and alive as never before.'"[22]

In this way the disciples' encounter with the risen Jesus caused a psychological displacement of divinity from the "old God" to the risen Lord. In reality the displacement of divinity was actually an extension of divinity. This monumental shift in consciousness was soon followed by the emergence of a larger trinitarian pattern.

The grass roots derivation of the Trinity

Moore also explores the process by which the trinitarian pattern dawns in the disciples' consciousness. The reappearance of Jesus was the birth of a new spiritual vitality of an astonishing kind. His death, in a sense, was their death. Now, with Jesus newly alive, the disciples too are newly alive, transformed by him. Risen from the dead, Jesus does what only God could do. Because of the vividness of the encounter with the risen Jesus and the experience of the death of God that preceded that encounter the first form of their experience of the resurrection was more like a *displacement* than an *extension* of divinity. In other words, in their encounter with Jesus newly alive they experienced God *in* Jesus. The old God, the God sealed off by guilt and now "dead" was effectively displaced. Jesus himself became for them the center of a new God-consciousness, "the next divine affective focus"[23] of their experience. In this way the first believers experienced a *re-centering* of their God-consciousness. Psychologically they experienced a displacement of divinity from the pre-paschal God into Jesus. The risen Jesus became the focus of a new liberated

---

[20]"Jesus the Liberator of Desire: Reclaiming Ancient Images," *Cross Currents* 40 (1990) 497.
[21]See also "Death as the Delimiting of Desire: A Key Concept in Soteriology" in Steven Kepnes and David Tracy, eds., *The Challenge of Psychology to Faith* (New York: Seabury, 1982) 51–56.
[22]*The Fire and the Rose are One* 81–82.
[23]Ibid. 83.

God-connection. In proclaiming Jesus as Lord they were giving expression to this new religious consciousness.

However, Moore explains that very soon the original God re-emerged, and wonderfully so. The Father who had "died" was now seen to have declared his love for us by enacting it in raising Jesus. The disciples then experienced the original God not as remote and overpowering but as loving and life-giving. Thus the initial displacement of divinity was now experienced instead as an *extension* of divinity from God to Jesus. As a fuller trinitarian picture emerged the initial sense of displacement of divinity into Jesus remained as the divinity of Jesus.

In addition, closely connected with their experience of Jesus as Lord was the experience, in a third resurrection shock wave, of the Holy Spirit as the other power center for the disciples' new experience of divinity, the "cyclic life-flow" between Father and Son. A vital conviction that the oneness of the Father and the Son, the Holy Spirit, is itself personal dawned in their consciousness. In what Moore describes as a further "extension of the divinity" the Holy Spirit emerged as the personal connection of the Father and the Son. The trinitarian differentiation within the Godhead is thus finally established in their consciousness:

> With this, the pattern becomes cyclic, a system, a flow of life between Father and Son through the Spirit. The three stages of shock-waves of the Resurrection encounter are thus these: displacement, extension, cyclic life-flow. . . . Thus the matrix of the images of the divine persons is the "infinite connection" as it undergoes the transformation of the encounter with the risen Jesus. The pre-religious concentration of divine energy takes, under the pressure of this encounter, the shape of Father, Son and Spirit.[24]

In this way Moore locates the "grass-roots derivation of the Trinity" in the process of psychological transformation the disciples experienced in the paschal mystery of Jesus' death and resurrection. Their paschal experience culminates in the revelation of the Father and the Son in the unity of the Spirit. Later this new consciousness would be articulated in the doctrine of the Trinity. Again Moore emphasizes that this "grass-roots derivation of the Trinity" depends on an understanding of our pre-paschal God-connection. That prior understanding of "God" is shaped by a person's psychological state of guilt. Guilt sees God as powerful, fearful, and dominating. The God of their guilt dies with the death of Jesus and the collapse of the Jesus movement. In the resurrection, liberated from guilt and guilt-projections, they experience the manifestation of God not as power but as love. However it is *only* then that God, as threefold differentiated love, can emerge in their consciousness:

> The attribution of divinity to Jesus comes from the deepest reaches of human consciousness when the love therein has been set free from guilt. Of this new

[24]Ibid. 83–84.

> liberated God-connection, Jesus is the focus. That is why "Jesus is Lord" is
> the rallying-cry, the "logo", of the liberated. "Jesus is Lord" is the expres-
> sion of a consciousness of God as purely generous and life-giving, a con-
> sciousness of God as ultimate yet not "Master", a consciousness of God as
> love and nothing else.[25]

Liberated from guilt, in the God encountered in the risen Jesus they experience God as love that is stronger even than death. Infinite power then reveals
itself as infinite love, and when the psyche perceives the infinite mystery as
love, not as power, everything changes. The religious psyche is radically
transformed. Only after the resurrection can the crucifixion be understood as
an act of love. The catastrophe of the cross and the failure of the Jesus movement make way for an understanding of the transforming event as the act of
God who is love: "The love that transforms is not the attitude of Jesus to the
disciples, regarded as *representing* the attitude of God, but is the loving presence of the infinite Mystery itself, its death a wonderful act of the lover's def-
erence to man who prior to this revelation could not contemplate God without
guilt."[26]

God is thus revealed in the depths of the disciples' consciousness not as absolute power, but as absolute love. At that very moment when the disciples are
floundering in the bewildering experience of God's weakness—because it is
only possible at that precise moment of utter desolation—God is revealed as
infinite love.

The conciliar formulation: experience brought to the bar of logic[27]

Moore recognizes that this liberation of desire and the revelation of the
threefold differentiation in God the disciples experienced in the death and resurrection of Jesus were inevitably to be brought to the bar of logic. This occurred at the Council of Nicea, which with amazing objectivity accepted the
realism that Jesus Christ was God. It was a case of accepting an unavoidable
judgment in spite of the difficulties it posed, as Moore explains: "The bottom
line of Nicaea was that Jesus had done for us what only God could do, had
given us what only God could give, and therefore had to be God, whatever the
awesome problems created by such an equation in the intellectual world."[28]

Moore identifies the Nicene proclamation as the intellectual recognition of
the original psychologically and spiritually revolutionary experience and thus
describes the conciliar formulation as "the appropriate witness of the intellect
to this liberation of the heart."[29] The doctrinal statement is the indispensable

[25]Ibid. 95.
[26]Ibid. 119.
[27]Ibid. 91, 94–96, 114.
[28]Ibid. 91.
[29]Ibid. xiv.

logical note to a belief whose substance is the disciples' experience of the risen Jesus in the Spirit. It represents the stark exigencies of belief in Jesus when brought to the bar of logic.

In his exploration of the emergence of the conciliar formulations Moore thus separates a consideration of the experiential meaning of Christianity's central belief in the Trinity from the conceptual structure in which the early councils expressed it. The correctness of the conciliar conceptual structure is not in question. However, doctrinal statements, and similarly classical trinitarian theology, are methodologically situated in terms of the exigencies of consciousness and culture. Their deficiencies are then understood in terms of cultural change, a shift in consciousness, and the need to respond to new exigencies and the emergence of a new kind of concern for meaning.

Turning then to contemporary culture Moore recognizes that now, as in the past, the question of Jesus' divinity continues to challenge the mind of the questioner, but that today theology faces a new question in terms of experience. In this way Moore diagnoses the need for a further transposition of Christian meaning in response to a new God-consciousness, as he explains:

> Whereas at the time of Nicaea those resources were centred in inquiry into the nature of the real, today they are centred in the exploration of human experience. There are many signs that this exploration is reaching a point where we ask: "How does human experience, in all its psychic depth, reflect objective reality?" . . . In other words, a new God-consciousness, a new trembling of consciousness in the presence of its constituting mystery, may be trying to be born. This may be the reason why the christological question, always an accurate barometer of changing culture, is beginning to be: "What conceivably could be that experience of God which would have to express itself in the words 'Jesus is God'?"[30]

Moore himself thus attempts a new expression of meaning that is more appropriate and meaningful to contemporary consciousness. Transposing the intelligibility of the trinitarian dogma from the terms of scholastic metaphysical analysis into the realm of interiority in order to meet the demands of the modern turn to the subject and its concern to ground truth in human experience, he attempts to address precisely the question of what conceivably could be that experience of God that would have to express itself in the words "Jesus is God." The conciliar formulae are not set aside; they are *complemented* in this way in order to communicate the mystery to contemporary consciousness.

Classical trinitarian theology as dogmatized mystical experience

Moore clearly intends his work as a complement, not a substitute, for the theoretic mediation of classical theology. When he does turn to consider

[30]Ibid. 132.

divine subjectivity—trinitarian theology as such—he does not set aside the
traditional explication of the immanent processions in terms of the classical
psychological analogy. In *The Inner Loneliness* Moore's reflection on human
self-awareness leads him to a retrieval of Aquinas's understanding of God as
Ipsum Esse Subsistens and its transposition into a distinctly experiential key.[31]
Moore argues that from this perspective Aquinas's analogy of the Trinity
proves to be surprisingly relevant.

Again, methodologically he separates a consideration of the experience
from its explication in a conceptual structure: the classical explanation of the
mystery thus emerges as "dogmatized mystical experience."[32] Hence he explores the Trinity in terms of the traditional categories of self-understanding
of the conscious being: knowing and loving. The eternal process of self-
affirming in self-love emerges as the structure of the all-originating mystery
of God, so he can write: "Thus the Trinity is the way it is because God is God.
Because God is the original mystery whence is all reality, knowing and loving which for us *reflect* reality *originate* for God. The divine 'processions' are
these originatings, these arisings, out of the depths of the divine nature, of that
knowing and loving which for us finite beings are ultimate and not derived
realities."[33]

Moore concludes that "the Trinity *is* the divine nature."[34] He argues that it
is the failure to perceive this that leads to the dichotomy between the Trinity
and the divine nature, resulting in a confusion whereby the Trinity is the
highly mysterious "inner life of God," somehow behind the divine nature.
However, the inner life of God in this sense is meaningless: "The 'mystery' of
the Trinity comes to mean 'how there applies in God an oversimplified and
lifeless model of knowing and loving.'"[35] Instead, the Trinity is the very mystery of the Godhead in its transcendence of knowing and loving. Knowing and
loving are the structure of God's reality, which *is* reality.

In taking up the classical psychological image Moore transposes it into a
distinctly psychological frame of reference. The Thomistic metaphysical
analysis of the faculties of intellect and will is replaced by an intentionality
analysis in terms of consciousness. Again interiority is not merely supplement
but foundation. Psychological categories are not just introduced in a somewhat extrinsic way but fully appropriated.

We note, however, that when Moore does come to a consideration of the
mystery of the Trinity categories drawn from the paschal mystery do not feature. While the paschal mystery provides the existential dynamic by which the
disciples' consciousness is transformed, the classical psychological analogy
shapes his understanding of the processes of subjectivity. Moore thus assumes

[31]*The Inner Loneliness* 103–114.
[32]Ibid. 103–109.
[33]Ibid. 113.
[34]Ibid.
[35]Ibid. 114.

the traditional treatment of divine subjectivity. He writes: "this statement [that God *is* knowledge and love], far from defining God as linguistically it appears to do, goes in the reverse direction, of making us wonder whether we know what knowing and loving are. This statement about the unknown, that it *is* knowing and loving, backfires onto what we took to be known, knowing and loving."[36]

Thus Moore almost reverses the traditional analogical procedure and applies an understanding of the Trinity as an eternal process of self-affirming in self-love to the human subject. The end point of his trinitarian theology, brief though it is, coincides with the end point of theological anthropology. Under the impulse of trinitarian belief Moore is thrown more deeply into the mystery of our own self-awareness.

The role of the paschal mystery in Moore's theology

We see that Moore's theological project is quite different from that of our other authors. Unlike them he recognizes that the problem with traditional trinitarian theology is not that it is expressed in terms of the psychological analogy or that it is removed from the biblical data as such but rather that it does not address the psychological dimension of conversion and so is not expressed in a way that is meaningful to contemporary understanding. Moore is not primarily concerned with an explication of trinitarian theology in terms, say, of the processions, the relations, the persons, the missions, nor does he address the question of the relationship between the immanent and economic Trinity. Rather he acknowledges the essential rightness of the conciliar statements and classical formulations. However, recognizing that sin and redemption are not just theological but deeply psychological realities, he attempts to transpose the classical statements of trinitarian theology into appropriately psychological terms. What is striking is that his effort to transpose the classical trinitarian doctrine gives him occasion to link the Trinity with the paschal mystery, prompting him to reclaim the original experience on which the doctrine is ultimately based.

Though Moore's theology is undoubtedly focused on the paschal mystery his attention is not directed toward the divine Three but rather to the disciples' experience. In effect Moore fixes his attention on a very different point of the paschal narrative: the disciples themselves and their experience of a transformation of consciousness and the irruption of new meaning. The paschal mystery emerges as the psychological pattern through which their consciousness is utterly transformed. While the paschal mystery provides the dynamic of displacement, extension, and cyclic life-flow, the classical psychological analogy remains as the determining feature in his properly trinitarian thinking; indeed

[36]Ibid. 110.

it remains as the primary image of trinitarian being in Moore's theology. In a way that is reminiscent of Augustine, Moore describes self-awareness as "the trace or vestige of God."[37] It is the process of subjectivity, not Jesus in his paschal mystery, that serves as the essential analogy for the Trinity. The paschal mystery and the trinitarian relations it discloses do not serve to provide categories for a trinitarian theology as such.

Assessment of gains for trinitarian theology

Despite our initial hesitation about including Moore's work in our study his attempt to reclaim the original experience out of which the New Testament was created and so to unlock the meaning of Jesus' paschal mystery by way of psychological mediation of the mystery is manifestly an original and creative contribution to contemporary theology. In the disciples' experience of Jesus' paschal mystery Moore finds the experiential ground for the proclamation that God is Father, Son, and Holy Spirit, and the later theoretical transposition of that experience into trinitarian doctrine. The result is a highly evocative and imaginative theological construction, one that is consciously designed to evoke a psychological appropriation of Christian faith in its readers.

There is no doubt that Moore's work is deeply informed by the classical doctrines. The originality of his contribution lies in his effort to re-express the meaning of Christian faith in a modern cultural context, marrying the emphasis on human experience of contemporary theological anthropology with the basic insights of classical theology. Traditional trinitarian theology is assumed but the foundation shifts from objective theory as such to the subjectivity of the conscious self. The metaphysical categories of faculty psychology give way to self-awareness of the human subject in terms of knowing and loving as the classical psychological image is taken up and transposed into a more experiential key. Note again that interiority is no mere supplement but the foundation of Moore's theology.

Predictably Moore's highly creative psycho-historical reconstruction of the disciples' experience of Jesus' paschal mystery has drawn a good measure of comment and criticism.[38] Methodologically the psycho-historical reconstruction remains problematic. As his critics are not slow to remark, Moore's reconstruction is based on a minimum of scriptural data. It is in effect a highly imaginative projection onto the biblical data. Stephen Duffy among others takes issue with Moore at the level of the "knowability" of the experience of the disciples. Duffy comments: "His reconstruction, while appealing, even ingenious, appears a conjectural and skewed extrapolation of his second order

[37]*The Fire and the Rose are One* 120.
[38]See "Review Symposium: Sebastian Moore's *Jesus the Liberator of Desire,*" *Horizons* 18 (1991) 93–123.

psychological appropriation of the Easter story."[39] The reconstruction as such has little explicit warrant from the New Testament sources. The obscure is explained by the more obscure, Duffy comments. Are the disciples' Easter experiences too elusive a mooring? Duffy asks. Yet as Moore's critics, including Duffy, admit, spiritually and emotionally Moore may indeed know something about the disciples through the resonance with his own experience and what he draws from the mystical tradition.

On one level Duffy's criticism is valid, yet we must ask whether he gives full weight to the realm of interiority within which Moore works, so missing the essential point of the construction. Moore is not concerned simply with the scriptural data but with the subjective experience of the transformation and emergence of the self. For Moore, following Lonergan, "objectivity is simply the consequence of authentic subjectivity."[40] In other words objectivity resides not in the data but in the authentic self-transcending subject attending to the data. The authentic self-transcending subject in question is Moore himself. His reconstruction is thus founded on the basis of an appropriation of his own experience of conversion in the paschal mystery. That is "the upper blade" with which Moore reads the data of the scriptural narratives and builds his contemporary theological reconstruction of the disciples' paschal experience.

William Loewe on the other hand describes Moore's retelling of the story of the disciples' experience as "a theological construct, a distinctly contemporary narrative informed by both modern psychology and also very markedly by the classical mystical tradition. In forging such a narrative Moore stands quite directly in the tradition of the gospel writers themselves."[41] However, the comparison Loewe draws between Moore and the gospel writers obfuscates rather than clarifies the matter. It fails to advert to the fact that Moore is operating in a quite different stage of meaning than the gospel writers. They operate in the realm of meaning whereby the transcendent is mediated through narrative and symbolic discourse. Moore operates in the realm of interiority. His is no naïve or precritical return to a narrative form of theology but rather a postcritical retrieval that cannot simply be equated with the work of the gospel writers. Moore's postcritical religious consciousness is quite different from the consciousness that produced the gospels even if the phenomenon of "conversion" is common to both, indeed even though they share the common goal of mediating religious meaning to their respective contemporary consciousnesses.

Admittedly Moore's methodology has its problems. His theology is anthropocentric and narrowly western. It is fragmentary, sketchily developed, in many ways written for the converted or those on the very edge of religious conversion. It actually pays little attention to the actual scriptural data about the Three. Its terminology is loose. The psychological categories seem rather

[39]Ibid. 105.
[40]Bernard Lonergan, *Method in Theology* 265.
[41]"Review Symposium" 123.

"soft" and call for further development and refinement. Control of meaning is clearly a problem in Moore's theology. There is a "looseness" and "softness" in the construction that invites justifiable criticism and calls for a more critical grounding and a greater depth of conceptual clarity in his work.

Despite these problems Moore, I believe, enjoys a considerable measure of success in attempting to render the dynamics of conversion and to retrieve the experiential component so drastically attenuated in the classical formulations. His reconstruction of the disciples' experience, admittedly based more on a generalized notion of the religious psyche than on data explicitly drawn from the New Testament, results in a symbolically and emotionally plausible account of the dynamic of the believer's personal transformation and conversion to Jesus as Lord even as it moves far beyond any metaphysically-fashioned theology. In agreement with Duffy I consider that despite its problems the reconstruction is heuristically most valuable in achieving its goal.[42]

Methodological observations: a shift to interiority as foundation

While admitting some problems we may still ask what methodological shifts Moore effects. First we should emphasize again that his starting point is not the biblical data strictly speaking; it is rather an intentionality analysis of human subjectivity together with a psychologically informed analysis of the human situation. Moore only then turns to the biblical data for verification of the structure of conversion in the effect of Jesus' life, death, and resurrection on the disciples. His aim is to speak coherently not so much about what they came to proclaim as how they came to know what they then proclaimed as true. The basic categories are therefore those of intentionality. In this sense the biblical data come in second place in Moore's theology. The primary datum in his retrieval of the "grass-roots derivation of the Trinity" is the actual experience of the disciples on which the biblical data are based, which is reconstructed on the basis of his own self-appropriation. It is this that lies "behind" the text, chronologically and logically prior to it. The biblical text itself is in some measure second-order, based on that original experience of transformation.

In shifting foundations from metaphysical theory to interiority Moore certainly issues a challenge to traditional theological method. Negatively he challenges, at least implicitly, any theology that would proceed as if the structures of interiority did not exist. Positively Moore challenges traditional theological method to respond to the specific exigencies and existential concerns of contemporary culture in order to mediate the transcendent to it. The implications for the way in which the theological task is envisaged are considerable. To repeat, it is not that the theological method of classical tradition is repudiated; rather traditional theological method is recognized as no longer appropriate or adequate to the demands of modern consciousness. In Moore's theology the

[42]Ibid. 111.

paschal mystery and the Trinity thus come together in a way that poses critical questions for the prevailing systematic theological tradition.

What we see in Moore's work is what he himself describes as a challenge to traditional theological method, the demand that theology be "authentically autobiographical."[43] It is to become *biographical* in the sense that the task of theology in the third stage of meaning is to understand and mediate the way in which the story of Jesus interacts with and liberates the story of the person it thus converts. It becomes *autobiographical* in the sense that the process necessarily begins with and is grounded in the theologian's own self-appropriation. The evidence proper to systematic theology is only accessible to the degree that the theologian has been converted. The foundational thus grounds the doctrinal and the systematic. Moore explains: "Systematic theology only begins when the theologian has been converted, and being converted to Christ is nothing else than allowing my story to be opened up and to flower in the Jesus story. To be a theologian is to thematize, to explicate, this event, that cries out with the psalmist *'Dilatasti cor meum.'* Thus theology is far more than finding new words for old."[44]

Moore, like Lafont, recognizes that narrative theology is not enough to mediate Christian faith to modern consciousness.[45] However, unlike Lafont, Moore also recognizes that a theoretical way of speaking about the mystery that comes, as it were "from the outside" is also inadequate. There is no going back on the turn to the subject. Rather, in the third stage of meaning the initial dramatic-historical stage of mediation and the later theoretical stage of mediation are appropriated as phases in the one process of self-appropriation of the mystery of our salvation. They are taken up into the realm of interiority where theology becomes profoundly autobiographical, where the theological task consists in cultivating and expressing a sense for "my story resonating the saving story of Jesus."

In conclusion we could describe this theology as a subject-conscious, subject-centered, personal theology. David Tracy, in the fly-leaf, describes Moore's work as a "spiritual theology." Moore retorts: "I wish people wouldn't call this stuff spiritual theology. It is a somewhat gauche attempt to do real theology in a world whose intellectual climate is still divorced from feeling."[46] Undoubtedly Moore's theology is much more than merely a spiritual theology; it is a genuine attempt to heal the schism between the existential and the theoretical in theology, the fruit of a refined methodological awareness of the dynamics of consciousness, expressed with literary skill.

[43]Moore, "Four Steps Towards Making Sense of Theology" 87.
[44]Ibid. 88.
[45]Ibid. 89.
[46]Ibid. 81.

CHAPTER FIVE

Thematic Gains for Trinitarian Theology

After examining the role of the paschal mystery in the trinitarian theologies of Durrwell, Lafont, von Balthasar, and Moore, we are now prepared to pose the question: how does this new development compare with the traditional explication of the mystery of the Trinity, in particular the Augustinian-Thomistic paradigm? In the Introduction I observed that in privileging the psychological analogy the Augustinian-Thomistic treatment holds itself relatively remote from the concrete events of salvation history. Indeed, Karl Rahner commented rather provocatively that psychological speculation in classical trinitarian theology has

> the disadvantage that in the doctrine of the Trinity it does not really give enough weight to a starting point in the history of revelation and dogma which is within the historical and salvific experience of the Son and of the Spirit as the reality of the divine self-communication to us, so that we can understand from this historical experience what the doctrine of the divine Trinity really means. The psychological theory of the Trinity neglects the experience of the Trinity in the economy of salvation in favor of a seemingly almost gnostic speculation about what goes on in the inner life of God.[1]

In contrast the authors whose works we have studied, far from speculating on the inner life of God, take up their trinitarian reflections precisely at the point of the Trinity's involvement with us in the events of the economy of salvation. Theirs is no a-historical inquiry: the mystery of the Trinity is approached as none other than the mystery of this God who has saved us. The resultant trinitarian theology differs in significant ways from its classical antecedent.

[1]Karl Rahner, *Foundations of Christian Faith: An Introduction to the Idea of Christianity,* translated by William V. Dych (New York: Crossroad, 1987) 135.

We want now to draw out the specific features of the trinitarian theology that emerges when the mystery is approached in this new way. Clearly there are myriad possibilities for comparison and contrast in this thematic analysis. Let us highlight the general features of these trinitarian theologies we have studied and then attend in to their two salient features: the soteriological context of this trinitarian theology and what I shall refer to as the "paschal character" of divine being.[2]

General features of these trinitarian theologies

Considerable convergence is immediately evident in the features of the trinitarian theologies our authors present to us. As already explained, Moore's interest when interconnecting the mystery of the Trinity with the paschal mystery is not so much the explication of a trinitarian theology as a description of the experience of conversion on which such an explication is based. When he does turn to an explication of the trinitarian processions his thinking is apparently not directly informed by the paschal mystery.[3] It is therefore the works of Durrwell, Lafont, and von Balthasar that are the subject of our attention here.

1. A convergence in starting point

Despite differences in perspective and approach to the interconnection of the mysteries there is considerable convergence in our authors' starting points and concerns:

a. With regard to trinitarian theology they all clearly assent to the conciliar christological and trinitarian statements. Indeed, their concern to be in conformity with the classic Christian doctrine acts as counterbalance to the dangers inherent in their respective approaches.

b. While all identify themselves as standing within the tradition, they express a certain dissatisfaction with traditional Latin trinitarian theology and its expression of the intelligibility of the trinitarian mystery. They consider that a fuller explication of the mystery is both possible and necessary.

c. They recognize that the dynamic character of the divine being, traditionally expressed in terms of processions, relations, and missions, has been weakened in traditional Latin trinitarian theology. A tendency to essentialism has obscured the dynamism inherent in the description of God as Pure Act, resulting in a rather abstract and immobilist trinitarian theology with a fixed

---

[2]We owe the expression "paschal character" to John McDade in "The Trinity and the Paschal Mystery" 175–191.

[3]See ch. 4 above, "Classical trinitarian theology as dogmatized mystical experience" 103–105.

order of relations that fails to convey the biblical sense of the liveliness and vitality of the interpersonal relations. It is the interpersonal, indeed paschal dimension of divine being that our authors seek to reclaim for trinitarian theology. All especially wish to render more fully the dynamism of divine love that the biblical data so strongly attest.

d. With regard to the paschal mystery all see a unity in Jesus' death and resurrection. Certainly different aspects of the mystery emerge with different emphases in their theologies, be it the death (Lafont), or the resurrection (Durrwell), or indeed the descent (von Balthasar), but all have a vital sense of the unity of this one mystery. For Durrwell and von Balthasar this unity is symbolically expressed in the image of the Slain Lamb who sits at the right hand of the Father.[4]

e. In connecting the paschal mystery with the Trinity they recognize that the paschal mystery is not just redemptive but revelatory of the trinitarian mystery. It emerges in these theologies as the enactment (that is, the divine act of being) of the Trinity in creation.

2. A vitally differentiated trinitarian theology

What stands out immediately with signal clarity in the resultant trinitarian theologies is the diversity and uniqueness of the divine persons, Father, Son, and Holy Spirit. Clearly a vitally renewed sense of the *differentiated* Trinity of three distinct divine persons emerges when the mystery is approached in this way. God is expressed not as a homogenous divine subject but in terms of a trinitarian communion and communication of persons both within God's being and in relation to us. We recall that the Thomistic *ordo doctrinae* begins with a treatment of the divine essence: a consideration of undifferentiated divine being precedes a consideration of the Trinity. Such an approach is certainly not unjustified and can be defended on biblical grounds, the Old Testament revelation of the one God preceding the New Testament revelation of the Trinity. However, in these theologies God is first treated not as one undifferentiated being but as a dynamically threefold differentiated being.

Similarly there is no prior consideration of the divine attributes. Instead we find that when consideration is given to the perfections of the divinity they are derived from reflection on God as revealed in these three persons. Consequently the notion of the divine essence or nature is cast in a very different light in relation to traditional trinitarian theology. The divine unity is presented primarily as a communion of these three persons, not as one nature or substance. The Three, in their relationship to each other and in relationship to creation, express the divine essence, each in a unique way as is proper to the specific person. The Augustinian-Thomistic strategy of appropriation

[4]See above, ch. 1, n. 29 (Durrwell); ch. 3, n. 96 (von Balthasar).

whereby substantial characteristics and roles are *appropriated* to the divine person although they are not in fact "proper" in a formal sense to that person[5] is superfluous from this perspective. Durrwell almost collapses the notion of divine nature entirely.[6] In his theology the divine attributes are personalized in the Holy Spirit: the Holy Spirit is, in person, the divine unity. There is no implication of a divine essence that is somehow prior to or separate from the Trinity of the divine persons.[7]

Certainly there is no risk of modalism in such vitally differentiated trinitarian theologies. Indeed the problem, to the extent that there is a problem as such, is not how to explain the tri-unity but rather how to preserve the unity of God. In fact none of our authors addresses in any systematic way the question of the way in which these three constitute one God and not three gods. The statement of doctrinal orthodoxy, *tres personae una substantia*, is assumed, not defended or explained. That they are one God, not three gods, is presupposed. An explication of trinitarian theology that better conveys the biblical data is their concern.

A renewed sense of the *perichoresis* (or circumincession) also emerges.[8] In these theologies the divine persons do not just exist in relation to each other but *in* each other, and dynamically so. This dynamic intimate indwelling that our authors' use of the notion of the trinitarian *perichoresis* intends moves beyond the Augustinian-Thomistic treatment of the divine persons and the relations.[9] Indeed, in the theologies we have examined the divine *perichoresis* serves to maintain and convey the dynamic unity of the Three while simultaneously allowing each of the three persons a distinct identity and specific role. In other words instead of the traditional notions of unity of essence, nature, or substance, God is these Three—Father, Son, and Spirit—existing in an eternal perichoretic communion of life and love.

We find that in these trinitarian theologies the notion of the divine *perichoresis* emerges as having greater significance than the traditional notion of the divine substance. It is in the *perichoresis* that the divine unity effectively consists. However, the notion of *perichoresis* not only allows our authors to avoid tritheism as well as subordinationism: it points the way to transcending the opposition between essentialist and personalist categories to which Durrwell refers.[10] An understanding of the divine unity in terms of *perichoresis* in fact allows a shift to the application of relational categories to describe the divine essence or nature, to which traditionally only substantial categories

[5]See Thomas Aquinas, *ST* Ia. 39, 7.
[6]Durrwell, ch. 1 nn. 58–61, 79–80.
[7]Durrwell, ch. 1 n. 61.
[8]Durrwell, ch. 1 nn. 53, 54, 69; Lafont: ch. 2 nn. 16, 46, 72.
[9]Aquinas does not use the term *circumincessio* at all in the *Summa Theologiae* although he does address the question of "Whether the Son is present in the Father and vice versa" in *ST* Ia. 42, 5.
[10]Durrwell, ch. 1. n. 62.

were applied.[11] For this reason the shift is, I suggest, a most significant one, for when one describes the divine unity in terms of *perichoresis* personalist categories may be applied both to the unity and the tri-unity of God.

3. The three divine persons: their identity and proper roles

In this return to the narrative of the paschal mystery the three *dramatis personae,* Father, Son, and Spirit, emerge with clearly distinct identities and roles. In traditional Latin trinitarian theology the Three are distinguished within the unity of the divine essence by means of relations of opposition or origin, and as a counter to any charge of subordinationism their equality and consubstantiality is stressed. In Thomistic terms they are subsistent relations within the divine being. However, the notion of subsistent relation remains somewhat abstract and a-historical. Although it has ontological precision it lacks *personal* depth and existential reference. The persons as persons do not emerge clearly. In contrast, though our authors continue to describe the divine persons in terms of relations their treatment of the persons is concretely situated in the context of the events of salvation history. The divine persons thus emerge as *dramatis personae* with considerable vitality and clarity, something the traditional description does not convey with such vibrancy and concreteness.

A number of similarities in our authors' treatment of the *dramatis personae* are evident. We turn briefly to summarize the traits and roles of the divine persons that emerge. We begin with the Son, for in connecting the paschal mystery and the Trinity our authors recognize that it is through the person of the Son, his personal characteristics and role, that we apprehend the other two divine persons, Father and Holy Spirit.

a. The Son
Obedience and receptivity emerge as utterly central characteristics of the Son.[12] They are not simply traits that the incarnate Son adopts in a kind of extrinsic way in order to execute his mission and achieve our salvation. Rather our authors perceive that these characteristics are hypostatic traits expressive of the Son's very being as the eternal Son. In the eternal act of generation the Son receives his being from the Father. In the economy, in obedience to the trinitarian will that he receives from the Father and through the Holy Spirit, the Son becomes incarnate and dies on the cross. For von Balthasar Jesus' obedience to his mission finds its climax when he descends into the God-

---

[11]See Augustine, *DT* V. In the Augustinian-Thomistic framework for trinitarian theology the distinction between substantial and relational categories allowed for distinction between the Three (in terms of relational categories) and the unity of the one God (in terms of substantial categories).

[12]Durrwell, ch. 1 nn. 40, 41, 58; Lafont, ch. 2 nn. 43, 44, 53; von Balthasar, ch. 3 nn. 26, 27, 41–45, 62, 65, 88–91.

forsakenness of hell. In the resurrection he receives his being as the risen Christ from the Father. Each movement of the paschal mystery expresses his unreserved obedience to the trinitarian will and a receptivity that is characteristic of, and proper to, the person of the Son. This obedience and receptivity does not imply any subordination of the Son in relation to the Trinity. Von Balthasar identifies this potential problem and explains the Son's obedience and receptivity, as demonstrated in the economy, as the "modality" or "kenotic translation" of the Son's eternal self-surrendering love for the Father.[13]

The mission of the Son, which he receives from the Trinity and executes in obedience, is also recognized as expressive of his unique person.[14] Aquinas's notion that any of the Three could have become incarnate and accomplished the redemptive mission is quite alien to our authors' understanding.[15] The mission of redemption, which climaxes in the death on the cross and the descent into hell, is formally and properly the mission of the person of the Son, not of the Father or of the Spirit. Here too the image of the Risen Son as Slain Lamb who bears the stigmata of his suffering and death is particularly significant. It expresses the mission of the Son as uniquely his own.

b. The Father

All three authors, but particularly Durrwell and von Balthasar, interpret the resurrection of Jesus in terms of the Father's eternal generation of the Son.[16] The Father's begetting of the Son is thus the primordial mystery in these trinitarian theologies. Indeed Durrwell, who apprehends both processions within the one act of the Father's generation, goes as far as to say that "God is essentially Father."[17] Von Balthasar presses farther still and considers the nature of the love whereby the Father begets a coequal other. To use von Balthasar's expression, in the generation of the Son the Father makes himself destitute of all that he is and has to generate his coequal and consubstantial Son.[18] The Father's generation of the Son implies that the Father is characterized by unreserved self-giving love. Fatherhood in God emerges as the total self-giving to the Son of all that the Father has and is.

In von Balthasar's theology the Father also clearly emerges as Creator and Judge.[19] In the paschal mystery the Father, as Judge, sends his Son into the world and into the depths of hell in order to give all judgment to him. In the descent the Son takes the full measure of all that is opposed and alien to God. However, precisely in this way the Father as Creator also takes responsibility for creation, including all the contingencies of created freedom, even the

---

[13]Von Balthasar, ch. 3. nn. 46, 89.

[14]Durrwell, ch. 1 n. 39; von Balthasar: ch. 3 nn. 47–53.

[15]*ST* 3a. 3, 5.

[16]The correspondence between the resurrection and the eternal generation of the Son, while noted by Lafont, is not developed by him to any great degree: Lafont, ch. 2 n. 70.

[17]Durrwell, ch. 1 n. 79; see also n. 77.

[18]Von Balthasar, ch. 3 n. 20.

[19]Von Balthasar, ch. 3 nn. 34, 64.

possibility that finite freedom may reject God.[20] This is the essential meaning of the descent, where the Son in the weakness of love accompanies the sinner in the desolation of hell. In each movement the Father acts in self-giving love, giving what is most deeply his own.

The Father's abandonment of the Son on the cross figures large for both von Balthasar and Lafont.[21] Lafont identifies the apparent abandonment or withdrawal as "the mysterious face of fatherhood," the meaning of which is revealed in the resurrection: abandonment *by* the Father allows for the possibility of abandonment *to* the Father and entry into communion with him. Von Balthasar, assiduously avoiding the univocal attribution of mutability to God, recognizes the abandonment—at Gethsemane, on the cross, in the descent—as another modality from among the infinite number of possible modalities of trinitarian love as it expresses itself in the economy.[22]

c. The Holy Spirit

In contrast to the oft-commented obscurity of the Holy Spirit in traditional Latin theology the Holy Spirit emerges in these theologies with singular vitality. Indeed, among the most remarkable features of the trinitarian theologies before us is the theology of the Holy Spirit they present. This is particularly evident in Durrwell's theology where the Holy Spirit emerges as the begetting in person, personifying the divine perfections traditionally attributed to the divine essence.[23] In contrast, a sense of the person of the Holy Spirit emerges least clearly and vividly in Lafont's theology. Lafont, unlike Durrwell, stays relatively close to the traditional trinitarian framework and works at a higher level of abstraction, somewhat farther from the data. He struggles to identify the role of the Spirit and consequently gives little emphasis to the third divine person in his trinitarian thinking.[24]

As in traditional trinitarian theology the Holy Spirit emerges as both bond that unites Father and Son in their love for each other and as fruit and personification of their love.[25] In the paschal mystery the Holy Spirit holds the Father and Son in unity in the death and in the descent, and it is in the Spirit that the Son is resurrected. It is not that the properties and role of the person of the Holy Spirit are substantially different from those traditionally understood, but rather that a more vivid sense of the person of the Holy Spirit emerges.

For both Durrwell and von Balthasar it is particularly significant that the Holy Spirit is sent into creation upon the Son's return to the Father and that the reunion of Father and Son thus appears as the condition for the sending of

---

[20] Von Balthasar, ch. 3 nn. 71, 74.
[21] Lafont, ch. 2 n. 66; von Balthasar: ch. 3 nn. 38–39.
[22] Von Balthasar, ch. 3 nn. 24, 89.
[23] Durrwell, ch. 1 nn. 58–61, 78–79.
[24] Lafont, ch. 2 n. 81.
[25] Von Balthasar, ch. 3 nn. 26, 27, 100, 101, 104–106.

the Spirit into the world. In their theologies it follows that the Spirit proceeds from the Father *and* from the Son *(filioque)*.[26] Von Balthasar also considers that the unanimity of will between Father and Son, so evident in the paschal mystery, attests their common spiration of the third divine person.[27] In contrast to the traditional Latin understanding however, Durrwell stresses that the Spirit proceeds from Father and Son not as from an *undifferentiated* principle but from their *differentiated* communion, the Father acting as Father, the Son as Son, each acting in a way that is uniquely and properly his own.[28] Again a vitally differentiated treatment of the mystery of the Trinity is evident.

Such are the ways in the theologies before us in which the divine persons emerge with unique identities and with proper and distinct roles both within God and in relation to the economy of salvation. Again we find no strategy of appropriation of substantial attributes to particular divine persons. Instead, the attributes of the divine persons are those that are proper to the particular divine person as revealed in and through Jesus in his paschal mystery. Indeed, we find no discussion of substantial categories when the Trinity is considered in this way. The distinction between relational and substantial categories, while not dispensed with, is far less significant than in the traditional Augustinian approach where it served to meet a need to distinguish between the divine unity and the tri-unity.[29] Here, as we have noted, the divine unity is conveyed principally by means of the notion of *perichoresis*. The distinction between substantial and relational categories thus recedes in importance, enabling a new way of imagining the trinitarian mystery.

4. The Three as "persons"

Augustine settled somewhat reluctantly on the term "person" to designate the three hypostases.[30] Moreover, no psychological overtones were present in the patristic use of the term *hypostasis*. It was strictly a metaphysical, not a psychological term, which it has now largely become. Aquinas, on the other hand, after consideration of the trinitarian processions and relations appropriated with some modification Boethius's definition of the person as an "individual substance of rational nature."[31] We find no such strategy here. There is no question in our authors' considerations of "what" the Three are. That they are appropriately designated as "persons" is presupposed. Indeed, instead of a

---

[26]Durrwell, ch. 1 nn. 63–70; von Balthasar: ch. 3 n. 103.

[27]Von Balthasar, ch. 3 n. 104.

[28]Durrwell, ch. 1 nn. 70–72.

[29]*DT* V.

[30]*DT* V, 9–10; VII, 7–11. Augustine's dissatisfaction with the Greek term *hypostasis* and what became its Latin equivalent, *persona,* to denote the threefold distinctions within the Godhead is partly due to the fact that both are technically terms of substance rather than of relation.

[31]*De persona et duabus naturis* 3 (MPL 64:1343).

consideration of whether the notion of person is appropriately applied to the hypostases, such as we find in Augustine and Aquinas, we find that the reasoning is reversed and our authors, particularly von Balthasar and Durrwell, consider the trinitarian relations among the Three in terms of how this is expressive of what it means to be a person. It is not that a notion of person drawn from human intrasubjective or interpersonal experience is applied analogically to the divine Three. Rather the divine persons as persons reveal what it is to be a person: it is not just to possess intellect and will, but to have a mission (von Balthasar).[32] It is to be in relationship with others, as is most clearly demonstrated in the Holy Spirit who is, in person, the bond of communion and relationship (Durrwell).[33] Even Lafont, working within the traditional scheme, recognizes in the paschal mystery "the law of spiritual being," that personhood is realized in unreserved gift of self in the trinitarian communion[34] (even though he also employs a more traditional analogical procedure when he introduces the notion of the reflexive construction of the personality).[35]

Personhood is therefore a primary category in these trinitarian theologies. A theology of the divine persons is by no means subordinate to a theology of divine essence as appears in the traditional treatment. The three persons emerge in uniqueness and distinction, with proper—not just appropriated—characteristics and roles in salvation history. Aquinas could at least countenance the prospect that any of the Three could have become incarnate, but this speculative question does not arise when the Trinity is approached from the paschal mystery. In these theologies we have studied the missions are primarily expressive of the divine persons. Thus, indeed, von Balthasar can speak of the mission as actually identical with the person.[36] The redemptive mission is the accomplishment of Jesus' *personal* mystery.[37]

5. *God as love*

Perhaps most striking of all is our authors' emphasis on God as love, as radical excess of *agapē*. Far from any juridical understanding of the mystery of our salvation, the paschal mystery reveals how lovingly the Trinity has entered into our world to meet and deal with the problem of evil in creation. God as *Actus Purus* is thus more richly rendered in these theologies as *Ipsum Amare Subsistens*. As von Balthasar expresses it so poignantly, "love alone is credible."[38] For von Balthasar and Durrwell love alone is "that than which

[32]Von Balthasar, ch. 3 nn. 54–55.
[33]Durrwell, ch. 1 nn. 74–75.
[34]Lafont, ch. 2 nn. 29–31.
[35]Lafont, ch. 2 n. 39.
[36]Von Balthasar, ch. 3 n. 52.
[37]Durrwell, ch. 1, "The paschal mystery as Christ's personal mystery" 19–20; von Balthasar, ch. 3 nn. 42–53.
[38]Von Balthasar, ch. 3 n. 8.

nothing greater can be thought." As we have noted, both firmly resist the psychological analogy on the grounds that no human analogy could adequately express the glory, the excess of the mystery of love that is revealed here in the paschal mystery.[39]

This emphasis on God as love results in some very untraditional and rather unorthodox ways of speaking about the divine being and its perfections.[40] The divine attributes are not those deduced in abstract *a priori* fashion as the perfections of the metaphysically-conceived Godhead; rather, consideration of the divine perfections follows a consideration of the Three who are revealed in the paschal mystery, the mystery of love. Thus by avoiding the tyranny of an overly philosophical and deductive approach to God these authors achieve a far richer theology of the nature of God and the divine attributes as the qualities of love that pushes beyond the boundaries of traditional philosophical-theological inquiry. We shall later return to consider this feature of these theologies when we consider the "paschal character" of divine being that emerges.

The Trinity as mystery of our salvation

A striking feature of the theologies we have studied is that in contrast to its classical antecedent trinitarian theology is cast and reconstituted in a very different and distinctly soteriological context. This shift in context dramatically affects both the trinitarian theology and the soteriology that ensues.

1. Trinitarian theology is cast in a soteriological context

Unlike Thomistic trinitarian theology which is fashioned without any apparent direct reference to the events in which God is actually revealed as these Three, an explication of the mystery of the Trinity, when interconnected with the paschal mystery, is firmly rooted in the events of the economy and in fact right at the point of its engagement with us in our greatest struggle, death. The mystery of the Trinity is thus found and contemplated not in isolation from us but rather in its involvement with us, and there at the very "rock of atheism," the problem of evil.

In this new development we therefore find a highly significant shift in the context within which the trinitarian mystery is addressed. A profound recasting and reconstitution of trinitarian theology results. It is not that essentially different trinitarian categories are employed. After all, processions, relations, persons, and missions still serve to designate the reality we are attempting to express, but we have a very different context—a soteriological context—and the traditional categories are refashioned to serve it.

---

[39]Durrwell, ch. 1 nn. 55, 56, 77; von Balthasar: ch. 3 n. 108.
[40]Von Balthasar, ch. 3, "The divine attributes" 83–85.

Consider, for example, the missions. Aquinas, following Augustine, allows for both visible and invisible missions.[41] In the visible missions the Son becomes incarnate and the Spirit is given at Pentecost. However, Aquinas's consideration of the Son's visible mission extends only to the point of the incarnation; the death and resurrection do not figure at all at this point in the *Summa Theologiae*. Not only do the death and resurrection not feature: Aquinas's treatment of the visible missions tends to be overshadowed by consideration of the invisible missions. In contrast our authors contemplate the missions in the paschal mystery precisely at their point of exposure to our problem of evil, where the (visible) missions express in very concrete ways the redeeming and liberating presence of God in our world. Thus trinitarian theology, constructed by connecting it with the paschal mystery, is recast and so moves beyond the conceptual boundaries of the more abstract and a-historical Thomistic treatment. The obedience of the Son to his mission, the Father's raising of the Son that brings his mission to completion, and the pentecostal outpouring of the Spirit emerge as the differentiated expressions of the determination of the divine being to be God-for-us in the midst of sin and evil.

The theologies of Durrwell and von Balthasar are so deeply soteriologically shaped that from their perspective traditional trinitarian theology fails to render the most crucial aspect of the revealed mystery. The Latin trinitarian scheme does not convey the mystery of the Trinity in terms of its loving engagement with us in the world of suffering. It does not convey adequately either what was accomplished or what was given in Jesus' paschal mystery, so profoundly transformative of creation. For Durrwell and von Balthasar much more is at stake in the explication of the mystery of the Trinity than is expressed in the traditional treatment. For them trinitarian theology is a vital expression of soteriology. The Trinity is the mystery of our salvation, of how it is that we are saved, of that in which our salvation consists, and of who this God is who enters into human existence to save us, incorporating creation into God's divine life of love.

Seeking a fuller expression of the mystery of the Trinity, these authors emphatically reject the classical psychological analogy as an inadequate elucidation of the mystery and insist that the immanent processions be understood not as the processions of intellect and will but of love.[42] It is a procession of love that issues in the Son who enters into creation and descends into the depths of hell. It is a procession of love that issues in the person of the Holy Spirit, spirit of the love of Father and Son. Both processions are processions of love. In this way von Balthasar and Durrwell suggest a newly fashioned trinitarian ontology in which love and the relationality of love, as distinct from substantiality, have primacy in explicating the mystery.

---

[41]*ST* Ia. 43.
[42]Durrwell, ch. 1 nn. 55, 56, 77; von Balthasar, ch. 3 n. 108.

2. *Soteriology is cast in a trinitarian context*

Not only is the mystery of the Trinity located in a soteriological context when interconnected with the paschal mystery: soteriology is correlatively cast in a trinitarian context. Recall, for example, that in Durrwell's theology God's salvific action is expressed in terms of raising Jesus and all in him. Creation, in Christ, "inhabits" the Trinity. Salvation is thus the incorporation of creation in the person of the Son and in his begetting in the Trinity. It is in this sense a genuine divinization, a cosmic transformation.[43] Von Balthasar also understands that creation is taken into the sphere of the Trinity; even hell exists "within" the Trinity.[44] However, in contrast to Durrwell who tends to stress the elevation of creation and its incorporation into the Trinity, von Balthasar stresses how deeply the Trinity has entered into creation in Jesus' descent. Where Durrwell focuses on the resurrection von Balthasar uses the descent into hell to express the mystery of our salvation and to explore the kenotic nature of the triune love of God who accomplishes it for us. However, both clearly reject any notion of salvation as simply achieved by Jesus in a way that is almost extrinsic to us, to him, and to God.[45]

In contrast to juridically-fashioned theologies of redemption, salvation in these theologies is not some apparently intra-divine crypto-economic transaction that is effected in the death and resurrection of Jesus, with creation a mere stage on which this transformation takes place. Much more than just redemption from sin, salvation is a trinitarian event and a trinitarian reality whereby through Jesus' paschal mystery creation is incorporated into the trinitarian communion. A radically new relationship is thus offered, and alienation and isolation overcome by God freely and graciously coming to meet us, choosing to connect Godself to us, effecting the incorporation of creation into God's own trinitarian relationality.

Salvation is thus a rebirth: it is a birth in Jesus into the trinitarian *peri-choresis*.[46] As Durrwell expresses it salvation is *parousia,* for it is the coming of the risen Jesus that permits this communion.[47] Von Balthasar dramatically presses farther still. Salvation is God coming to us in our lostness, not judging us from the outside, as it were, but sending the Son to bear our sin, judging our sin as it must be judged, but in infinite compassion and unalienable love for the sinner. Above all it is this mystery of incorporation into the life and love of the Trinity that our authors, especially Durrwell and von Balthasar, seek to convey in their trinitarian theologies.

---

[43]Durrwell, ch. 1 n. 35.

[44]Von Balthasar, ch. 3 n. 73.

[45]Durrwell, ch. 1, "The paschal mystery as Christ's personal mystery" 19–20.

[46]Durrwell, ch. 1 nn. 33, 35, 36.

[47]Durrwell, ch. 1 nn. 4, 30.

3. Soteriology is cast in a cosmic context

Soteriology emerges as a trinitarian reality. Moreover, it is cosmic in scale. Durrwell and von Balthasar clearly share an understanding of salvation as an event whereby all creation is taken into the primordial "event" of the love of the Father for his coequal Son in the Holy Spirit.[48] It is that same trinitarian love that creates a world in love and gives it genuine freedom, freedom even to reject the love that brought it into existence. In God's coming to redeem it no part of creation is left in isolation from God's love, not even hell, as von Balthasar depicts so dramatically. The enactment of trinitarian relationality in the economy is the consummation of creation. All of creation becomes filial, assumed in Jesus Christ into the love of the Father for the Son in the Holy Spirit.

The object of the trinitarian will to salvation is not just the human person or humankind but all creation, the whole cosmos.[49] Salvation is thus presented on a scale of cosmic proportions. Far from any notion of salvation as an individual or private event, what emerges is a much more social and relational soteriological reality. Salvation is not merely individual but corporate, indeed cosmic in scale, embracing the totality of creation. In the paschal mystery the Trinity enters into creation, so that all creation enters into God's trinitarian being.

An interconnection of the mysteries of Trinity, soteriology, and creation is thus achieved by our authors in their exploration of the interconnection of the paschal mystery and the Trinity. The paschal mystery, as the achievement of the summit of creation, is placed in the context of a doctrine of creation. The physical universe is by no means extrinsic to the history of salvation; it is no mere stage on which the drama of the salvation of humankind is played out. Salvation history culminates in the salvation of the whole cosmos that through the visible missions of the Son and Spirit enters into the trinitarian communion.

In contrast to the Thomistic treatment that tends to emphasize the invisible over the visible mission we find no great emphasis on the invisible missions in these theologies we have studied. Here too we see that their focus is not so much on the individual but on the whole cosmos and the universal ramifications of God's engagement and enactment of trinitarian relationality in creation. In this theological imagining all creation is embraced in the trinitarian indwelling. Here a new horizon dawns for theology, with new possibilities for a more cosmologically and ecologically attuned reflection and interconnection of the mysteries of Christian faith.

For Lafont, too, salvation is the entry of creation into the trinitarian communion.[50] For him also salvation is not a denial or negation of creation but its

---

[48]Durrwell, ch. 1, "The resurrection as a divine generation" 16–19; von Balthasar, ch. 3, "The inner-trinitarian 'event'" 60–63.

[49]Durrwell, ch. 1 nn. 35–36.

[50]Lafont, ch. 2 nn. 21, 70.

accomplishment. However, in Lafont's theology history finds its meaning in a *transfiguration* through and beyond death.[51] Here is Lafont's originality. Unlike Durrwell and von Balthasar he stresses this aspect of mortification and transfiguration in the paschal mystery. Salvation is entry into the mystery of Jesus' death as well as that of his resurrection. It is entry into his permanent filial invocation of the Father that attains its perfection in the moment of death and thus achieves entry into the distinctly paschal dynamic of innertrinitarian being.[52]

In some ways, rather like Moore, Lafont attends to the existential dimension of soteriology: the process by which the human person is incorporated into Christ. Like Moore's, his focus at this point is more individual and anthropocentric than cosmological in scope. For both Moore and Lafont, each of whom addresses this profoundly personal and existential aspect of salvation, death is utterly crucial to the experience of new life, liberation, salvation. Moore describes the process in terms of liberation from guilt and self-disesteem and the liberation of our desire for its infinite object.[53] For Lafont death is freely consented loss of self in and for the other, the supreme act of renunciation of any autonomy of self in preference for communion.[54] However, at this point Lafont also meets von Balthasar, for the question of freedom is central to both although explored in different ways. Lafont stresses that this radical self-transcendence to which the human person is called and that finds its ultimate expression in death is proposed, not imposed.[55] Von Balthasar on the other hand explores the radical possibility of human freedom to reject God's love. In his theology hell remains as the ultimate entailment of genuine human freedom.[56] What is particularly significant in Lafont's theology, however, is that the paschal dynamic of death and resurrection signifies not only the nature of the process by which the human person responds to the offer of communion with God but also something that is anteriorly and eternally true of God's trinitarian being.

The paschal character of divine life

While the soteriological context profoundly shapes these trinitarian theologies, the mystery of the Trinity is more than a soteriology. We find that our authors, but particularly Lafont and von Balthasar, perceive that the paschal mystery is revelatory of the very nature and character of trinitarian relationality itself. Lafont refers to the paschal mystery as "icon," "perfect image" of

[51]Lafont, ch. 2 nn. 17, 18, 21, 70.
[52]Lafont, ch. 2 nn. 65, 70.
[53]Moore, ch. 4 nn. 16, 17, 20, 22, 25, 26.
[54]Lafont, ch. 2 n. 20.
[55]Lafont, ch. 2 nn. 19, 28–31.
[56]Von Balthasar, ch. 3, "The reality of human freedom" 70–72.

the proper reality of the Trinity.[57] For von Balthasar the paschal mystery is the "form" *(Gestalt)* of God's triune love for the world.[58] In other words our authors perceive that Jesus' paschal mystery is not just redemptive but revelatory of God's mode of acting and God's mode of being, not just in relation to us and our salvation but as it is in itself in eternity.

Lafont and von Balthasar recognize that it is no accident that this enactment of the mystery of the Trinity in the realm of the economy takes place in the dynamic modality of Jesus' paschal mystery, and indeed that it is intrinsically appropriate to the divine being to express itself in precisely this way. They perceive that the paschal movement therefore somehow conveys the eternal trinitarian relations in a paradigmatic way, that it is essentially expressive of the eternal trinitarian relationality. From this perspective it appears, then, that there is a *paschal* mystery *because* there is a trinitarian mystery.[59]

The emphasis on the death and resurrection as having properly theological and not just redemptive significance profoundly affects trinitarian theology. The nature of the divine subjectivity that our authors express in their theologies is characterized by a certain "paschal character." By "paschal character" I mean that the dynamic of death and resurrection, but particularly the aspect of death, is incorporated into the nature of the trinitarian relationality as our authors perceive it. A new understanding of the divine being and love thus emerges and correspondingly a very new understanding of the divine perfections. Hence because of their interconnection of the mystery of the Trinity with the paschal mystery our authors' trinitarian theologies are not only situated in a soteriological context. The nature of the divine being emerges with a distinctly paschal character. This too stands in contrast to the classical antecedent where, as we have noted, the death and resurrection of Jesus are treated quite separately from a consideration of the mystery of the Trinity under the rubric of redemption, and where the nature and perfections of God are treated in an *a priori* fashion before a consideration of the Trinity and the mystery of love it reveals.

Consider, for example, Lafont who first identifies in Jesus' death a moment that "corresponds and responds"[60] to the offer of divine communion and thus distinguishes between a consideration of the "anthropological" aspect (the aspect of human response) and the "theological" aspect (the aspect of divine offer) of Jesus' paschal mystery.[61] He then asks why it is that trinitarian life finds its expression in the paschal dynamic of Jesus' death and resurrection and concludes that since we have the Son of God at the heart of Jesus' paschal mystery the renunciation and self-dispossession his death so radically expresses signify something of the proper and eternal reality of God, the interior

[57]Lafont, ch. 2 nn. 16, 22–24, 71.
[58]Von Balthasar, ch. 3 nn. 1–5.
[59]Lafont: ch. 2 n. 25; von Balthasar: ch. 3, "The innertrinitarian 'event'" 60–63.
[60]Lafont, ch. 2 n. 15.
[61]Lafont, ch. 2 n. 16.

modality of trinitarian life. They are revelatory of the eternal trinitarian exchange.[62]

For Lafont death expresses the utter being-for-another character of the divine persons as first and foremost gift of self, sheer other-directedness, other-centeredness. In creation death is the modality of this unreserved gift of self to the other that is the perfection of spiritual being. Death is thus the paradigmatic expression of the ecstatic (out-going) aspect of the trinitarian relations. It is not that the negativity of death as such is an aspect of the divine being, for no negativity is attributed to the divinity. Rather, it is that the negativity of death paradigmatically expresses the positivity of trinitarian love, albeit somewhat paradoxically. It expresses the self-dispossession in regard to the other that is positively and essentially constitutive of the trinitarian relations. Something analogous to death is thus attributed to trinitarian relationality and being.

Lafont does not develop this insight further in terms of the divine attributes. His concern is how best to designate the divine persons. Nonetheless, based on his insight that the death of Christ "corresponds and responds" to the gift of God, Lafont in effect if not quite explicitly broaches an understanding that being—human and divine—is intrinsically paschal being. To be is to be utterly for the other. It is death to absolutely any other reality. That is the essential meaning of the paschal mystery. Indeed, this is *why* it is a *paschal* mystery. It is a *paschal* mystery *because* it is the mystery of the Trinity as it engages with us and incorporates creation into its own paschal being.

Something similar emerges in von Balthasar's theology. The strategy of situating the paschal mystery in terms of the primordial "event" of the Father's generation of the Son not only allays the problem of mutability that a consideration of the events of salvation history inevitably raises but also profoundly affects von Balthasar's understanding of the nature of divine love and the perfections attributed to God. Recognizing a divine *kenosis* implicit in the Father's generation of the Son, von Balthasar is led to recognize *kenosis* as an essential characteristic of divine love. He therefore explicates the very nature of the divine reality, both the divine mode of acting *ad extra* and the divine mode of being *ad intra,* in terms of *kenosis.* Thus what I have described in rather more general terms as the "paschal character" of divine being finds expression in von Balthasar's theology in terms of the kenotic character of divine love.

In dialogue with kenotic christologies[63] von Balthasar describes this characteristic of divine love in terms of *kenosis.* In this analysis I have chosen instead to describe this aspect of divine being in terms of a "paschal" character on the grounds that the latter term, I suggest, better conveys the fullness and unity of the paschal mystery, the mystery of death *and* resurrection. *Kenosis,*

---

[62]Lafont, ch. 2 nn. 22, 26.
[63]Von Balthasar, ch. 3 n. 119.

on the other hand, tends to emphasize self-dispossession without acknowledging so clearly the reception of being that is also inherent in the process. *Kenosis,* while dramatically conveying the unfathomable depths of divine love, does not render quite so explicitly the positivity intrinsic to the paschal dynamic.

The divine attributes that emerge from von Balthasar's reflection on the divine being from this paschal perspective are very different from those traditionally expressed.[64] They are not the attributes that follow from a philosophically-fashioned consideration of the perfection of the one almighty God—simplicity, immutability, impassibility, and so forth. Indeed such notions are profoundly challenged in the light of the God who is revealed in the paschal mystery of Jesus Christ. While none of our authors actually develops to any significant extent the ramifications of the interconnection of the paschal mystery and Trinity for an understanding of the divine attributes in any systematic thematic way, nevertheless the implications of the approach are patently clear: a radical reshaping of our understanding of the divine perfections as the attributes of self-giving is intimated.

In contrast to the work of von Balthasar and Lafont, the full paschal character of divine being is less apparent in Durrwell's theology. Like them he recognizes that the paschal mystery is not just redemptive but revelatory of divine being. However, unlike Lafont whose focus is the death and von Balthasar who highlights the descent, Durrwell's focus is the resurrection. Death is the necessary passing over into the resurrection.[65] The paschal character of the divine being is consequently somewhat overshadowed. Nevertheless the image of the risen Jesus as the Slain Lamb who bears eternally the stigmata of his suffering and death is of pivotal significance to Durrwell.[66] He recognizes that the death and resurrection correspond to the filial dynamism of Jesus Christ. Dying to self, yielding to the other, self-surrendering in love: all these express what it is to be the Son, and by implication Father and Holy Spirit. The paschal mystery thus expresses, again in a paradigmatic way, the dynamic of sonship. Hence though Durrwell's treatment is less explicit, in his theology too death is somehow at the heart of reality, both human and divine. However, in contrast to Lafont and von Balthasar, Durrwell identifies the paschal dynamic with the person of the Son and leaves its implications for the other two divine persons, and for trinitarian being, relatively undeveloped.

We find that for each of our four authors, though in different ways, death has a crucial role in the paschal mystery not only in effecting our redemption but in revealing a certain paschal character in the divine being itself, manifesting the nature of divine love and the trinitarian relations. Not to be found in the traditional treatment, this sense of the paschal character of divine being

[64]Von Balthasar, ch. 3, "The divine attributes" 83–85.
[65]Durrwell, ch. 1 nn. 31–33.
[66]Durrwell, ch. 1 n. 29.

is in my assessment *the* most profound insight in regard to the divine being that emerges when the Trinity is approached from the paschal mystery. It adumbrates a radical recasting of our understanding of God within a very new horizon, a re-imaging of God that will be, I suggest, far more responsive to contemporary questions of God in a suffering world.

The relationship between the immanent and economic Trinity

We have seen that none of our authors shrinks from daring to speak of God as God is *in se*. Indeed, von Balthasar in particular speaks about God in very imaginative and daring ways. We come then to the question of the relationship between the economic and the immanent Trinity and their interrelatedness in the paschal mystery. As we noted in our introduction, this distinction between the immanent and economic Trinity has become the source of considerable debate in contemporary theology, having been raised to some prominence by Karl Rahner.[67] The question is fundamentally whether one can legitimately speak, not just meaningfully but truly, about God *in se*.

We first note that our authors maintain the "immanent/economic" distinction implicitly if not explicitly. For each the immanent Trinity remains as the absolute and transcendent reality of God. There is no indication that it is reduced to or dissolved into the economic Trinity. To collapse the immanent into the economic Trinity would be to risk denying the utter freedom and gratuitousness of God's salvific engagement in creation and, indeed, in the paschal mystery itself, and thus denying the glory of divine love that our authors seek to convey in their trinitarian theologies. Rather than being a description of the character of divine life that is somewhat removed from the events of God's engagement in salvation history (with which the opponents of the notion of the immanent Trinity tend to identify it and to which they rightly object) the notion of the immanent Trinity, God *in se,* enables our authors to designate the freedom of the divinity as acting *ad extra.*

While our authors hold that the immanent and economic Trinity are not, strictly speaking, identical, and while they clearly distinguish the two, they do not separate them. They recognize that the economic and immanent Trinity are inextricably related: the economic Trinity is the epiphany of the immanent Trinity, corresponding to the innermost mystery of God. Hence it is, as we have noted, that none of our authors hesitates to speak of God *in se,* for the economic Trinity is none other than the immanent Trinity realized in the realm of the economy. In other words the distinction between the immanent and economic Trinity is not an ontological distinction. It is the same triune God of whom we speak, be it *ad intra* or *ad extra;* it is indeed one and the same divine act of being. Hence in speaking about God in the paschal mystery we are in fact speaking of God.

[67]Rahner, *The Trinity* 21–24.

Durrwell, while not employing the terminology of immanent and economic Trinity, explains the distinction between the act of divine being (theology) and the act by which creation is taken up into the divine life (economy) as a distinction between two different interpretations of this one event in which triune relationality is expressed.[68] From this perspective the economic Trinity is the immanent Trinity under a soteriological aspect. Durrwell's distinction in terms of two interpretations of this one event, both valid but addressing different aspects of the mystery, is a useful one. In effect it establishes the distinction at the level of meaning without creating a rift between the two at the level of ontology. It admits an understanding of the paschal mystery of Jesus as the realization in creation of the eternal dynamic interchange constituting the divine life. Therein lies its interpretation in terms of the immanent Trinity. At the same time it admits the paschal mystery as the event by which creation is brought to share in the self-giving of the Son to the Father in the union of the Holy Spirit. This is its interpretation in terms of the economic Trinity. In this way Durrwell situates the distinction in epistemological terms, distinguishing between our experience of knowing (epistemology) and God's being (ontology).

Von Balthasar makes a similar kind of distinction between the primordial event of trinitarian being and the modalities of the divine love as it expresses itself in creation.[69] Thus though they employ different terms we find a profound convergence in our authors' thinking on the relationship between the immanent and economic Trinity. Whereas some contemporary authors propose that the distinction be abandoned,[70] our authors maintain the distinction and insist that the immanent Trinity not be reduced to the economic Trinity. They effect a closer connection between but not a collapse of the immanent and economic Trinity. In these theologies the paschal mystery corresponds to the immanent Trinity as icon in the truest sense. However this correspondence is not a tautology; the distinction is neither superfluous nor dispensable.

Interestingly, while we have raised this issue in examining our authors' works because of its prominence in contemporary theology we find that the immanent/economic distinction does not have for any of our authors the significance that some modern writers in trinitarian theology would give to it. It simply remains in these theologies, and relatively unobtrusively at that, as a necessary distinction enabling coherent discourse about God who is with us and for us, allowing a framework for securing the freedom and

---

[68]Durrwell, ch. 1 n. 82.

[69]Von Balthasar, ch. 3 n. 24.

[70]See, for example, Catherine LaCugna, *God For Us: The Trinity and Christian Life* (New York: Harper Collins, 1991) 223; eadem, "The Trinitarian Mystery of God" in Francis Schüssler Fiorenza and John Galvin, eds., *Systematic Theology: Roman Catholic Perspectives* 1 (Minneapolis: Fortress, 1991) 149–192. See also Thomas Weinandy's review of *God For Us* in *The Thomist* 57 (1993) 655–666.

transcendence of God together with the meaning and significance of the economy of salvation.[71]

Recall that the contemporary concern for the connection between the immanent and economic Trinity arose in reaction against traditional trinitarian theology's attention to the immanent Trinity and the inner-trinitarian processions and relations in a way that was seemingly remote from the events of salvation history. One of the virtues of this new development is that the interconnection of the Trinity with the paschal mystery firmly anchors trinitarian theology to its economic and soteriological roots, thus averting the problem endemic in the traditional approach. The paschal mystery of Jesus is the point from which our authors speak both of the immanent Trinity and the economic Trinity, implying that the paschal mystery is a kind of economic "enactment" of the immanent Trinity. The mystery of the Trinity is thus approached and presented, under its soteriological aspect, precisely as what occurs for us in the history of Jesus in his redemptive mission. This allows our authors to speak of the transcendent God who is intimately involved with us, and right where it matters most to us, in our experience of suffering and death.

Overall assessment of thematic gains for trinitarian theology

As we draw to a conclusion our thematic consideration of the salient features of the interconnection we have studied, what assessment of the development, from a thematic perspective, do I commend to the reader? I suggest that the development does indeed yield very significant thematic gains for trinitarian theology that can be summarized as follows:

1. The mystery is securely grounded in its economic roots. This development in trinitarian theology serves to balance the Augustinian-Thomistic treatment that tends to leave the mystery of the Trinity rather removed from the biblical data.

2. The result is a vitally concrete trinitarian theology in which the three divine persons, their hypostatic characteristics and proper roles, emerge clearly. Moreover the mystery is manifestly a mystery of love.

3. When trinitarian theology is set in the context of the paschal mystery, the mystery is cast in a distinctly soteriological context. In this way trinitarian theology is reconstituted. The traditional trinitarian categories remain but are recast and reprioritized as the mystery is approached from a soteriological perspective.

4. Soteriology is correlatively cast in a cosmic context. As Simone Weil asks, "how can Christianity call itself catholic if the universe itself is left out?"[72] By no means left out in these theologies, the whole universe, all of

---

[71]See Kathryn E. Tanner, *God and Creation in Christian Theology: Tyranny or Empowerment?* (Oxford: Basil Blackwell, 1988). Tanner's is a well-argued case for the rules that govern coherent discourse about the relationship between God and the world.

[72]Simone Weil, *Waiting for God* (London: Routledge and Kegan Paul, 1950) 100.

creation, is embraced in this theological vision of the trinitarian indwelling. The way is thus opened for a more cosmologically and ecologically attuned theology, a richer and more expansive imagining of the wholeness and interconnectedness of all reality.

5. Setting trinitarian reflection in the context of the paschal mystery also serves, I suggest, as a healthy corrective to a tendency in contemporary discussions to overemphasize the significance of the distinction between the immanent and economic Trinity, and to succumb to a new form of abstraction. Without giving undue attention to the distinction this new approach to trinitarian theology reconnects the mystery of the Trinity with the events of salvation history and so meets the concern that prompted Karl Rahner's criticisms in regard to the non-functionality of traditional trinitarian theology.

6. In light of the development of the biblical renewal movement and growing dissatisfaction with the classical Thomistic synthesis the interconnection between the mystery of the Trinity and the paschal mystery is not really so surprising a development. However, what was not perhaps to be expected is the very new understanding of the nature of God and of the divine perfections that results. The paschal character of the divine being *in se* represents, in my judgment, a remarkable advance offering new possibilities for meeting a contemporary stumbling block with philosophically-fashioned notions of divine immutability and impassibility. In plumbing the depths of the divine love more deeply it provides a richer and far more existentially satisfying understanding of being, both human and divine. Here too, a wholly new horizon dawns for the theological imagination, a horizon for exploration of the meaning and ramifications of divine being as intrinsically paschal being.

CHAPTER SIX

Methodological Shifts
and Their Meta-Methodological Significance

We turn now to consider what emerges from our study for theological method. Though we find a number of areas of convergence in our authors' methods we also find some notable areas of divergence that are worthy of comment because they pose deeper methodological questions to us. Let us first attend to the methodological shifts to be observed in these authors' approach to and explication of the mystery in relation to the traditional Latin approach to trinitarian theology. Our aim here is not so much to evaluate the methodological shifts but to bring them to the reader's attention and point to their deeper significance.

Points of convergence in theological method

A certain complexity confronts us as we approach the task of identifying the points of methodological convergence. Recall that we have already distinguished between the work of Moore and that of Durrwell, Lafont, and von Balthasar. We saw that Moore's intention in interconnecting the Trinity and paschal mystery is not so much to explicate divine subjectivity but rather to describe the process of conversion in human subjectivity on which such an explication is based. When he does attend to trinitarian theology he appropriates the psychological analogy, transposed from the metaphysically-fashioned faculty analysis into modern categories of intentionality analysis.[1] We also noted that Lafont's concerns are more confined and have a rather more specific focus and that in this sense his trinitarian theology is less developed than those

[1]Moore, ch. 4, "Classical trinitarian theology as dogmatized mystical experience"103–105.

of Durrwell and von Balthasar. Although Lafont's reflections on the paschal mystery profoundly affect his theology of the divine persons his considerations are *inserted* into the traditional Thomistic approach. On the other hand, in contrast to Lafont, Durrwell and von Balthasar adopt a very different approach to trinitarian theology than the traditional one. Thus even at a preliminary stage of analysis we can identify distinctly different methods of approach. Despite these significant differences, however, we find a number of points of methodological convergence in the theologies before us. The shifts are essentially those identified in our consideration of Durrwell's pioneering study.[2]

1. A shift in starting point from metaphysical system to biblical narrative[3]

In classical Latin trinitarian theology, as we have noted, a philosophically-fashioned consideration of the unity and perfections of God's being precedes an explication of the mystery of the Trinity. In contrast our four writers set aside the traditional metaphysical framework and approach. They are averse to adopting a philosophical system and then applying it to the biblical data. Each (even Lafont) returns to the biblical narrative as primary source with the express intention of giving primacy to the data. Admittedly they do this in different ways and attend to different aspects of the data; they even bring different understandings as to what qualifies as data. However, to this degree they converge in their starting point and in this respect their method of approach to trinitarian reflection differs markedly from the traditional one.

The shift in starting point is highly significant. Negatively, it represents a correction both to traditional trinitarian theology's philosophical bias and to its relative isolation from its moorings in historical revelation. Positively, when the classical metaphysical framework from which the trinitarian mystery is traditionally approached is set aside one is freed to enter into the data anew and to perceive them with new eyes. Thus von Balthasar perceives Jesus as the "form" *(Gestalt)* of God and constructs a theological aesthetics in which perception is the primary act. In a similar way Lafont, in his second volume, expresses the primacy of the founding narrative, stressing that the hearing of the narrative, chronologically and logically, has precedence over interpretation and construction of meaning. Moore brings intentionality analysis to bear on the data to reconstruct the disciples' paschal experience. Thus returning to the biblical data in these new ways, our authors are not caught up in a metaphysical scheme that would effectively predetermine their approach to the data.

---

[2]Durrwell, ch. 1, "Assessment of gains for trinitarian theology" 30–32.

[3]We encounter some difficulty in describing this shift because our authors both start from the biblical data (roughly equivalent to the biblical narrative) yet they also employ narrative form in their theologies in order to construct more refined narratives. As prime examples of this dual role of narrative in these theologies consider the narrative of the descent (von Balthasar) and that of the disciples' paschal experience (Moore).

Methodologically the result of this shift in starting point from doctrine to data, from metaphysical system to narrative, is a reordering of trinitarian theology that points to a radical revision of the whole *ordo doctrinae* of Latin Catholic theology. Such a revision is arguably more appropriate to contemporary more empirically-oriented culture and sensibilities. However, the change in starting point not only affects theology's attempt to meet contemporary exigencies and effects a revision of the traditional *ordo doctrinae*; it profoundly affects the understanding of divine being that emerges, as we have seen.

2. A shift in focus from the incarnation to paschal mystery: from Christmas to Easter

Our authors not only shift the starting point from system to data and stress the reclamation of the narrative in which the experience was first communicated. They shift their focus from the incarnation in a restricted sense to the paschal mystery of Jesus Christ, thus from Christmas to Easter; the result is a fuller sense of the incarnation. As we noted in our introduction to this study, classical trinitarian theology took shape in the fourth-century controversies that centered on the status of the Logos or Son. However, this concern for the status and origin of the Son, while of fundamental importance to Christian faith, focused attention not on the Son's *relation* to the Father or on what *function* he performed apart from the Father, but rather on the definition of the Son's ontological status. The problem for Nicea was how to express that the Son is God, equal in divinity to the Father. In the philosophically-refined milieu in which this controversy raged theological reflection was prompted to shift from the biblical, functional level of language to adopt a metaphysical or ontological terminology in order to express and, indeed, to protect the realism of Christian faith. In the process trinitarian theology, to the degree that it made any direct contact at all with the person of Jesus, turned to consider questions raised by the incarnation. In contrast our authors shift the focus of attention from the incarnation to the paschal mystery. They address the question of the nature of this God who is revealed in the death and resurrection of Jesus. The consequence of this shift in focus, as we saw in the previous chapter, is that trinitarian theology is cast in a distinctly soteriological framework.

It is important to note that this shift does not establish a counter-theology; instead we find a refinement of and a complement to traditional trinitarian theology. In this new approach to the mystery of the Trinity the incarnation—and creation itself—is the necessary *a priori* for the supreme revelation of God in the paschal mystery. It too, from the perspective of the paschal mystery, is revelatory of the paschal character of God's being. In von Balthasar's terms the creation is another modality of the *kenosis* of God *ad extra*. Its possibility, like that of the paschal mystery, is grounded in the primordial *kenosis ad intra*. Nor is creation a mere *a priori* in these theologies: in the paschal mystery creation is brought to its full accomplishment. In a genuine divinization, it enters into trinitarian communion.

By no means are the paschal mystery and the incarnation set at odds; instead the paschal mystery is the incarnation brought to full expression, its completion and consummation. A fuller and richer sense of the incarnation results. This is especially evident in Lafont's theology where explorations of the anthropological and theological meaning of the paschal mystery converge in an understanding that being, human and divine, is intrinsically paschal.

One of the consequences of this shift in starting point from the incarnation to the paschal mystery is that the biblical categories of sonship and fatherhood, rather than those of God and Word, tend to predominate in these trinitarian theologies. The relationship between Father and Son becomes the focus of attention while, to some extent at least, the image of the Second Person as the Word is overshadowed. From this perspective the classical psychological image of trinitarian theology is even farther removed from these authors' trinitarian reflections. This, I suggest, points to an area worthy of further development for scripturally-inspired trinitarian theologies. An appropriation of the full range of the biblical data in regard to trinitarian relationality (such as that offered, for example, in the baptism-anointing of Jesus)[4] promises an even fuller explication of the mystery of the Trinity. A reclamation of the God-Word symbolism also offers possibilities for meeting the feminist critique that these theologies before us, focusing as they do so heavily on the Father-Son relationship and terminology, must inevitably face. I shall return to this point in the conclusion.

3. A reversal of ordo doctrinae in trinitarian theology

The Thomistic *ordo doctrinae* in treating the mystery of the Trinity commences with a consideration of the unity of God and then proceeds to the Trinity *ad intra*. After the unity and attributes of divine being comes a consideration of the immanent processions, and the equality and consubstantiality of the Three is carefully established. The Thomistic approach then proceeds to the relations, thence to the persons, and finally to the missions. Consideration of the visible missions extends only to the incarnation and Pentecost. Aquinas's highly systematic consideration of the Trinity is thus conducted in apparent isolation from the other events of salvation history. His treatment of the mystery of Jesus' life, death, and resurrection, and the mystery of our salvation that it effected, figures much later in the *Tertia Pars* of the *Summa Theologiae*, quite separate from his considerations of the mystery of the Trinity.

In the trinitarian theologies of Durrwell and von Balthasar, however, we find a very different order of approach. They do not set out with a prior con-

---

[4]We shall later, in our concluding chapter, address David Coffey's work in this regard.

sideration of the divine unity and its perfections. They also reverse the Thomistic *ordo doctrinae* and adopt an order of approach whereby the Trinity *ad extra*, not the Trinity *ad intra*, is starting point for reflection. In other words their trinitarian reflections commence with a consideration of the Trinity as revealed in the missions and the concrete events of salvation history. Aquinas's way of exposition, *via doctrinae*, is thus replaced by the way of discovery, *via inventionis*, as our authors return to the biblical data that record the experience on the basis of which the early Church was led to proclaim the trinitarian and christological dogmas.

While our authors share a common starting point in the experience of the Trinity *ad extra* as witnessed in the New Testament we find among them different orders of approach in treating the mystery of the Trinity. This is perhaps hardly surprising since none intends a properly systematic synthetic statement of trinitarian theology of the kind Aquinas envisaged. In addition to different orders of treatment of the mystery of the Trinity different aspects of the biblical narrative are accorded different emphases. Nonetheless our authors, including Lafont, clearly converge in espousing the economic way of approach. In doing so they avoid the problem inherent in the immanent way of approach to trinitarian theology, a tendency to sever the mystery of the Trinity from its economic roots. On the other hand these trinitarian theologies, approached from the perspective of the paschal mystery, must eventually contend with the problems that inevitably arise in the economic way—particularly the problems of tritheism, subordinationism, and, indeed, anthropomorphism.

All in all, in this reversal of the traditional *ordo doctrinae* in trinitarian theology we find a radical challenge to the traditional order of Latin Catholic trinitarian theology that left the paschal mystery as "empirical residue"[5] in regard to a consideration of the mystery of the Trinity. Instead of beginning with the existence of God and the divine attributes and thence proceeding to a consideration of the Trinity these authors firmly ground a consideration of God's triune being in a reflection on the Trinity as revealed in salvation history. The doctrine of the Trinity is not appended to that of God's essence and attributes. The divine attributes are considered in the light of, not prior to reflection on the Three who are revealed in the paschal mystery.

Undoubtedly the *ordo inventionis* is a part of theology, a very valuable part, and the authors whose theologies we have studied have employed it most powerfully and evocatively. The question remains, however, whether a strict reversal of the *ordo doctrinae* constitutes properly *systematic* theology.

4. A shift from metaphysical to psychological categories

Setting aside a prior philosophical consideration of God's essential nature and attributes, our authors also eschew substance-based metaphysical categories

---

[5]Introduction, 2 n. 2.

to explicate the mystery of the Trinity. The validity of substance-based metaphysics is not denied although its adequacy and appropriateness in the contemporary context is. Moore in particular is acutely conscious and appreciative of the role of the theoretic mediation of meaning that scholastic theology represents and at the same time of the need for a new form of mediation. The traditional framework for understanding the mystery is no longer disclosive or persuasive in a culture that is neither competent nor confident in the realm of classical metaphysics. Thus without repudiating the classical approach, and resituating trinitarian theology within a soteriological context, our authors effectively rework the traditional metaphysically-fashioned categories of trinitarian theology and attempt to render the difference-in-unity that is inherent in traditional trinitarian theology in more dynamic and relational terms.

Metaphysically-fashioned categories are replaced by psychologically-fashioned categories. The category of relationality becomes central. Traditional substance categories recede in importance and yield to more affective personalist and relational categories. This is particularly evident, for example, in our authors' understanding of the divine essence and unity. It is not explicated in terms of substantial categories but in terms of *perichoresis*, and that of a distinctly psychological kind. Mission is recast in more personal terms. Recall, for example, Durrwell's and von Balthasar's emphasis on the redemptive mission as uniquely and properly the Son's, expressive of his person as Son.[6] Personhood is explicated in specifically relational terms.[7] Similarly the divine persons are not explicated in a rather abstract a-historical way as subsistent relations, but as dynamically interacting subjects.[8] The relations are not somewhat immobilist relations of opposition or origin, but are instead expressed in more psychological terms as dynamic relations of interpersonal love. Finally, the processions are not elucidated in terms of a faculty analysis but rather in terms of the relationality of love.[9] Throughout we find a refashioning of traditional metaphysical categories in more personalist and relational terms.

We have also observed that our authors convey more vividly the essence of God's being in terms of love. The ramifications of this shift are particularly evident in a consideration of the divine perfections. There we find a substantial modification of the traditional account of the divine attributes and, I suggest, a far more adequate answer to the modern protest against an understanding of God as immutable and impassible. However, the significance of this transposition of trinitarian theology into the categories of love and the reconstitution of the mystery in a soteriological context is that it affords what, in Lonergan's terms, we would describe as "a higher viewpoint"[10] for theologi-

---

[6]Durrwell, ch. 1 n. 39; von Balthasar: ch. 3 nn. 47–53.
[7]Durrwell, ch. 1 nn. 73–74; Lafont: ch. 2 nn. 29–31; von Balthasar: ch. 3 nn. 54, 55.
[8]Lafont, ch. 2 nn. 33–56.
[9]Durrwell, ch. 1 nn. 55, 56, 77; von Balthasar: ch. 3 n. 108.
[10]Durrwell, ch. 1 n. 85.

cal reflection, a vantage point from which to effect a more wide-ranging integration of theological themes. In von Balthasar's theology in particular we see the extensive interconnection of themes that this higher viewpoint affords. Pneumatology, christology, soteriology, creation, and ecclesiology all find their point of connection in the mystery of the Trinity. Conceived in this way the mystery of the Trinity, far from being somewhat esoteric and peripheral to the major concerns of theology, emerges as the centerpiece in which the others find their meaning and point of connection.

Points of divergence in theological method

Despite all this we also find notable differences in method among the four scholars that are worthy of attention.

1. Differences in methodology

We first find considerable differences in methodology and methodological awareness in our authors. Durrwell approaches trinitarian theology by way of a biblical theology and does not engage in considerations of historical or methodological factors. Indeed, David Stanley comments that the value of Durrwell's study of the resurrection would have been enhanced considerably by some attention to the historical development of this most important New Testament theme.[11] In contrast, in his historical survey of the development in trinitarian theology Lafont recognizes changes in theological methodology over the centuries[12] but lacks a meta-methodological framework within which to situate and interpret those methodological developments. Von Balthasar's work is undoubtedly grounded in a carefully considered and meticulously constructed methodological framework but it is one that is uniquely, even idiosyncratically, his own. Although von Balthasar is deeply acquainted with the tradition, his work too appears to lack a meta-methodological awareness of his own project in relation to theological development generally. On the other hand Moore, despite the rather sketchy character of his theology, is acutely aware of methodological differences and clearly situates them in the meta-methodological framework developed by Bernard Lonergan. Moore operates consciously in the realm of interiority, the realm of conscious psychological experience; the intentional operations of the *human* subject are his focus. When he comes to consider the immanent processions of the divine subject the intentional processes of the human subject then serve as an analogy,

---

[11]David Michael Stanley, *Christ's Resurrection in Pauline Soteriology.* Analecta Biblica Investigationes Scientificae in Res Biblicas 13 (Rome: Pontifical Biblical Institute, 1961) 16 n. 81.

[12]Recall that Lafont devotes the first part of *PCDJ* to a study of the post-Nicene tradition. See *PCDJ* 31–167.

as they do in the traditional Thomistic treatment, although there in a meta-physically-grounded framework.[13] In contrast to Moore, von Balthasar is deeply suspicious of any turn to the subject. His determinedly revelation-centered theology refuses to incorporate the classical psychological analogy or its modern transposition. He effectively addresses the interiority of the *divine* subject as the intending subject in the paschal mystery.

Our authors' methodologies affect the choice, development, and use of trinitarian categories. While we see in each a shift from the substance-based metaphysical categories of traditional trinitarian theology to more personalist and relational categories to describe the mystery of the Trinity, psychological categories are employed in rather different ways. Durrwell applies psychological categories in an essentially uncritical "common sense" fashion.[14] Lafont, operating basically within the traditional approach, applies them somewhat extrinsically.[15] In his theology psychological categories are introduced to serve theory. In contrast the application of psychological categories is *intrinsic* to Moore's treatment. His application of psychological categories is grounded in an intentionality analysis of the conscious subject.[16] Interiority is not just supplement but ground for his theological exploration. In short he not only applies, but *appropriates* psychological categories, inviting his readers to a critical, religious self-appropriation.

2. What qualifies as data

Differences are clearly evident in our authors' use of data. Recall that we observed that our authors privilege different narrative points, be it the death (Lafont), the descent (von Balthasar), or the resurrection (Durrwell). However, differences emerge not only in the use of the data by these authors but in their understanding of *what qualifies as data* for trinitarian theology. Moore pushes the question to the limit in his reconstruction of the disciples' experience, his own imaginative post-critical construction of data. This raises the question: what legitimately constitutes data for theological reflection? Moreover, if such a reconstruction is to be admitted how are we to verify its meaning and assess its validity? The question of objectivity clearly becomes crucial when metaphysical theory no longer serves to control theological meanings. I will return to this issue in the conclusion.

A further question arises concerning the relationship between the data and the discussion of the meaning of the data, that is, between experience and explication. Durrwell's biblical theology and his determination to confine his theologizing within the realm of biblical terms and categories fundamentally raises the question whether the terms of the biblical data determine the terms

---

[13]Moore, ch. 4 n. 10.
[14]Durrwell, ch. 1 n. 74.
[15]Lafont, ch. 2 nn. 39, 48–51.
[16]Moore, ch. 4, "Moore's resources: narrative, psychology, and intentionality analysis" 94–95.

of theological discussion regarding the meaning of the data. Durrwell, as we have noted, retrieves the biblical narrative of the paschal mystery in what is basically a pre-critical manner, apparently untroubled by the exegetical problems inherent in such a biblical synthesis or by metaphysical questions in regard to the divine being. Though his emphasis on the biblical data as the starting point for theology cannot be contested, the critical question is whether or not the point of entry also defines and determines the terms of the discussion about God's being. This was essentially the point at issue in the Nicene proclamation of *homoousios,* when a non-biblical term was introduced into theological discourse in order to express the meaning of the biblical data and thus to protect the realism of Christian faith. Durrwell's biblical theology fundamentally raises the same sort of question Nicea was called to address. The Council's answer, the proclamation of *homoousios,* was a recognition that biblical terminology does not suffice, that non-biblical terminology is legitimate and, indeed, given the philosophical milieu in which the question was raised, necessary to affirm the mysteries of Christian faith. Ultimately, then, a systematic theology cannot be constrained to the terms and categories of the biblical data. Though invaluable to the theological enterprise, biblical theology in Durrwell's sense is no substitute for technical systematic explication of the mysteries of faith.

Nicea marked the point of entry of incipiently metaphysical terminology and conceptuality into Christian theology. Today, however, it seems that theology faces a new challenge in its task of affirming the realism of Christian faith. Where Nicea employed *metaphysical* categories in response to the questions of its time, contemporary theology faces the challenge of employing *psychological* categories. What we see, in effect, before us in this new development in trinitarian theology is the entry of distinctly psychological terminology and conceptuality into theology. This introduction into theological discourse of psychological, as distinct from metaphysical terminology and categories is another significant feature of the originality of this new development in trinitarian theology.

In contrast to Durrwell's pre-critical approach to the data both Lafont and Moore recognize that a simple return to the narrative form of the data alone is not sufficient. In *God, Time and Being* Lafont stresses that the narrative unaided cannot respond to ontological questions the narrative itself inevitably raises—as, for example, in Durrwell's theology that implicitly raises the question of change in God. Lafont understands that the interpretation of the narrative demands the principle of analogy. However as a corrective to traditional theology, so strongly focused on the principle of analogy and correspondingly far removed from the biblical data, Lafont insists that the narrative always has primacy and serves to inspire, direct, and challenge analogical interpretation of the narrative and construction of meaning.[17]

[17]Lafont, ch. 2 nn. 59–64.

Moore, who approaches the narrative with what we could describe as a post-critical sensitivity, also recognizes that the narrative alone is not sufficient, but for very different reasons from those of Lafont: his point is that the narrative cannot answer *existential* questions of meaning. Neither can theory and systematically formulated doctrine suffice, necessary and correct though the dogma and formulations of doctrine are. Something more than the narrative itself, and something more than metaphysical theory, is required. The narrative and the theory do not and cannot tell the believing self what the paschal mystery means "for me" personally and existentially. At this point Lafont's distinction between narrative and construction of meaning and the principle that productions of meaning are to be judged in the light of whether and to what extent they evoke conversion (that is, do they have the effect of the founding narrative on its hearers?)[18] is helpful. It provides the acid test, a means by which to justify and assess Moore's rather provocative project. From Lafont's perspective Moore's reconstruction is justified as a production of meaning to the extent that it facilitates Christian conversion. At this juncture Lafont meets Moore, for the facilitation of conversion is precisely Moore's objective.

Lafont's principle also provides justification for von Balthasar's extraordinary account of the descent into hell. As in the case of Moore's psychological reconstruction of the disciples' experience, there is little direct biblical warrant for von Balthasar's extraordinary emphasis on this aspect of the paschal mystery. However, as in Moore's case, von Balthasar's is no pre-critical reclamation of the narrative. On the contrary, this is theology in a highly refined post-critical constructive mode. It is justified, in Lafont's terms, if it prompts the conversion the founding narrative prompted.

3. The use of the paschal mystery as analogy

Among the more remarkable and truly novel features of the theologies we have examined is the recognition that the paschal mystery is not only redemptive but revelatory. Where the traditional approach accords a redemptive meaning to the death and resurrection of Jesus, here the paschal mystery is recognized as having properly theological meaning, shedding light on the divine being itself, revealing God's inner triune relationality. Whereas the traditional Thomistic approach to trinitarian theology had its understanding mediated through the psychological image explicated in very theoretical way, we find our authors, Durrwell and von Balthasar in particular, focusing on the paschal mystery not merely as metaphor but as analogy, properly speaking, of trinitarian life. Instead of looking for an analogy from human experience to describe the trinitarian being they focus on Jesus in his paschal mystery.

Both von Balthasar and Durrwell expressly reject the classical psychological analogy and insist that both processions be understood as processions of

[18]Lafont, ch. 2 n. 64.

love.[19] At the very least they challenge the hegemony of the psychological analogy in traditional Latin trinitarian theology. However, more than this, they construct their trinitarian theologies on the basis of the trinitarian relationality that is revealed in the paschal mystery itself.

Admittedly Lafont effectively locates a consideration of the paschal mystery *within* the classical approach. However, the paschal mystery profoundly affects his treatment of the divine persons. Thus although he incorporates a consideration of the paschal mystery into the traditional framework it is the gift of self, the loss of self in the other that is revealed in the paschal mystery, the law of spiritual being he finds expressed there that prompts Lafont to modify the traditional approach in a remarkable way. Indeed, in my judgment his treatment of the interconnection and the paschal character of being, both human and divine, that emerges from the paschal mystery is the most subtle of the approaches before us, a careful adjustment to the traditional Thomistic scheme. In Lafont's treatment the paschal mystery becomes *intrinsic* to the system. Here lies the striking originality of his contribution.

Moore, on the other hand, to the degree that he considers the mystery of the trinitarian processions transposes the psychological image into the terms of intentionality analysis—the cognitive and affective experience of the conscious subject. Transposed in this way the psychological analogy becomes newly relevant, no longer remote from our experience but firmly grounded in an appropriation of the experience of intentional subjects.[20] Moore's reappropriation of the psychological analogy is a salutary reminder that this classical analogy continues to enjoy considerable explicative power and is more in need of being complemented than replaced. Fundamentally the *hegemony* of the psychological image in the tradition is being challenged in these theologies, not its legitimacy or value. Indeed, in effect Moore implies that it is the *balance* of knowing and loving that needs attention in trinitarian theology. From this perspective we can recognize that these renewed trinitarian theologies focusing as they do on the paschal mystery as mystery of love function to redress an imbalance in this regard in the traditional method of explication.

4. The use of metaphor

Not only do we find in these authors a new sense of paschal mystery as analogy, but also more general use of analogical thinking employing metaphor, traditionally designated as "analogy of improper proportionality." Recall that one of the remarkable features of von Balthasar's theological method is that he quite deliberately employs the full spectrum of speech, from metaphor through to analogy, about God. He expressly attempts to combine the use of

---

[19]Durrwell, ch. 1 nn. 55, 56, 77; von Balthasar, ch. 3 n. 108.

[20]Moore, ch. 4, section "Classical trinitarian theology as dogmatized mystical experience" 103–105.

metaphor with properly analogical speech.[21] His work stands to challenge those who would hold that metaphor has no place in systematic theology. Certainly there is no difficulty in admitting metaphor into *descriptive* or *explanatory* theological discourse. The communication of trinitarian doctrine has long been served by this practice. However, here the issue fundamentally turns on whether metaphor can serve not simply for the explanation and communication of faith but in its proper *systematic* expression. That metaphor can and, indeed, should serve in the systematic explication of faith: this is the methodological challenge von Balthasar's work poses. While recognizing that metaphor needs to be set within a strong ontological framework and complemented by strictly analogical speech, he insists that metaphor is indispensable to systematics.

Still, as his critics respond and we must agree, the use of metaphorical language is highly problematic. It is inherently imprecise because it relies on the context in which it is used for clarification of its meaning and at the very least on a strong ontological framework to control that meaning. Highly prone to ambiguity, it is vulnerable to misinterpretation, yet despite the dangers it is very evocative and manifestly highly apt for the expression of "the beautiful," as von Balthasar realizes. This, indeed, is its virtue. We can agree with O'Hanlon who, after a thorough and careful study of von Balthasar's theology in regard to the question of divine immutability, concludes: "I believe that the main thrust of his [von Balthasar's] position on theological discourse is acceptable; he has argued persuasively that a combined conceptual and metaphorical approach is needed to evoke a response in us to the scriptural presentation of mystery."[22] If, again, we invoke Lafont's principle that any construction of meaning is to be judged according to whether it brings about the conversion provoked by the founding narrative von Balthasar's use of metaphor, employed within the full spectrum of theological language and adequately grounded in an ontological framework, can be justified. To the degree that it can be, so much of his treatment of, say, the descent and the trinitarian relations, makes sense.

These, then, are the general methodological issues that arise in the theologies before us. Interconnecting the paschal mystery with the Trinity, our authors pose a remarkable challenge to the traditional method of approach to trinitarian theology. The gains they achieve in their trinitarian theologies ultimately turn on the shift in starting point, for in setting aside a metaphysical approach and privileging the biblical narrative they open up a new horizon within which to perceive and, indeed, receive the revelation given in the paschal mystery. New ranges of data come forward for consideration and prompt new ranges of analogical speech in which to express the meaning of

---

[21]Von Balthasar, ch. 3, "From metaphor to analogy: use of the full continuum of language in theology" 87–89.

[22]O'Hanlon, *The Immutability of God* 143.

the data. The hegemony of the classical psychological analogy, which has for so long dominated considerations of the immanent Trinity, is overturned as attention turns to the paschal mystery as paradigmatically revelatory of trinitarian relationality. Certainly, the psychological analogy can continue to serve to elucidate the mystery, as Moore's work clearly demonstrates, but in this reconstruction of trinitarian theology the status of the psychological analogy is, in effect, relativized in relation to the paschal mystery.

A meta-methodological inquiry

Our four authors share much in common in their dissatisfaction with traditional Latin trinitarian theology, in their return to the biblical data and in particular to the paschal mystery, and in the essential features of their respective trinitarian theologies. Nevertheless we also observe notable differences among them in their particular methodologies, the data they employ, the technical terms and categories they use, and their appropriation of traditional trinitarian theology. We want now to consider deeper methodological issues and try to give some explanation of these differences.

Clearly the differences among our authors' works could be explained at least in part in terms of different cultural backgrounds, religious formation, education, theological training, and formative influences. However, while such distinctions would undoubtedly assist in accounting for the ways in which, for example, Durrwell's theology differs from that of Lafont, this level of explanation hardly addresses the deeper questions that arise when their works are compared. Is there not something more intrinsic to the person, a more refined framework allowing for not merely external influences on the theologian but including all the more tacit dimensions of consciousness? After all, any theology is the work of a person's mind, heart, and imagination. It should in principle be possible for us to describe the mentality that produces a particular work and thus to account for pluralism of the kind we have observed in our study. Clearly we must approach the task of describing a writer's consciousness with some caution. There is so much in the formation of any particular person's consciousness, the values that inform it, the images that inspire it, of which we are unaware. Yet some explanation is surely possible. The theologies before us present the data in terms of divergences in methodology, use of data, and use of categories. These differences constitute data for a meta-methodological inquiry.

Here Bernard Lonergan's analysis of the self-transcending character of human subjectivity is useful.[23] On the basis of an analysis of the intending

---

[23]See especially William F. J. Ryan and Bernard J. Tyrrell, eds., *Method in Theology. A Second Collection: Papers by Bernard J. F. Lonergan, S.J.* (London: Darton, Longman and Todd, 1974); Frederick E. Crowe, ed., *A Third Collection: Papers by Bernard J. F. Lonergan, S.J.* (New York: Paulist, 1985); *Collection; Understanding and Being;* Bernard Lonergan, *The Way to Nicea: The Dialectical Development of Trinitarian Theology.*

consciousness of the human subject Lonergan constructs a transcendental method, a method intrinsic to all potential methods. As he explains: "Transcendental method is not the intrusion into theology of alien matter from an alien source. Its function is to advert to the fact that theologies are produced by theologians, that theologians have minds and use them, that their doing so should not be ignored or passed over but explicitly acknowledged in itself and in its implications."[24]

Lonergan attends to the very sort of question we are asking here. His analysis considers the theologian as intending subject. The theologies before us are the fruit of four different minds attending, at least *prima facie,* to the same question, the interconnection of the mystery of the Trinity with the paschal mystery. With Lonergan's assistance we may therefore indicate something about the mentalities at work in the theologies before us.

1. Lonergan's analysis of intentionality and the sources of cognitive pluralism

Lonergan, by means of an analysis of intentionality, is able to trace pluralism in theological expression and meaning to its roots in conscious subjectivity. He explains:

> There are three sources of pluralism. First, linguistic, social, and cultural differences give rise to different brands of common sense. Secondly, consciousness may be undifferentiated or it may be differentiated to deal expertly with some combinations of such different realms as common sense, transcendence, beauty, system, method, scholarship, and philosophic interiority. Thirdly, in any individual at any given time there may exist the abstract possibility, or the beginnings, or greater or less progress, or high development of intellectual or moral or religious conversion.[25]

Lonergan thus locates the source of pluralism in terms of (1) different "brands" of common sense, (2) differentiations of consciousness, and (3) conversion. While authentic subjectivity always remains beholden to the transcendental precepts—be attentive, intelligent, reasonable, responsible[26]—the numerous brands of common sense, the various differentiations of consciousness, the different forms of conversion, and the various possible combinations lead to the manifold diversity that is pluralism, such as is evident in the theologies we have studied.

In terms of our study, given that we have confined our investigation to Catholic theology in the Western-Latin tradition we may, I propose, set aside

---

[24]Lonergan, *Method in Theology* 24–25.
[25]Ibid. 326.
[26]Ibid. 268.

the category of "common sense." Our four authors work within one theological tradition. There is a high degree of mutually shared understanding of the questions at hand, the traditional approach to the question, and the terminology and methodology of classical trinitarian theology. We may therefore consider that our four authors work within the one essentially Western-Latin "common sense" of Christian faith.

However, the category of differentiations of consciousness is, I suggest, potentially a most useful one in understanding cognitive pluralism such as our chosen authors present to us.[27] Clearly the presence of different differentiations of consciousness will result in a diversity in the expression of theological meaning. Consider, for example, the way an aesthetically differentiated consciousness, as distinct from a scientifically differentiated consciousness, would express itself: the data to which it would attend, the categories and images it would employ, and the values it would espouse. Thus it would appear that the category of differentiations of consciousness may enable us to account, at least to some degree, for the differences we see in our study.

Lonergan also identifies a form of development that is not simply differentiation, but conversion. Conversion, unlike differentiation of consciousness, involves not merely a development but a radical transformation of the subject. With conversion something quite new emerges in the subject that profoundly affects the subject's intentional operations, for it determines the very horizon within which the subject exercises his or her intentionality: "Conversion involves a new understanding of oneself because, more fundamentally, it brings about a new self to be understood. It is putting off the old man and putting on the new. It is not just a development but the beginning of a new mode of developing."[28]

Lonergan identifies three moments of conversion: intellectual, moral, and religious.[29] In later writings he adds affective conversion as another horizon of integrity and authenticity. Robert Doran, appropriating the resources of depth psychology, argues that psychic conversion should take its place alongside Lonergan's foundational conversions.[30] These conversions locate us within a

[27]For Lonergan's understanding of differentiations of consciousness see *Method in Theology* 81–85, 257. He describes the development of differentiations of consciousness in terms of different exigencies that give rise to different modes of conscious and intentional operation that then give rise to different realms of meaning. In other words a differentiation of consciousness occurs in the formation of a new realm of meaning as a response to a specific exigency. Lonergan identifies four realms of meaning in fully differentiated consciousness: the realm of common sense, the realm of theory, the realm of interiority, and the realm of transcendence.

[28]Lonergan, "Unity and Plurality: The Coherence of Christian Truth" in *A Third Collection* 247.

[29]*Method in Theology* 237–247, 318, 338.

[30]See in particular Robert M. Doran, *Subject and Psyche: Ricoeur, Jung, and the Search for Foundations*; idem, *Psychic Conversion and Theological Foundations: Towards a Reorientation of the Human Sciences*; idem, *Theology and the Dialectics of History*. Doran maintains that Lonergan's analysis of intentionality does not represent a full appropriation of human subjectivity and omits the affective-psychic drama that accompanies the operations of each intentional level. He proposes that human consciousness is twofold in its constitution. In addition to the

horizon of knowledge that, through their presence or absence in different combinations, differentiates us radically from one another. Conversion, profoundly affecting the horizon within which a theologian works and thus the categories that are then employed, would appear to be another potentially valuable meta-methodological category to bring to bear in our inquiry.

2. *Situating this new development in terms of intentionality analysis*

Equipped with categories from Lonergan's method, we can first situate this new development in trinitarian theology generally in terms of self-transcending subjectivity responding to the transcendental precepts (be attentive, be intelligent, be reasonable, be responsible), thereby manifesting the consciousness pertaining to each level of intentionality. Thus we can observe that:

(a) in attending to forgotten data in the biblical narrative of the paschal mystery an empirical consciousness is evident (be attentive);

(b) in the new theological meanings our authors find in the paschal mystery, an intellectual consciousness (be intelligent) is found;

(c) in the newly-fashioned categories, new ranges of analogical speech, in new evidence and argument they adduce, they manifest a rational consciousness (be reasonable); and

(d) in a readiness to advance, so to carry forward the tradition, a moral consciousness (be responsible) is evident.

There is also a more profound and radical transformation of consciousness that is shared by them in their interconnection of the paschal mystery and the Trinity and that, I suggest, can be described in terms of conversion, in effect "a conversion to the paschal mystery." In the new horizon for trinitarian thinking that emerges in these theologies we can discern a conversion that is

(a) religious, for a new sense of the divine mystery is clearly manifest in these theologies,

(b) intellectual, for a new Christian realism emerges, involving new meanings for Christian faith not hitherto explored, new analogies—

---

spiritual dimension of intentionality there is the sensitive psychic component of consciousness. While the integrity of the intentional aspect consists in the disinterested orientation of consciousness to the transcendental objectives of intelligibility, truth, goodness, and love, this aesthetic dimension participates in intentionality itself and constitutes the sensitive orientation to the beautiful. Fletcher observes that Lonergan himself conceded that there is a lacuna in his own work in terms of the psychic dimension of interiority and the appropriation of the symbolic. (See Frank Fletcher's unpublished D.Theol. diss., "Exploring Christian Theology's Foundations in Religious Experience" [Melbourne College of Divinity, 1982] 303.) Fletcher also notes that Lonergan spoke approvingly of Doran's work and accepted psychic conversion as a necessary fourth conversion ("Exploring Christian Theology's Foundations" 304). Doran thus offers a distinctly psychological complement (not a correction, he emphasizes) to Lonergan's theological foundations.

preeminently the paschal mystery—and a new sense of the interconnectedness of the Christian mysteries; and finally

(c) moral, for a new sense of Christian responsibility in a world afflicted with an excess of evil also emerges.

In this way, then, we can situate this new development in trinitarian theology generally in terms of its foundations in the intending consciousness of the converted subject. Nonetheless, while each of our authors is beholden to the same transcendental precepts and the processes of intentionality they clearly adopt very different perspectives and methods.

3. An application of Lonergan's category of differentiations of consciousness

Lonergan's method not only allows us to situate the development in general terms in the processes of authentic self-transcending subjectivity. We can press further and describe, in a more refined and discriminating way, the consciousness our different authors manifest. In Lonergan's category of differentiations of consciousness we find a means to describe these differences and account for them in terms of the polymorphic structure of consciousness. As we have mentioned, an aesthetically differentiated consciousness will express itself in quite different categories from a theoretically differentiated consciousness or an interiorly differentiated consciousness or, indeed, an undifferentiated consciousness. Let us turn now to consider our four authors separately in order to identify the differentiation of consciousness manifested in the works we have studied, thus to render some account of the differences and facilitate a deeper understanding of the contribution each represents.

Durrwell's theology: a relatively undifferentiated consciousness with respect to theory

As we have noted, Durrwell's work, confined as it is to the realm of biblical theology, resists engagement with systematic questions. Admittedly Durrwell does at times show that he is aware of systematic questions in relation to trinitarian theology. However, his treatment of theoretical and metaphysical considerations is episodic and on the occasions when he does address such questions it is essentially undeveloped because his theology resolutely avoids the use of non-biblical categories. Nevertheless, as we have also mentioned, questions such as that concerning change in God arising from the biblical data cannot be answered adequately by use of biblical categories alone. The method of biblical theology lacks the technical and conceptual apparatus to answer such questions. It eschews technical language and canons of method. It is concerned neither with issues of biblical criticism in regard to the texts employed nor with questions of theological foundations and systematics, content to leave such questions for other specialists. On the basis of these sorts of observations we can, with all respect for his work and the achievement it represents, describe Durrwell's work in Lonergan's terms as reflecting a relatively undifferentiated consciousness—undifferentiated, that is, with respect to theory.

Lacking a critical theoretical moment, Durrwell's approach is a rather intuitive one. His terminology is loose and begs for clarification and refinement. Effectively his method amounts to a pre-Nicene manner of theologizing. We could also say that his work is located within what could be described as the realm of the "common sense" of faith as distinct from the realm of theory. It is more interested in grounding the realism of Christian faith in its primary sources and in pastoral concerns. Recall, for example, his exploration of the procession of the Holy Spirit, which is motivated by an ecumenical concern.[31]

Undoubtedly this description of Durrwell's theology needs to be understood in the light of his overriding concern that the prevailing theology of his time was more dogmatic than biblical. In that context he attempted to correct an overly dogmatic emphasis by means of a return to the biblical data. This, indeed, is the virtue of his contribution. Nevertheless, the danger for this relatively undifferentiated "common sense" approach is that the interconnection of the paschal mystery and the Trinity is expressed and understood as merely "spiritual" or "homiletic" in form.

Lafont's theology: a theoretically differentiated consciousness

In contrast to Durrwell's work Lafont's theology is much more theoretical. Its primary concern is not pastoral or ecumenical but theoretical and systematic. It does not confine itself to the biblical field of reference but employs theoretical categories and analogies to address those concerns. Recall our observation that Lafont's exploration of the actual content of the biblical paschal narrative is relatively brief. Compared to Durrwell, in his interconnection of the Trinity and the paschal mystery Lafont moves to a higher level of abstraction from the biblical data, showing concern for systematic clarity and coherence in trinitarian theology. This is evident, for example, in his critique of Boethius's definition of person as it is used in Aquinas's *Summa Theologiae*. It appears, then, that a concern for theoretical coherence and conceptual clarity drives Lafont's work. Although he employs psychological categories he does this for the sake of theory. It is systematic control of meaning that prevails in his writings. On these grounds Lafont brings what we could describe, in Lonergan's terms, as a theoretically differentiated consciousness to the interconnection of the mysteries.

On the other hand, in contrast to Moore, Lafont's historical survey and analysis of the post-Nicene tradition shows a lack of the meta-methodological consciousness Moore demonstrates in his historical survey when he situates the stages of theological development in terms of the emergence of new exi-

---

[31]See Durrwell, "Foreword," *SFS* 10–11.

gencies for meaning in human subjectivity.[32] Though Lafont observes the development in theological method he lacks a meta-methodological transcendental framework within which to understand and account for the development. Here too it is evident that Lafont's work is primarily the fruit of a theoretically differentiated consciousness. He works, in effect, in what Lonergan describes as the second stage of meaning. Although consciousness is theoretical as well as common-sense in this second stage of meaning, theory is not sufficiently well advanced for the sharp distinction between the two realms of meaning to be adequately grasped. Hence Lafont is unable to advert to the meta-methodological significance of the theological developments he observes. An appreciation of the significance of the distinction between the two realms only comes in the third stage of meaning.[33] One is then able to return to the realms of common sense and theory with an ability to meet the methodological exigency. This is what we see in Moore's meta-methodological account of the development in trinitarian theology and it is precisely what Lafont is apparently unable to do.

What is particularly interesting, however, is that in recasting the notion of person Lafont appropriates a kind of consciousness or interiority. It is not the understanding of consciousness that Lonergan describes in far more detailed, sophisticated, and psychologically-informed fashion.[34] Nevertheless, the beginning of an interiority of some kind is evident here as Lafont re-situates the notion of person in terms of reflection on the intentionality of act. Person is thus understood in terms of interpersonal operations and described in personalist and relational categories. The shift adumbrates a full appropriation of a personalist or reflexive philosophy in trinitarian theology on the basis of a fully interiorly-differentiated consciousness. It foreshadows a transposition of the notion of person from substance-based metaphysical categories into psychological categories founded on an analysis of interiority. However, on the basis of the work we have before us Lafont's method is evidently not differentiated in the realm of interiority. He stays within the theoretic realm of meaning wherein Thomistic trinitarian theology is also generally situated. While he applies psychological categories in his trinitarian theology in designating the divine persons, that application is not consciously grounded in an appropriation of interiority and the data of consciousness; it is thus not intrinsic to his method. To that degree, rather like Augustine's psychological analogies, his application of psychological categories has a somewhat extrinsic character about it. Hence while we see a concern to shift away from classical metaphysical categories in designating the divine persons we do not see a fully developed shift to psychological categories that is the fruit of an interiorly-differentiated consciousness.

[32]Moore, ch. 4, "Theology in the 'third stage of meaning'" 95–96.

[33]Lonergan, *Method in Theology*, 93–96.

[34]Lonergan, *Insight: A Study of Human Understanding* (New York: Harper & Row, 1957); idem, *Method in Theology*.

Von Balthasar's theology: an aesthetically differentiated consciousness

We have noted that in their interconnection of the paschal mystery and the Trinity von Balthasar and Durrwell share a number of insights, but in fact the nature of their work is vastly different. Durrwell is concerned that theology be biblically, not dogmatically, fashioned. Von Balthasar is concerned that traditional theology has lost a sense of the aesthetic and dramatic dimension of God's salvific action in the world. Where Durrwell stays within the realm of the biblical reference, von Balthasar is deeply in dialogue with the secular as well, of course, as the tradition of Christian thought. His knowledge of the tradition is vast. He is particularly conversant with patristic literature. This is certainly no "undifferentiated consciousness" such as we described Durrwell's work. No naïve or uncritical "common sense" of faith is at work in von Balthasar's extraordinary corpus, a corpus of great sophistication and artistic sensitivity.

On the other hand, though in von Balthasar we have a highly refined consciousness and a deeply informed and cultivated intelligence, nonetheless his work is clearly not adequately to be described as one of a theoretically differentiated consciousness, as we have described Lafont's work. Certainly von Balthasar's method is theoretically differentiated, but there is manifestly something more involved.

Further light is shed on the characteristics of von Balthasar's consciousness by his theological aesthetics, where his understanding of Jesus in the paschal mystery as the "form" *(Gestalt)* of God is cast in terms of aesthetic theory.[35] In this application of aesthetic categories to Jesus as the "form" of God and the later application of dramatic categories to the drama of God's engagement with human freedom we can discern a highly refined *aesthetic* sensitivity at work. Hence I suggest that von Balthasar's is most appropriately described as an aesthetically differentiated consciousness.[36] His understanding of the act of faith itself is cast in terms of aesthetic theory: it is not primarily an act of belief or an act of understanding, but an act of *perception*. Believing is first be-

[35]O'Donnell has noted that this application of aesthetic categories is one of von Balthasar's major contributions to christology ("The Form of His Theology" 460). Note that von Balthasar carefully distinguishes between a "theological aesthetics" and an "aesthetic theology." See *The Glory of the Lord 1*, 79–117.

[36]Hilary A. Mooney in her doctoral study, *The Liberation of Consciousness: Bernard Lonergan's Theological Foundations in Dialogue with the Theological Aesthetics of Hans Urs von Balthasar*, Frankfurter Theologische Studien 41 (Frankfurt: Josef Knight, 1992) places Lonergan in dialogue with von Balthasar in order to develop the theological foundations objectified by Lonergan along the lines suggested by Hans Urs von Balthasar's theology. Introducing her dissertation, Mooney explains that "von Balthasar is introduced to play a 'catalyzing' role in the justification and amplification of a Lonerganian theological aesthetics" (p. 5). Thus Mooney in effect works in the reverse direction compared to what we are doing here. Where Mooney attempts an appraisal of the role of aesthetics in a Lonerganian foundational theology we are appraising von Balthasar's method in terms of Lonergan's categories of differentiations of consciousness in order to explicate and situate von Balthasar's project in the broader theological context.

holding, an act of active receptivity to and aesthetic contemplation of Christ's form. In von Balthasar's use of metaphor and of symbolic expression generally, particularly in his portrayal of the descent into hell, we have further evidence of an aesthetically differentiated consciousness. Such is definitely not a use of symbol and imagery that is spontaneous and uncritical in the manner pertaining to an undifferentiated consciousness. On the contrary, von Balthasar's use of symbol and imagery is the work of a conscious, explicit, and differentiated intentionality. By no means a regression to an undifferentiated pre-critical mode of thought, his dramatic, incarnationally-concrete rendering of the interconnection of the paschal mystery and the Trinity, which climaxes in the descent into hell, is a post-critical symbolic construction that is the work of a highly differentiated consciousness.

Moore's theology: an interiorly differentiated consciousness

Moore himself is able to situate his work in the meta-methodological framework described by Lonergan, as we have noted.[37] This meta-methodological awareness itself is evidence of an interiorly differentiated consciousness. It is a consciousness that is methodologically aware of the exigencies of the intending subject as they have emerged in the historical development of theology. Unlike our other authors Moore also understands the meta-methodological factors at root in the contemporary dissatisfaction with the traditional treatment of trinitarian theology. He apprehends the emergence of a new exigency in the human subject and a shift in the realm of meaning that is occurring, and thus of the need to transpose the old dogmas into new and meaningful doctrines.

Again some comparisons and contrasts are helpful. Moore clearly works within a very different realm of meaning from that of von Balthasar, for example. Moore is concerned to address the human subject's existential concerns for meaning in relation to the mysteries of Christian faith, whereas von Balthasar is not concerned for the human subject but is instead entirely focused on the divine subject in order that theology may more adequately convey the sheer glory of God.

On the other hand, unlike Lafont, Moore does not confine himself to the theoretical realm of meaning in which traditional trinitarian theology is expressed. Indeed it would appear that Moore's greatest weakness lies in the realm of theory. A theoretically differentiated consciousness is evident, but not highly developed. His theology is sketchy and lacks a certain rigor, precision, and refinement. He affirms the fundamental correctness of the traditional treatment and, on the basis of intentionality analysis, finds the classical psychological analogy once again relevant and appropriate. However, for Moore these theoretical concerns and the theoretic mediation of meaning that are the object of Lafont's attention are secondary to the experience of religious conversion itself. Moore is acutely aware that questions of understanding and

[37] Moore, ch. 4, "Theology in the 'third stage of meaning'" 95–96.

judgment of the data follow from personal experience of the data—indeed, experience in the depths of consciousness. It is the experience of conversion on which the biblical witness and later dogmatic formulae are based that Moore therefore seeks to reclaim and to evoke in his readers.

In other words, in terms of Lonergan's transcendental method, while Durrwell attends to the data of revelation but resists the systematic-theoretic task, Lafont and von Balthasar work at the explication of the Christian mysteries and Moore works at another level again, addressing the human subject's existential concern and the psychological process by which the subject comes to know that Jesus is Lord. Moore thus moves beyond concerns for explication and seeks to meet the contemporary existential concern for meaning. In seeking a psychological base in the religious psyche of the believer for the classic statements of Christian belief and searching for the psychological dynamics of the process of religious conversion he clearly locates himself in the shift to religious subjectivity as foundational for theology (as described by Lonergan). Here too we see that Moore's exploration of the interconnection of the paschal mystery and the Trinity, his "grass-roots derivation of the Trinity," is situated firmly within the realm of interiority, squarely grounded in the data of consciousness.

We find that in this way Lonergan's category of differentiations of consciousness is able to assist in describing and accounting for the differences our study presents to us. What is important here is that an application of this category, such as we have attempted here, is helpful not only in methodologically situating very different theologies, but in enhancing an assessment and understanding of their respective contributions and, moreover, furthering the possibility of theological dialogue.

4. Doran's notion of psychic conversion revisited

Returning once more to consider the development more generally one is struck yet again by the extraordinary nature of the development we have been investigating, and particularly so in the works of von Balthasar and Moore, whose highly imaginative constructions lie beyond what may be called the biblical data in any obvious sense. While Lonergan's category of conversion—religious, intellectual, and moral—is able to some degree to explain the development, our study prompts us to press even farther and to ask if there is not another factor at work in the deepest reaches of their consciousness that results in these rather striking constructions. Clearly neither Moore nor von Balthasar simply reclaims the biblical narrative. In their respective theologies each undertakes a highly creative construction. It would seem that something more than what Lonergan describes as pertaining to the intentional-spiritual realm of consciousness is at work. It seems to me that something of what Robert M. Doran describes in regard to the psychic realm of consciousness is involved.

Doran's notion of psychic conversion is a distinctly psychological contribution to Lonergan's methodological foundations and offers an even more refined terminology and methodology applicable to the deeper psychic reaches of theological subjectivity. Psychic conversion, he writes, is "a transformation of the subject, a change both illuminated and often mediated by modern depth psychology. It is a reorientation of the specifically psychic dimension of the censorship exercised over images and affects by our habitual orientations, a conversion of that dimension of the censorship from exercising a repressive function to acting constructively in one's shaping of one's own development."[38]

This notion would seem to be proportionately applicable to our authors, especially Moore and von Balthasar. Let us begin with a consideration of Moore's work from this perspective. We have seen that he attempts a psychological analysis of the actual process of transformation occurring in the event of Christian conversion. Drawing on the insights of modern psychology, he addresses the distinctly psychological dimensions of religious conversion in what he himself describes as "an aesthetic, imaginal effort, to have the events that have changed history forever enact themselves in the psychic roots of the desire to know."[39] In isolating the distinctly psychic dimension of religious conversion his work seems, therefore, more clearly to lie in the realm of affect, feeling, and symbol than in the realm of intentionality as such: the realm of the "psychic" rather than that of the "spiritual," as Doran expresses it. In this sense it would seem more appropriate to describe his project in terms of Doran's notion of psychic conversion. In fact Doran himself describes Moore's work as relying "at least in principle on what as a methodologist I call psychic conversion."[40]

Doran addresses in considerable detail the theological ramifications of his psychological complement to Lonergan's foundations.[41] He explains, for example, that this conversion in the realm of the psyche profoundly influences the theologian's choice as to what qualifies as data for theology.[42] Is this not in fact what we find in Moore's work, where the *disciples'* experience of the paschal mystery, based on Moore's appropriation of his own experience, becomes a primary source of reflection for him even though such a detailed description of their experience has little explicit biblical foundation? I think so. In his psycho-historical reconstruction we have a new sense of what qualifies as data for theology.

Doran also explains that psychic conversion affects the horizon that determines the theologian's view, the base from which the theologian engages in

[38]Doran, *Theology and the Dialectics of History* 9.
[39]Moore, "Jesus the Liberator of Desire" 496.
[40]Doran, *Theology and the Dialectics of History* 682 n. 11.
[41]See Doran, "Psychic Conversion and Hermeneutics," in *Theology and the Dialectics of History* 630–680.
[42]Doran, "Psychic Conversion," *The Thomist* 41 (1977) 236.

hermeneutics, and the ground from which theological categories and systems are derived.[43] He suggests that "such an appropriation and articulation will make possible the advent of that fully awake naïveté of the twice-born adult which Paul Ricoeur calls a second, post-critical immediacy."[44] It is not that a new set of theological doctrinal statements results but rather that new meanings attach to those statements. Is this not also what we see in Moore and, indeed, proportionately in our other authors? Classical trinitarian theology is not rejected as such, but new meanings and values are attached to the classical formulations and categories of traditional trinitarian theology. Thus in Moore's hands the doctrine of the Trinity, traditionally explicated in a highly theoretical fashion in terms of the psychological analogy, is transposed into the categories of intending subjectivity to emerge with deeply existential meaning. Recall Moore's "grass-roots derivation of the Trinity," where he takes the psychic dimensions of religious consciousness with full seriousness and casts the categories of sin, redemption, salvation, and liberation in distinctly psychological terms that then emerge with new meanings. As Vernon Gregson observes in relation to Moore's project: "In Lonergan's terms, it interprets the specific categories of Christian redemption in psychically grounded special theological categories. The terms of the central Christian mystery of redemption are interpreted, not in explanatory metaphysical terms, but in the explanatory terms of psychological theory."[45]

Moore's reconstruction of the disciples' paschal experience, consciously geared to facilitating religious conversion in modern consciousness, is far from being a regression to a pre-critical mode of thought: it is manifestly the fruit of a post-critical "fully awake naïveté." In Doran's words it is "the work of a theological consciousness that can express its meaning in symbolic terms, not because it is undifferentiated, but because it is differentiated precisely in the realm of the imaginal."[46]

Doran predicts that the generative power of foundations will be remarkably enhanced when psychic conversion is added to Lonergan's foundational conversions.[47] This is evident in Moore's work and arguably even more so in von Balthasar's. We turn at this point to attend to von Balthasar's work from this perspective. In direct reference to von Balthasar, Doran proposes that the psychological component of foundations that he advances could ground precisely the kind of theological discourse von Balthasar attempts in his theological

---

[43]The most obvious systematic-theological relevance of expanding the foundations by the addition of psychic conversion to Lonergan's scheme, as Doran comments, "is that symbolic categories and categories derived from authentic religious affectivity and sensibility can be employed in theology and even in systematics without any loss in rigour, since the base of these categories and the norms regarding their theological employment are found in interiorly differentiated consciousness" (*Theology and the Dialectics of History* 440–441).

[44]Doran, "Psychic Conversion" 236.

[45]Vernon Gregson, *Lonergan, Spirituality and the Meeting of Religions* 84.

[46]Doran, *Theology and the Dialectics of History* 61.

[47]Ibid. 647–648.

aesthetics. Moreover, Doran argues that without this critical grounding von Balthasar's theological project lacks the necessary methodical control factor for a properly systematic treatment. As Doran explains:

> The theological aesthetics of a von Balthasar (surely the most eminent figure to attempt a wholesale project of this kind), insofar as it is direct theological discourse—and its overall intent is to be such—is, strictly speaking, not a systematic theology, but a statement in aesthetic terms of Christian doctrine, and a massive collection of materials that can be employed in the communication of Christian constitutive meaning to people of a cultivated aesthetic and symbolic sensitivity. That is to say, in terms of Lonergan's functional specialities, von Balthasar's work, where it is more than interpretation, is a matter of doctrines and communications. And even here it is descriptive, not explanatory. The relevant methodical control factor needed to facilitate the systematic statement of the constitutive meanings affirmed and provided is not available in von Balthasar's general aesthetic theory.[48]

Certainly von Balthasar would argue that his application of aesthetic categories to Jesus and his use of metaphor and imagery can be grounded, and *is* in fact grounded, in a strong ontological framework,[49] but the critical question for Doran, schooled in Lonergan, is: what grounds the ontology in the dynamics of consciousness? Ontological grounding does not suffice. Doran proposes that the grounding is to be found in his distinctly psychological complement to Lonergan's foundations, a foundational conversion he calls psychic conversion. Moreover such a transcendental grounding for von Balthasar's project is also necessary, he argues, "if one is to avoid the arbitrary, indeed authoritarian, uses to which conservative theologians and church authorities have put von Balthasar's work."[50]

In other words psychic conversion adds to cognitional theory the necessary psychological grounding of an aesthetics such as we find in von Balthasar's theology. Foundational self-appropriation in the psychic realm of subjectivity thus provides that necessary control factor with which to address precisely the difficulties of ambiguity, imprecision, and lack of clarity we previously identified as problematic.[51] As Doran argues:

> That factor is provided only in a dimension of foundational self-appropriation where the theologising subject comes into articulate possession of the aesthetic, sensitive-psychic, elementally symbolic-productive dimension of *his or her own* subjectivity. Such a project within foundations not only partly validates and justifies, and partly criticizes, such a program as von Balthasar's

---

[48]Ibid. 641.

[49]Von Balthasar, ch. 3, "From metaphor to analogy: use of the full continuum of language in theology" 87–88.

[50]Doran, *Theology and the Dialectics of History* 167.

[51]See von Balthasar, ch. 3, "From metaphor to analogy: use of the full continuum of language in theology" 87–88.

theological aesthetics, but also enables the methodical move to systematics without the abandonment of the general ground available in the aesthetic appropriation of Christian doctrine.[52]

It remains to be seen how Doran develops more fully his meta-methodological understanding of von Balthasar's project from this perspective and particularly how von Balthasar's trinitarian reflections, focusing as they do on God as love, might in this way be integrated with the psychological analogy. Lonergan himself suggested how this might occur in a passing comment in one of his later writings. Beginning with God, who in the New Testament is named *ho theos* and *agapē* (1 John 4:8, 16), proceeding to the judgment of value and so to originated loving, we arrive at an understanding of the processions as proceeding from the higher synthesis of intelligence and love that is divine *agapē*: the Father as originating love, the Son as judgment of value expressing that love, and the Spirit as originated loving.[53] Such a top-down application, as it were, of the psychological analogy offers the possibility of a radical re-balancing of the analogy that in its bottom-up application (from the creature to God) has suffered an intellectualist distortion that von Balthasar and Durrwell, in particular, so vehemently reject.

From the point of view of our study Doran's notion of psychic conversion not only offers the possibility of a critical grounding for von Balthasar's theological aesthetics, the context within which we find his treatment of the interconnection of the Trinity and paschal mystery; it also points to a way in which to understand this extraordinary shift in focal image that inspires our four authors in their interconnection of the mysteries. "Behind" the differentiations that distinguish them one from another it does seem that there is a kind of psychic conversion at work, as a result of which a radically new horizon for trinitarian reflection has emerged. Indeed, the case of Lafont may be even more convincing. As noted, among the works of these four authors his theology is methodologically most closely in accord with the traditional Thomistic treatment of the Trinity, yet as we have previously noted his work is marked by a profound sense of the paschal character of the divine being. He broaches an understanding that it is a *paschal* mystery *because* it is the revelation of the mystery of the Trinity. Certainly a similar insight emerges in von Balthasar's work in his understanding of *kenosis* as a divine attribute. However, von Balthasar begins with the *kenosis* of the cross and, at least partly to avert the univocal attribution of mutability to God, posits a real ontological *kenosis* in the Trinity *ad intra* that then functions in his theology to ground all forms of *kenosis* of God *ad extra*. The notion of *kenosis* in the divine being thus serves a very important theological function in von Balthasar's work. Lafont, on the other hand, has no such agenda. His theology of the divine persons, which

[52]Doran, *Theology and the Dialectics of History* 641.
[53]Lonergan, "Christology Today: Methodological Reflections" in *A Third Collection* 93–94. I thank Robert Doran for his helpful comments in this regard.

stresses their dynamic interpersonal interaction and communication, could have been elaborated largely as it is without the distinctly *paschal* character. Thus the very occurrence of this paschal image of God, so manifest in Lafont's work, is strong evidence, I suggest, that a kind of psychic conversion of the kind Doran describes is involved. We sense that this quite profound insight in Lafont's theology arises from deep psychic reaches of consciousness and that a kind of conversion of the imagination, a liberation of images previously repressed and withheld from insight[54] has occurred in this new development in which the paschal mystery and the Trinity are interconnected. Why it is so may never be given to be known—contemplation perhaps, or a deeper awareness of evil in the world—but the fact is that Doran's notion of psychic conversion is at the very least a partial explicative category by means of which we can describe the development.

An emerging context for theology

There is one further point to pursue. Dare one suggest that our study points to a development in theology more generally? Recall the dissatisfaction expressed by our authors in regard to traditional trinitarian theology. This dissatisfaction involves more than merely functional questions concerning the *ordo doctrinae* or the apparent abstraction and remoteness of the traditional explication from the biblical data. Our authors' concerns, in fact, reflect the change of culture and of consciousness that has occurred, the corresponding breakdown of the scholastic theoretic mediation of meaning, and the emergence of theological pluralism. In Lonergan's terms we can describe this change as a shift into the third stage of meaning, where meaning is not expressed in theoretical categories but in terms of consciousness that is differentiated in manifold diversity.[55] Theology in this third stage of meaning will not be the systematic, rigorous, and logically exacting synthesis it is in the second stage where the exigency of theory prevails. It will, in contrast, be characterized by pluralism such as we see in our four authors, pluralism that

---

[54]Fundamental to Doran's notion of psychic conversion is the role of "censorship" in the psychic realm of consciousness. Psychic conversion is thus a conversion from a repressive to a constructive functioning. Doran writes: "Psychic conversion is a transformation of the psychic component of what Freud calls 'the censor' from a repressive to a constructive agency in a person's development. The habitual orientation of our intelligence and affectivity exercises a censorship over the emergence into consciousness of the images that are the psychic representation and conscious integration of an underlying neural manifold [which depth psychology calls the unconscious]. But the censorship can be either constructive or repressive. The censorship is constructive when one wants a needed insight and so is open to the emergence of the images required for that insight. The censorship is repressive when one does not want the insight and so excludes from consciousness the images required if the unwanted insight is to emerge" *(Theology and the Dialectics of History* 59–60).

[55]Lonergan, *Method in Theology* 85–99.

is the fruit of variously differentiated converted consciousnesses addressing and expressing the Christian mysteries. As the converted self becomes foundational for theology in this new stage, new categories will emerge to express the meaning of Christian faith and a deeper foundation will ground the new categories.[56]

Why this new development? Ultimately it is cultural change that, marginalizing traditional trinitarian theology, demands the development of new theological method and style, one that is in continuity with its classical antecedent but one that meets all the genuine exigencies of Christian faith and of contemporary philosophy, science, and scholarship.[57] In Lonergan's terms: "The worthy successor to thirteenth-century achievement will be the fruit of a five-fold [i.e., *fully*] differentiated consciousness, in which the workings of common sense, science, scholarship, intentionality analysis, and the life of prayer have been integrated"[58]—and, prompted by von Balthasar, we would add: art and the beautiful. Until then pluralism will prevail. What grounds the diversity and pluralism in this new stage of meaning is not a theoretical system as in the age of scholasticism, but rather a meta-method that grounds this pluralism in the intending human subject. This is what we have attempted to indicate in our meta-methodological survey.

Such a meta-methodological understanding of theology in this newly emerging stage of meaning also grounds the possibility that different theologians, working in different realms of meaning according to different differentiations of consciousness, may enter into genuine dialogue with each other. Pluralism does not mean the end of communication. However, communication is also grounded not in the framework of scholasticism, now superseded, but in the framework of a meta-method that is able to account for manifold pluralism.

---

[56]Lonergan explains: "One type of foundation suits a theology that aims at being deductive, static, abstract, universal, equally applicable to all places and to all times. A quite different foundation is needed when theology turns from deductivism to an empirical approach, from the static to the dynamic, from the abstract to the concrete, from the universal to the historical totality of particulars, from invariable rules to intelligent adjustment and adaptation" ("Theology in its New Context," *A Second Collection* 63–64).

[57]For an analysis of cultural change and the challenge of historical consciousness see Michael H. McCarthy, *The Crisis of Philosophy* (Albany, N.Y.: SUNY Press, 1990).

[58]Lonergan, "Unity and Plurality: The Coherence of Christian Truth" in *A Third Collection* 247. Other differentiations of consciousness are not excluded. Lonergan explains in a footnote that the listing of the differentiations of consciousness is not intended to go beyond the needs of this particular paper.

Conclusion

Why has this rather extraordinary development in trinitarian theology occurred and at this stage? After all, the psychological analogy has enjoyed
an esteemed status in trinitarian theology over the centuries. It is well en-
trenched as common doctrine, affirmed in the catechism of the Council of
Trent and in numerous papal documents. Moreover, there is no doubt that the
traditional treatment of the mystery of the Trinity, which reaches its apogee in
Aquinas's explication, is an extraordinary feat of logic, coherence, and systematic exposition. None of the theologies we have examined in this study
matches the rigor, comprehensiveness, and theoretical refinement of the
Thomistic treatment.

Evidently, however, systematic rigor and refinement do not in and of themselves suffice to render theology meaningful. The Thomistic mediation of
meaning has clearly broken down. The classical treatment of trinitarian theology is no longer effective in mediating religious meaning. Needless to say,
we live in a very different world and a very different culture than did Aquinas.
He lived in an age where cultural theism prevailed, but we live in an age where
the question of the existence of God is itself problematic and where theism is
hard won, all the more so in face of the enormous problem of evil. In the wake
of the twentieth century horrors of Auschwitz and the Gulag, to name only
these two, a sense of the *absence* of God is a deeply determining feature in
contemporary culture. In other words, what was unproblematic for Aquinas is
acutely problematic for us.

This change in cultural milieu and the emergence of new exigencies must
inevitably and profoundly affect the theological enterprise. Recall, for example, the shift in the treatment of the trinitarian missions. In Aquinas the
missions do not obviously connect with our need for redemption. In contrast

these modern approaches resituate the meaning of the missions in the very context of the problem of evil. In his death on the cross and in his descent into hell Jesus comes face to face with the manifestly concrete reality of evil. In the context of his paschal mystery the missions communicate the excess of trinitarian love to a world afflicted by an excess of evil. In this way, then, contemporary theology attempts to meet the present demand for evidence of God and of the very plausibility of Christian faith. The paschal mystery in particular offers a tangible point of entry into the reality of God who is with us, for us, involved with us in our struggle with evil.

Not only do we not live in a culture of theism: contemporary culture is no longer confident or competent in the realm of classical metaphysics, the foundation on which Aquinas built his *Summa Theologiae*. Aquinas's metaphysically refined theology, although an elegant exercise in analogical thinking, depends on a metaphysics of being, soul, natures, and faculties that is simply no longer comprehensible, let alone congenial to modern empirically-organized culture. The medieval method itself is no longer adequate or appropriate; it lacks persuasive and disclosive power. Contemporary culture, not content with logically and metaphysically satisfying statements of Christian faith, demands existentially satisfying religious meanings. The primary task of theology has shifted from the maintenance of theoretical rigor and systematic synthesis to that of fostering meaning for the emergence of authentic human beings. A new theological method and style are necessary, continuous with the old yet meeting the exigencies of contemporary self-understanding. In Lonergan's terms, a newly differentiated consciousness is required to meet the contemporary need for meaning and appropriate expressions of it. Classical doctrines are not replaced but rather need to be transposed into more experiential and existentially meaningful terms.

Nonetheless, despite the challenge of the absence of a culturally mediated notion of God together with the rejection of classical metaphysics, contemporary theology is in fact offered new freedom. It is released from the constraints of a prior metaphysical theory that has become antiquated. It is freed to return to its sources with new eyes, open to new stages in the self-transcending process of apprehending the revealed mystery. Theology is thus both liberated from the limitations of its classical antecedent and prompted to return to the data anew in order to meet the contemporary demand for existential meaning. All these factors, then, contribute to the emergence of the development we have been studying.

We have seen that this new way of approaching the mystery of the Trinity restores the soteriological dimension to our understanding of the mystery and grounds the mystery in its economic roots in the events of salvation history. In this way trinitarian theology is recovered as an intelligible way of articulating the mystery of our salvation, of what it means to say that we are saved by God through Christ in the power of the Holy Spirit. The three divine persons emerge in their uniqueness and distinction, in all the concreteness of their engagement with us. Classical trinitarian theology, on the other hand, tended to move the doctrine of Trinity away from the concrete details of our salvation. The shift in focus resulted in a gradual deemphasis on the economy of salvation in theology and a rather abstract a-historical explication of the mystery of God's triune being. In the process trinitarian theology also became increasingly isolated from other areas of theology, almost secondary or peripheral to the major tracts. A far richer, fuller, and more existentially meaningful trinitarian theology results when the mystery of the Trinity is approached via the paschal mystery. Trinitarian theology from this revelation-centered perspective is not isolated from salvation history but deeply rooted in it. It is not simply concerned with *theologia,* God *in se,* although as we have seen it does not shrink from speaking about God *in se.* However, God *in se* is considered precisely from the perspective of the God who is revealed in the events of salvation history. A very different understanding of God and of the divine attributes emerges. Firmly grounded in the events of salvation history and expressed in more personalist and relational psychological categories, this refashioned trinitarian theology responds more aptly to the demands of contemporary religious thought.

The new development is however justified not only in terms of an attempt to respond more adequately to contemporary culture and its exigencies, although this is an important stimulus that prompts it: undergirding it is a closer reading of the biblical data, a reading informed by contemporary developments in phenomenology and in biblical scholarship. Furthermore, the three traditional theological techniques expressed by Vatican Council I are very evidently realized in this development. As the Council wrote, "If human reason, with faith as its guiding light, enquires earnestly, devoutly and circumspectly, it does reach, by God's generosity, some understanding of the mysteries, and that a most profitable one. It does this by analogy with the truths it knows naturally, and also from the interconnection of the mysteries with one another, and in reference to the final end of man."[1]

In retrospect the traditional western approach to trinitarian theology, so strongly focused on psychological categories, tended to concentrate on the technique of analogy. That technique is now being applied to the paschal mystery itself but, as our study has highlighted, we find in this recent development a far greater concentration on the interconnection of the mysteries with one another as the Trinity is connected with the paschal mystery. Moreover, in reflecting on trinitarian theology from the vantage point of the paschal mystery we find the third technique to which Vatican I refers ("in reference to the final

---

[1]*Constitution on Divine Revelation (Dei Filius),* DS 3019. The decrees of Vatican I were formulated in the nineteenth-century context of the debates on the relationship between "faith" and "reason" but they continue to serve to express the mainline Catholic theological tradition (for example, the analogical thinking of Aquinas) and to affirm contemporary Catholic theologies such as those we examine here.

end of man") as trinitarian theology is situated in a soteriological and ultimately an eschatological context.

Parallels in contemporary Protestant trinitarian theology

In spite of the affirmation and encouragement provided by the Vatican I
statement attesting the validity of various theological techniques, in particular
that of interconnection of the mysteries, one is struck by the novelty of the development before us and the weight of the task of assessing its theological
value in light of its formidable classical antecedent. Let us now look farther
afield in order to ascertain what affinities and resonances in contemporary theology and philosophy might lead us to even greater assurance that this development in trinitarian theology marks a genuine advance.

Taking this wider perspective we first find that this refashioned trinitarian
theology has a strong affinity will parallel developments in contemporary
Protestant theology where trinitarian theology is also enjoying a renaissance,
following Karl Barth who, in his *Church Dogmatics,* made this doctrine the
cornerstone of his revelation-centered theology. Jürgen Moltmann's treatment
of the connection between the cross and the Trinity is arguably the most
widely known of all.[2] More accessible than von Balthasar's thought and style,
and promptly translated into English and circulated world-wide, Moltmann's
theology of the cross is a veritable *tour de force* in the field. It is located at
the very cutting edge of contemporary theology, and its impact has been
considerable.

Is theology even possible after Auschwitz?[3] This is the nub of the question
for Moltmann. The suffering of the innocent, indeed any incomprehensible
suffering, calls the very idea of a righteous and loving God into question. At
the rock of suffering and injustice theism meets its match, for if God is the
omnipotent and gracious author of history how could such horrific travesties
occur? Roused by such questions, modern protest atheism staunchly rejects
the God of classical philosophical theism, repudiates as utterly inimical a God

---

[2]Among the works of Jürgen Moltmann see in particular *The Crucified God,* translated by R.
A. Wilson and John Bowden (London: SCM, 1974); idem, *The Trinity and the Kingdom of God:
The Doctrine of God,* translated by Margaret Kohl (London: SCM, 1981); idem, *History and the
Triune God,* translated by John Bowden (London: SCM, 1991); idem, "The Unity of the Triune
God," *St. Vladimir's Theological Quarterly* 28 (1984) 157–171; idem, *The Coming of God:
Christian Eschatology,* translated by Margaret Kohl (London: SCM, 1996). For a helpful
overview of Moltmann's work see Douglas Meeks's review, "Jürgen Moltmann's *Systematic
Contributions to Theology,*" together with "Reflections" by Jürgen Moltmann in *Religious Studies
Review* 22 (1996) 95–105. See also W. Waite Willis, Jr., *Theism, Atheism, and the Doctrine of the
Trinity: The Trinitarian Theologies of Karl Barth and Jürgen Moltmann in Response to Protest
Atheism* (Atlanta, Ga.: Scholars Press, 1987) and Richard Bauckham, *The Theology of Jürgen
Moltmann* (Edinburgh: T & T Clark, 1995).

[3]See *History and the Triune God* 26–30. See also pp. 165–182 for Moltmann's illuminating
review of his theological method and development.

who is removed from history, unrelated and unaffected by suffering. But is this the only God there is? Indeed, is this God? That is the question. For Moltmann, who stands in the Lutheran reformed tradition, the solution to the dilemma is nothing less than a revolution in our concept of God. He writes: "The question of theodicy is not a speculative question; it is a critical one. It is the all-embracing *eschatological question*."[4] He seeks a theological response that is both adequate to the critique of protest atheism and consistent with Christian revelation.

Dissatisfied with the traditional rendering of trinitarian theology and particularly critical of a theology that is detached from the historical dimension of the Christian understanding of God, Moltmann reminds theology that God is known where God is self-revealed: on the cross. Moltmann recognizes that the cross demands that the classical theistic understanding of God as absolute, omnipotent, without potentiality, immutable, impassible, with no real relation to creation, be abandoned. In contrast, in the crucified Jesus he finds a God who participates in the suffering of creation. As he explains: "To take up the theology of the cross today is to go beyond the limits of the doctrine of salvation and to inquire into the revolution needed in the concept of God. Who is God in the cross of the Christ who is abandoned by God?"[5] The cross reveals that the Christian God is not the essentially impassible and immutable God of classical theism, but the God of Jesus Christ, a God who enters into history in the event of Jesus and who suffers in time. It reveals God's love as suffering love.

In this way Moltmann understands that Jesus' death on the cross is fundamental to our understanding of God, and indeed to human hope. A theology of the cross necessarily leads him to trinitarian theology. "The content of the doctrine of the Trinity is the real cross of Christ himself. The form of the crucified Christ is the Trinity."[6] There on the cross God is known as Father, Son, and Holy Spirit. Indeed, Moltmann argues that the event of the cross can only be understood in trinitarian terms: "If a person once feels the infinite passion of God's love which finds expression here, then he understands the mystery of the triune God. God suffers with us—God suffers from us—God suffers for us; it is this experience of God that reveals the triune God. It has to be understood, and can only be understood, in trinitarian terms."[7]

Jesus' agonized cry of dereliction in Gethsemane together with his cry from the cross reveals the trinitarian differentiation within God, the distinction between Father and Son, the distinction between God and God. As Moltmann explains:

> The more one understands the whole event of the cross as an event of God, the more any simple idea of God falls apart. In epistemological terms it

[4]*The Trinity and the Kingdom of God* 49.
[5]Ibid. 4.
[6]*The Crucified God* 246.
[7]*The Trinity and the Kingdom of God* 4; see also 21–60.

takes, so to speak, trinitarian form. One moves from the exterior of the mystery called "God" to the interior, which is trinitarian. This is the "revolution in the concept of God" that is manifested by the crucified Christ.[8]

On the cross the Father delivers up the Son. The Father abandons the Son. But Moltmann understands that it is not just the Father who delivers Jesus up to die: the Son gives himself up. There is in this sense a double delivering-up, but at the point of their greatest separation, in the God-forsaken death of Jesus on the cross, Moltmann recognizes a conformity of will between Father and Son. In other words the cross event contains both community in separation and separation in community.[9] Herein lies the mystery of the Holy Spirit, the third trinitarian differentiation, later fully disclosed in the outpouring of the Spirit at Pentecost.

Most strikingly of all, and critical to his response to the theodicy question, Moltmann recognizes the pain and grief of the Father at the death of the Son. For Moltmann the Father, who loves the Son, clearly suffers the death of the Son, and suffers deeply. What then does the cross of Christ mean for God? Moltmann would persuade us that it means that God suffers: "To recognize God in the cross of Christ, conversely, means to recognize the cross, inextricable suffering, death and hopeless rejection in God."[10] The cross means that suffering is in God. In other words, Jesus' cry of dereliction has inner-trinitarian significance for Moltmann; it is an event of suffering within God.

In this way, then, Moltmann responds to the anguish that finds expression in protest atheism. His answer: God suffers. Suffering and God are thus no longer contradictions, for Moltmann's theology of the cross understands that precisely because God is love God's being is in suffering and that suffering, the voluntary suffering of love, is intrinsic to God's being. "Even Auschwitz is taken up into the grief of the Father, the surrender of the Son and the power of the Spirit."[11] It is not that the horror of Auschwitz is in any way justified or diminished, but rather that it is taken up in the cross and into the trinitarian history of God, God in Auschwitz and Auschwitz in the crucified God. Moltmann thus finds a basis for a hope that is able to face the terrors of history.

Moltmann, like von Balthasar, takes seriously Jesus' cry of abandonment on the cross. Jesus is handed over into God-forsakenness. He writes:

> Jesus died crying out to God, "My God, why hast thou forsaken me?" All Christian theology and all Christian life is basically an answer to the question which Jesus asked as he died. The atheism of protests and of metaphysical rebellions against God are also answers to this question. Either Jesus who was abandoned by God is the end of all theology or he is the beginning of a

---

[8]*The Crucified God* 204.
[9]Ibid., *The Crucified God* 243–244. See also *The Trinity and the Kingdom of God* 82.
[10]*The Crucified God* 277. See also *The Trinity and the Kingdom of God* 83.
[11]*The Crucified God* 278.

specifically Christian, and therefore critical and liberating, theology and life.[12]

Whereas von Balthasar grounds the event of the cross in the eternal primordial trinitarian event whereby the Father begets the Son, and understands the cross as the form or modality in the realm of creation of that supra-temporal inner-trinitarian event of mutual self-giving and self-yielding love, Moltmann understands that divine being is ruptured on the cross in a drama that is constitutive of God's being and history. As Moltmann explains: "What happened on the cross was an event between God and God. It was a deep division in God himself, in so far as God abandoned God and contradicted himself, and at the same time a unity in God in so far as God was at one with God and corresponded to himself."[13]

For von Balthasar, however, the separation of Father and Son in the cross is eternally allowed for, included and exceeded in the eternal supra-temporal drama of trinitarian life. It is not that divine being is rent asunder in the event of the cross, as Moltmann would have it, but rather that in the cross event the triune God of love, who in love has ever allowed for the radical separation and differentiation of freedom, enters the very hiatus of our death and draws creation into God's own life. Moltmann, on the other hand, understands that "the cross is the beginning of trinitarian history of God."[14] It is the event of the cross that is constitutive of God's triune being. In Moltmann's theology God is *this* trinitarian event, the event of the cross: the Father who delivers up his Son, the Son who is abandoned, the Holy Spirit who is the bond of union between them. The death on the cross takes place in the history between the Father and Son. It is "the concrete history of God," the event of the love of the Son and the grief of the Father from which the Spirit opens up the future and creates life.[15]

In Moltmann's theology of the cross God suffers. Suffering, abandonment, God-forsakenness, rejection, and death emerge as intrinsic to God's being. This, then, is Moltmann's response to protest atheism: that we can understand our own history, a history of suffering and of hope, in the history and suffering of God. The history of the world is the history of God's suffering. In contrast von Balthasar, while coming within a hair's breadth of attributing suffering to God, assiduously avoids such an attribution. Suffering and death *ad extra* are not attributed univocally to God *ad intra*. Von Balthasar attributes no more than something *analogous* to suffering to the divine being. He argues that the grounds for the possibility of what takes place *ad extra* are to be found in God *ad intra*. In other words God does not become what God was not: God is, in the paschal mystery, what God is eternally. The crux of the matter, as

---

[12]Ibid. 4.
[13]Ibid. 244.
[14]Ibid. 278.
[15]*The Trinity and the Kingdom of God* 90.

von Balthasar would persuade us, is that in and through the paschal mystery all creation is incorporated into God's trinitarian love, that love alone is credible, that the mystery we behold in the paschal mystery is not the mystery of God's suffering but the mystery of God's inexhaustible and ever-creative love. Moltmann, on the other hand, maintains that it is the suffering of the Trinity in their common love for the world, their mutual differentiated suffering, that overcomes creation's estrangement and God-forsakenness. In Moltmann's theology it is precisely through suffering that God redeems creation and liberates it for its participation in God's eschatological joy.[16]

Perichoresis is a very strong element in Moltmann's theology of the Trinity.[17] In the New Testament narrative Moltmann finds multiple forms of the trinitarian *perichoresis*. He recognizes, for example, a *perichoresis* of suffering among the three divine persons. Moltmann understands the divine unity in terms of *perichoresis*, as do Durrwell and von Balthasar. However, in Moltmann's radical eschatological understanding of God *perichoresis* is understood as in effect a moral union, a union of intention, with the divine unity achieved at the eschaton. Such an understanding of *perichoresis* stands in contrast with the classical understanding of the divine unity, but for Moltmann the unity of the Trinity is not an ontological question but rather an eschatological one: the divine unity is finally achieved when God is fully united with creation at the eschaton, when God will be "all in all."[18] He explains: "If one conceives of the Trinity as an event of love in the suffering and the death of Jesus—and that is something which faith must do—then the Trinity is no self-contained group in heaven, but an eschatological process open for men on earth, which stems from the cross of Christ."[19]

The notion of *perichoresis* effectively serves as the linchpin of Moltmann's trinitarian theology. Moreover, in the dynamic, non-hierarchical, perichoretic community of the three divine persons Moltmann finds a radical challenge to monarchical monotheism, together with its derivatives, patriarchal theology and patriarchalism, which, in Moltmann's view, ultimately reside in a metaphysics of substance. Negatively, a substance-based metaphysics is staunchly rejected. Positively Moltmann's trinitarian theology, firmly grounded in the notion of the trinitarian *perichoresis,* demands expression in a praxis-oriented eschatology.

Love, *perichoresis,* relation, mutuality and community are fundamental categories in Moltmann's understanding of the Trinity, as we found in our study of recent Catholic trinitarian theology. However, we find a strong measure of Hegelianism in Moltmann's theology: God is and becomes God

---

[16]Ibid. 59–60.

[17]Ibid. 174–176.

[18]Ibid. 148–150. See also "The Unity of the Triune God," *St. Vladimir's Theological Quarterly* 28 (1984) 157–171.

[19]*The Crucified God* 249.

through the events of history, a history that is centered on the cross of Jesus, a history to be consummated at the eschaton.[20] As Moltmann explains:

> The relationships in the Trinity between Father and Son are not fixed in static terms once and for all, but are a living history. This history of God or this history in God begins with the sending and delivering up of the Son, continues with his resurrection and the transference of the rule of God to him, and only ends when the Son hands over this rule to the Father. The delivering up on the cross is the central point of this history in God, not its conclusion. Only with the handing over of rule to the Father is the obedience of the Son, and thus his Sonship, consummated.[21]

In this sense the ontological completion of the Trinity *ad intra* will occur at the eschaton with the completion of the mission of the Trinity *ad extra*.[22] Again one is struck by the radical eschatological orientation of Moltmann's theology. He insists that we must see the Trinity as event, the event of the cross, and then think of it as history open toward the eschatological. "For eschatological faith, the trinitarian God-event on the cross becomes the history of God which is open to the future and which opens up the future. . . . [T]he divine Trinity should not be conceived of as a closed circle of perfect being in heaven. . . . [O]ne should think of the Trinity as a dialectical event, indeed as the event of the cross and then as eschatologically open history."[23]

The goal of history is the completion of God's own history: the eschatological glorification of the Trinity. It is the radically new future that Jesus' resurrection adumbrates, promises, and sets in train. In other words the eschaton will be not only the end of world history but the consummation of the trinitarian history of God. It is God's future as well as that of creation.

In Moltmann's theology the economic Trinity not only reveals the immanent Trinity; it has a retroactive effect on it.[24] "The economic Trinity completes and perfects itself to immanent Trinity when the history and experience of salvation are completed and perfected. When everything is 'in God' and 'God is all in all', then the economic Trinity is raised into and transcended in the immanent Trinity."[25] Indeed Moltmann suggests that the traditional distinction between immanent and economic Trinity be surrendered.[26] In that

---

[20]Note, however, that in Catholic theology there are signs of reevaluation and indeed reappropriation of the Hegelian contribution to theology. See, for example, the work of Emilio Brito who, inspired by the dialectic of the Ignatian Spiritual Exercises, has undertaken a distinctly paschal interpretation of the dialectic of Hegel in *La Christologie de Hegel: Verbum Crucis*, translated by B. Pottier. Bibliothèque des Archives de Philosophie Nouvelle Série 40 (Paris: Beauchesne, 1983).

[21]Moltmann, *The Crucified God* 265.

[22]Ibid. 256–266.

[23]Ibid. 255.

[24]*The Trinity and the Kingdom of God* 160.

[25]Ibid. 161.

[26]Ibid. 151–154, 158–161.

case, however, two questions remain: how to preserve God's freedom and, second, how to avoid an understanding that God needs history in order to realize Godself. Despite this, from Moltmann's perspective there is no question of a process theology at work here because his theology recognizes that God acts out of love, not out of a need for creatures, in order to realize Godself. In fact Moltmann argues that process theology is inadequate as Christian theology precisely because it lacks the trinitarian dimension.[27]

Recall, in contrast, that von Balthasar maintains a clear distinction between the immanent and economic Trinity. The economic Trinity does not constitute the immanent Trinity, nor does the economic Trinity retroactively affect the immanent Trinity. There is, however, not only an ethical but an ontological connection between the economic and immanent Trinity. For von Balthasar, and indeed for Durrwell, the event that is constitutive of God is not the cross but that primordial event of love whereby the Father engenders the Son in the love that is the Holy Spirit. In contradistinction to Moltmann's view the paschal event is not regarded as constitutive of God; it is rather an icon of God's eternal triune being: it is analogy, properly speaking.

In Moltmann's theology, through the cross God's inner-trinitarian suffering reaches the godless and God-forsaken with God's love. His theology of a suffering and crucified God is, however, held in careful balance with his understanding of the redemptive significance of the resurrection. Moltmann's theology is not only a theology of a crucified God but a theology of hope and promise. Hope is grounded in the suffering of God who raises Jesus from the dead. For Moltmann, without a suffering God there is no hope and no promise; the suffering, however, is possible because of the resurrection and the redemptive resurrecting activity of God. It is the resurrection that makes Christian faith eschatological. The definitive event of eschatological promise, the resurrection sets in train a historical process in which the promise already affects the world and moves it in the direction of its future promise. Here again we find the strong proleptic character of Moltmann's theology whereby the present is characterized by the future, where past and present are part of and shaped by the future in an eschatological framework that transcends linear time and necessarily demands a certain dialectical character in our God-talk. In contrast von Balthasar's theology is characterized by a sense of the paradoxical.

This all too brief discussion of the trinitarian theologies of Moltmann and von Balthasar begs a much more careful and detailed comparison of their work. What is unarguable, however, is that both grapple, albeit from very different perspectives, with the reality of God's genuine engagement in the life, the struggle, and the suffering of the world. Von Balthasar ultimately maintains the divine transcendence through a primordial originating, Moltmann through an eschatological originating. What is striking is the remarkable similarity of the conclusions derived from such radically different perspectives.

[27]*The Crucified God* 255–256.

Moltmann's theology of the cross has proved a foundational work in the field of trinitarian theology, providing rich and fertile ground for advances in contemporary theology, both Protestant and Catholic. His critical theology of the cross in which historical liberation and eschatological redemption are inextricably linked, together with his strident critique of monarchical monotheism, inevitably lead him to a critical theology of Church and society. Here the influence of Moltmann's theology has been decisive, contributing in no small measure to developments across a range of theologies of liberation including Latin American liberation theologies, black theologies, feminist theologies, and political theologies.

The trinitarian theology of Eberhard Jüngel is also highly significant in regard to this new development we have been studying.[28] Here too we find a number of resonances with developments in recent Catholic trinitarian theology. Moltmann and Jüngel—and also Wolfhart Pannenberg,[29] although he does not explore the Trinity from the paschal mystery as such—emphasize that a consideration of the Trinity should be rooted in the events of the economy of salvation. Jüngel and Pannenberg too reject the traditional approach to the Trinity that is based on a prior consideration of the divine essence and attributes. Similarly we find a shift away from the traditional metaphysical categories of classical trinitarian theology. For Jüngel as for Moltmann the doctrine of the Trinity serves as a starting point for a critical re-examination of the understanding of the relationship between God and the divine attributes as articulated in classical theology, and between God, time, and history. Colin Gunton, from the United Reformed Church in England, represents another example from the Protestant tradition. Although his work is somewhat difficult to classify, nevertheless what is pertinent to our study is that in his explorations in trinitarian theology we also find a strong emphasis on the relational.[30]

Resonances in contemporary neo-Thomism

The shift from substance-based metaphysical categories toward more personalist and relational psychological categories certainly challenges the emphasis in classical trinitarian theology on substance-fashioned categories and the use of a metaphysical framework in which substantiality has primacy over

[28]For the work of Eberhard Jüngel see in particular *The Doctrine of the Trinity: God's Being is in Becoming*, translated by J.C.B. Mohr (Edinburgh: Scottish Academic Press, 1976); idem, *God as the Mystery of the World: On the Foundation of the Theology of the Crucified One in the Dispute between Theism and Atheism*, translated by Darrell L. Guder (Grand Rapids: Eerdmans, 1983).
[29]Wolfhart Pannenberg, *Systematic Theology* 1, translated by Geoffrey W. Bromiley (Grand Rapids: Eerdmans, 1991).
[30]Colin E. Gunton, *The Promise of Trinitarian Theology* (Edinburgh: T & T Clark, 1991); idem, *The One, the Three and the Many: God, Creation and the Culture of Modernity* (Cambridge: Cambridge University Press, 1993).

relationality. The renewed Christian metaphysics that will therefore be adequate and appropriate to this new development will clearly be one that addresses this now crucial aspect of being and personhood. It will be one where relationality is regarded as a primordial aspect of being. William Norris Clarke, S.J., standing firmly in the Thomistic tradition but alert to modern phenomenology, offers a metaphysical foundation that is able to contribute to this renewal of trinitarian theology.[31] He recognizes that a renewed ontological model must adequately express the emerging awareness of person as an essentially relational being. It must incorporate relationality as intrinsic to and constitutive of the person.[32] He insists, however, that it must not deny person as substance, for person is not simply relation. Without the dimension of substance the notion of person loses its metaphysical grounding. The challenge, from this perspective, is to construct an ontological model of being in which substance and relation are each primordial modes of reality.

Describing his project as a "creative retrieval and completion"[33] of Aquinas's own work, Clarke draws out the dynamic and relational notion of person that, he maintains, is implied in Aquinas's metaphysics of being as existential act *(esse)*. As he explains, it is not that such a notion is foreign to Aquinas but rather that relationship is more significant to us now than it was in Aquinas's time. Aquinas's task was to explain the distinction between person and nature required for the explication of the trinitarian and christological doctrines and to identify the root of the "incommunicability" or uniqueness of each person as distinct from the common nature the persons shared. In the process the relational, self-communicative dimension of the person, flowing from its very status in being, was overshadowed. In other words, while Aquinas has an explicit, powerfully dynamic notion of being as intrinsically self-communicative and relational through action he did not apply this in an explicitly thematized fashion to his philosophical notion of person, holding instead with some modification to Boethius's definition of person.

[31]William Norris Clarke, *Person and Being.* The Aquinas Lecture, 1993 (Milwaukee: Marquette University Press, 1993) 1; idem, "Person, Being and St. Thomas," *Communio* 19 (1992) 601–618; idem, "To be is to be self-communicative: St. Thomas' view of personal being," *Theology Digest* 33 (1986) 441–454; idem, "The 'We Are' of Interpersonal Dialogue as the Starting Point of Metaphysics," *The Modern Schoolman* 69 (1992) 357–368; idem, "Thomism and Contemporary Philosophical Pluralism" in Deal W. Hudson and Dennis W. Moran, eds., *The Future of Thomism* (Notre Dame, Ind.: American Maritain Association, University of Notre Dame Press, 1992) 91–108. See also Gerald A. McCool, "An alert and independent Thomist: William Norris Clarke, S. J.," in Gerald A. McCool, ed., *The Universe as Journey: Conversations with W. Norris Clarke* (New York: Fordham University Press, 1988) 13–47; idem, "The Tradition of St. Thomas since Vatican II," *Theology Digest* 40 (1993) 324–335.

[32]Clarke notes that this development of a relational notion of person has also been suggested by Cardinal Joseph Ratzinger in his *Introduction to Christianity,* translated by J. R. Foster (New York: Seabury Press, 1969); idem, "Concerning the Notion of Person in Theology," *Communio* 17 (1990) 439–454.

[33]Clarke, *Person and Being* 1.

Clarke recognizes that the challenge is a different one today. Existential phenomenologists and personalists of various schools, as well as contemporary schools of psychology and psychotherapy, have developed rich phenomenological analyses that stress the relational aspects of personhood. Suspicious of, even hostile toward the notion of person as substance, they call for the explicit philosophical thematizing of the relational, interpersonal dimension of personhood that was eclipsed in the classical tradition. However, as Clarke observes, the tendency now is to explain the being of the person so one-sidedly in terms of relation and systems of relations as to exclude the dimension of the person as self-identity, interiority, and "in-itselfness":

> Hence we are faced, on the one hand, with a richer older metaphysical tradition of the person that left the relational dimension underdeveloped and, on the other hand, the more recent phenomenological tradition that has highly developed the relational aspect of the being of the person but lost its metaphysical grounding. What is urgently needed is a creative integration of these two valuable but incomplete lines of thought into a more complete and well-rounded philosophy of the person.[34]

Clarke returns to Aquinas's understanding of real being as intrinsically active and self-communicative. This activity, self-communication, and dynamism are not just the consequence of being, but the very nature of being as such. However, while an understanding of the innate dynamism of being as overflowing into self-manifesting, self-communicating action is clear and explicit in Aquinas, what is not explicit (but implied) is the corollary that relationality is a primordial dimension of every real being, inseparable from its substantiality just as action is from existence. Being naturally flows over into self-communication, generating a network of relations. In other words, substantiality (the *in-itself* dimension of being) and relationality (the *towards-others* aspect) go together as two distinct but inseparable modes of reality. Substance is the primary mode, Clarke explains, in that all other aspects, including relations, depend on it as their ground. However since existence flows into action and self-communication, *to be* is to be *substance-in-relation*.[35] Clarke thus introduces the intrinsically relational aspect into both being and person and lays the philosophical ground on which to base contemporary phenomenological developments.[36]

Such a dynamic metaphysics is able to accommodate and ground the notion of receptivity as a divine attribute, so strong a feature of the theologies we have examined. Interestingly, in addressing this issue Clarke expresses his indebtedness to Hans Urs von Balthasar for whom, as we have seen, the notion of receptivity as a divine perfection derives from his reflections on the paschal

[34]*Person and Being* 5.
[35]Ibid. 14. Robert A. Connor is critical of Clarke in this respect: "The Person as Resonating Existential," *American Catholic Philosophical Quarterly* 66 (1992) 43.
[36]*Person and Being* 17.

mystery.[37] Without receptivity no communication can become act and be complete. Therefore, as Clarke explains, if self-communication is a fundamental aspect of real being, so too must receptivity be, as the complementary pole of self-communication: "[Receptivity] must therefore be a primordial dimension of reality as a whole, even though it follows upon the substantial and self-communication aspects of being in the ontological (not necessarily temporal) order of dependence and intelligibility."[38] Receptivity, from this perspective, is not a sign of imperfection, poverty, or potentiality but is a positive ontological perfection of being and predicable of God in its purest form.[39]

Another corollary of Clarke's retrieval of Aquinas's metaphysics is that real being, as intrinsically self-communicative and relational through action, tends naturally toward modes of being-together, that is, community. "To be" turns out to mean "to-be-together." Being and community are therefore inseparable. Here Clarke finds supporting data in the growing body of empirical evidence of the extraordinary interconnectedness of all things in the universe. He presses farther still, indicating that the perfection of the self-communicating dynamism of being at its deepest and most intimate level is not just community, but communion. At this point Clarke is able to ground metaphysically the perfect communion within God's triune being that is the trinitarian circumincession or *perichoresis*, where the unity and communion are total yet the distinction of persons remains. In a similar way his metaphysics is also able to ground the soteriology that emerges in our theologies, a soteriology that is expressed in terms of incorporation into the trinitarian communion.[40]

In such ways Clarke's metaphysics resonates with and indeed is able to ground the insights of the trinitarian theologies we have examined. First, it can ground an understanding of the nature of the divine being, even in its overflow into creation, as an ecstatic process that is beyond time and change, as self-communicating love: the Father, unoriginated possessor of the infinite fullness of the divine being, communicates ecstatically his entire divine nature to the second person, the Son or Word, in an act of loving self-knowledge, so that the only distinction between them is the distinction of two complementary but opposed relations, Giver and Receiver. The Father and Son together in a single act of mutual love pour forth the same divine being in all its fullness to the Holy Spirit, the third person. The inner life of God, the supreme fullness of what it means to be, is by its very nature *self-communicative love* and subsequently flows over freely in the finite self-communication that is creation, to be revealed and realized in creation in the paschal mystery.

---

[37]Ibid. 20–22; idem, "Person, Being and St. Thomas," 611–614.

[38]*Person and Being* 20.

[39]David Schindler is not convinced that Clarke has laid an adequate metaphysical foundation for this claim and asks how this receptivity translates into properly metaphysical terms: "Norris Clarke on Person, Being, and St. Thomas," *Communio* 20 (1993) 582–585. See also "Discussion: The Person, Philosophy, Theology, and Receptivity," *Communio* 21 (1994) 151–190.

[40]*Person and Being* 22–24.

Second, in the metaphysics Clarke proposes relationality is a primordial dimension of reality, together with substantiality. Relationality is grounded in the substantial act of *esse* itself. There is no need for an either-or dichotomy between substance and relation such as pertained in classical Aristotelian metaphysics. Indeed, Clarke warns, either alone leads to distortion. Once the notion of substance as center of activity—and receptivity—has been retrieved both substance and relation are equally primordial. Clarke is thus able to stress both the intrinsically relational dimension of all substance and the inherently substantial dimension of all relationship. Here, then, we find philosophical ground, a more relational metaphysics built on personalist foundations, on which to base the shift from substance-based to relational and personalist categories in the development in trinitarian theology we have examined.

Moreover, without an adequate ontology to support it theology runs the risk of imprecision and even confusion in understanding God's being and God's relations to the world. There are potential dangers in viewing the paschal mystery as effecting or realizing the self-relatedness of the divine being in creation. As John McDade describes so lucidly, the risk inherent in a reclamation of the biblical narrative in this way is a confusion between narrative theology and divine ontology.[41] In other words narrative discourse must not be confused with a narrative phenomenology of the divine being. Certainly narrative theology is an evocative and immensely fruitful mode of theological discourse, and indeed in commending this new development in trinitarian theology we are in effect making more space within the realm of theological reflection for narrative theology as a necessary complement to traditional, more metaphysically-fashioned theology. However, as McDade explains, it must neither be confused with nor used without an ontology of divine being. A clear understanding of the distinction between narrative theology and ontology is vital to the integrity of trinitarian theology when approached from the paschal mystery.

We have seen that both Durrwell and von Balthasar are critical of traditional explication of the divine processions, insisting that both processions are processions of love. They call for an ontology of the divine being that is explicated not in the traditional terms of being but rather in terms of love. We see the ontological element of Christian realism mapped out in von Balthasar's work. In a more traditionally systematic way Anthony (Tony) Kelly also attempts such a transposition.[42] He resituates the mystery of the Trinity in a framework of Being-in-Love, basing the transposition on Lonergan's analysis of intentionality wherein the peak state of consciousness is self-transcending being-in-love. The result is a revised ontology in which being is understood not in terms of substance categories but in terms of love.

---

[41]McDade, "The Trinity and the Paschal Mystery" 175–191.

[42]Kelly, *The Trinity of Love: A Theology of the Christian God.* New Theology Studies 4 (Wilmington, Del.: Michael Glazier, 1989).

In such a framework the concept of essence is not external to the category of relation. Indeed, in contrast to the traditional more substance-fashioned concept of the divine essence such an ontology shows that we can think of the divine essence precisely as epitomized in the personal relations among Father, Son, and Holy Spirit. Here too we find a high degree of convergence with the trinitarian theologies we have studied.

Such a trinitarian ontology sublates rather than negates its classical antecedent. As adumbrated by Moore and demonstrated by Kelly, being-in-love does not mean the exclusion of being. Nor should it mean the exclusion of being-as-knowing. To love and to know are not mutually exclusive. Both constitute the self-transcending subject. Here too we glimpse new possibilities for the psychological analogy when relativized and transposed in this kind of way and when introduced to *serve* an understanding of the God who is revealed in the paschal mystery of Jesus Christ. In Kelly and in Moore we have trinitarian theologies in which the psychological analogy is effectively taken from its hegemonic "idolic status" and made to work *with* the paschal mystery.

Parallels in Eastern Orthodox trinitarian theology

This refashioned trinitarian theology we have been studying also has a strong affinity to its Eastern and in particular its Greek counterpart.[43] The emphasis on the Trinity of hypostases (including the vital role of the Holy Spirit) rather than on the unity of the divine being is a feature that has long been understood to be a characteristic of Eastern trinitarian theology as distinct from its Western form. That we find no doctrine of appropriations such as occurs in Latin theology, following Augustine, also accords with the Greek tradition.

Even more striking in its affinity to Eastern theology is the understanding of soteriology. Recall that Durrwell, Lafont, and von Balthasar each understand the work of our salvation as the *personal* filial accomplishment of Jesus Christ. Durrwell and von Balthasar in particular are firm in their resistance to the tendency in classical Latin theology toward a juridically-fashioned understanding of redemption. The interpretation of soteriology that emerges is thus much broader and more inclusive than that traditionally rendered in Latin theology. Salvation not only means redemption or liberation from sin, or even reconciliation with God; it embraces the whole cosmos. Soteriology is understood on a fully cosmic scale. In these theologies all of creation, the whole universe, is incorporated into the mystery of the Trinity. The mystery of sal-

---

[43]For introductory discussions of Eastern trinitarian theology see Constantine N. Tsirpanlis, *Introduction to Eastern Patristic Thought and Orthodox Theology*. Theology and Life Series 30 (Collegeville: The Liturgical Press, 1991); John Meyendorff, *Byzantine Theology: Historical Trends and Doctrinal Themes* (London: Mowbrays, 1975); *The Oxford Dictionary of Byzantium* (Oxford: Oxford University Press, 1991).

vation is not merely the satisfaction of divine justice but being enfolded into the mystery of the Trinity, an entry into the trinitarian *perichoresis*. It is communion, re-creation, regeneration into the mystery of divine sonship, and in this sense truly deification *(theosis)*, divinization. Moreover this re-creation does not arise merely because humankind has sinned and creation is therefore sin-infected. The divinization is the culmination of God's creative plan and thus the crowning of creation. We thus find that in its soteriology, christology, and pneumatology this new development in Latin trinitarian theology approaches Greek theology much more closely than did its classical Latin antecedent.

We have seen that this new development in Latin Catholic trinitarian theology involves the use of more personalist categories and points to a more relational ontology. In this respect it finds a parallel development in contemporary Orthodox trinitarian theology. John Zizioulas's *Being as Communion: Studies in Personhood and the Church*[44] is a particularly noteworthy development in the contemporary Orthodox tradition. In his trinitarian theology the category of personhood has primacy over that of substance. He writes: "No substance or nature exists without person or hypostasis or mode of existence. No person exists without substance or nature, *but* the ontological 'principle' or 'cause' of being—i. e. that which makes a thing to exist—is not the substance or nature but the *person* or hypostasis. Therefore, being is traced back not to substance but to person."[45]

Zizioulas observes that whereas classical Latin theology treated ontology in terms of being and relation the traditional tendency in Greek trinitarian theology to insist on the monarchy of the Father served to maintain personhood as the highest ontological principle. In this way Orthodox theology more readily tends to a relational ontology, an understanding of being as being-in-relation, focusing on personhood, relationship, and communion as the modality of all existence. Zizioulas's work both exemplifies and develops this tendency in the Orthodox tradition of trinitarian theology. Primacy is accorded to personhood over being as substance. Communion is affirmed as the nature of ultimate reality. Here we find not merely a parallel development but a certain degree of convergence with the development we have studied in Latin Catholic theology.

These affinities, resonances, and convergences with developments in contemporary Protestant, neo-Thomist, and Orthodox theology are evidence that this development in recent Catholic trinitarian theology by means of reflection on its interconnection with the paschal mystery is not ill-founded or ill-directed. The new development represents a sincere effort to render the biblical witness *more fully* than the traditional Latin treatment and in ways more attuned to

---

[44]Zizioulas, *Being as Communion: Studies in Personhood and the Church*, with a Foreword by John Meyendorff (Crestwood, N.Y.: St Vladimir's Seminary Press, 1985).

[45]*Being as Communion* 42 n. 37.

contemporary exigencies. It is neither repudiation nor reiteration of the classical treatment, but an attempt to express the Mystery of the Trinity in a richer and fuller and ultimately more persuasive way. That we find a considerable degree of convergence with the trinitarian theology and soteriology of the Orthodox tradition and parallel developments in modern Orthodox and Protestant theology supports the thrust of the development as well as promising an enriched possibility of theological dialogue and trans-confessional communication.

Resonances in postmodern philosophical thought

Setting aside the classical metaphysical approach to God to return anew to the data of revelation, the theologies we have studied occupy what we could describe as "a new space," a space that is both deconstructive and constructive. It is constructive in the sense that it insists on a return to the data. It is deconstructive in the sense that our authors in their exploration of the interconnection of the paschal mystery and the Trinity effectively combine, in a postmodern kind of way, to undo any attempt to absolutize reason and "being" in theology. Jean Luc Marion observes that this theological insistence on revelation resonates with French postmodern philosophical thought, and in his *God Without Being: Hors-Texte*[46] takes up the discussion of this revelation-based strategy, this shift from system to revealed given, at a philosophical level.

Clearly influenced by von Balthasar,[47] Marion recognizes that God's self-disclosure as the radical excess of *agapē* demands that every route to thinking about God via the notion of being must be rethought. In the paschal triduum divinity appears as *kenosis*; its logic is the logic of love. What is peculiar to love is that it gives itself as gift. Marion therefore questions whether any transcendental (for example, Rahnerian) or metaphysical reflection can provide an assured route forward for theology. The problem as he describes it is that a metaphysical determination of God imposes itself on what is still designated under the (disputable) title of "God." The notion of "God" in philosophy arises less from God as revealed than from metaphysics: God as supreme being, ground of all other derived beings.[48] Indeed Marion recognizes that this imposition of metaphysical names onto God actually obscures the mystery of God.[49] The result is a conceptual idol.[50]

---

[46]Jean Luc Marion, *God Without Being: Hors-Texte*, translated by Thomas A. Carlson, with a Foreword by David Tracy (Chicago: University of Chicago Press, 1991).

[47]Ibid. xix, 193.

[48]Ibid. 34.

[49]In *The Trespass of the Sign: Deconstruction, Theology and Philosophy* (Cambridge: Cambridge University Press, 1989) Kevin Hart also proposes that "rather than thinking of God as a particular kind of being, and therefore as a metaphysical entity, let us explore the possibility that it is metaphysics which compels us to regard God as a particular kind of being." (p. 76).

[50]Marion writes: "the conceptual idol has a site, metaphysics; a function, the theo-logy in onto-theology; and a definition, *causa sui*." (*God Without Being* 36).

Marion rejects a metaphysical determination of God in terms of being. Because God comes to us in and as gift God is best considered not in terms of being but in terms of love. "For the gift does not have first to be, but to pour out in an abandon that, alone, causes it to be; God saves the gift in giving it before being."[51] Only love does not have to be, Marion argues.[52] God's self-revelation as love demands that one allow God to be God, and not some idol created by modern or ancient reflection on being. From this perspective even Aquinas's understanding of God as *Ipsum Esse Subsistens* is brought into question as a route for understanding God revealed as Love. True theology, Marion argues, needs "God without Being." It needs to cease being modern theo-*logy* in order to become *theo*-logy. He explains: "Theology can reach its authentically *theo*logical status only if it is does not cease to break with all theo*logy*."[53] Marion therefore attempts to sketch a philosophy and a theology of "God without Being," an understanding of God that is free from the traditional metaphysical constraints. In other words he seeks to free God from the question of being.

In this way Marion provides a postmodern philosophical structure within which to situate this methodological shift from system to data that we have observed. He insists that revelation is the only possible and necessary foundation of any theology. The phenomenological difference between the idol and the icon is crucial to his thought.[54] Whereas ontologically-fashioned metaphysics can become a conceptual *idol,* revelation, centered in forms of visibility, can become an *icon* for thought.[55] Reason, although undoubtedly crucial for developing rigorous philosophical-theological concepts for understanding the "gift" of God's self-disclosure is, on its own, not an "icon" but an "idol". Reason, Marion explains, though capable of thinking being is not capable of iconically disclosing God. In contrast true theology is focused iconically on God's excessive self-revelation as love. It therefore needs to abandon all the metaphysics of the subject that have defined modernity and also to abandon the onto-theo-logical horizon that confines an understanding of God in terms of being.

David Tracy describes this alternative Marion proposes as "a revelation-centered, non-correlational, postmetaphysical theology."[56] Face, excess, gift, idol, icon, *agapē*, and goodness[57] emerge as categories through which to understand and express the reality of God's self-disclosure as love, as Marion

[51]Ibid. 3.
[52]Ibid. 36.
[53]Ibid. 139.
[54]Ibid. 7–24.
[55]Recall von Balthasar's stress on faith as an aesthetic act, an act of perception.
[56]*God Without Being* xii.
[57]Marion takes the notion of goodness as having primacy among the divine names from Pseudo-Dionysius's theology of the divine nomination. He argues that Aquinas inverted the primacy of goodness over being: *God Without Being* 73–83.

outlines a postmodern philosophical grounding for this new development in theology. Following in the footsteps of Hans Urs von Balthasar, Marion attempts a rigorous and coherent theological strategy focused on the reality of God's revelation as pure gift. Whether or not Marion succeeds in his attempt is a question we must leave to others to decide. We introduce his contribution here because it exemplifies the kind of philosophical grounding available within which to situate the methodological shift from system to data we have documented. Moreover, Marion's work is also indicative of the resonances this theological development has in postmodern philosophical thought. There too we have a radical questioning of metaphysics and a critique of onto-theological determinations of God.

Pluralism and objectivity

Recall that in concluding our meta-methodological inquiry we suggested that this new development in trinitarian theology and the theological pluralism it expresses is indicative of the newly emerging face of theology. However, a problem immediately surfaces: where is objectivity to be located in such manifold pluralism? There remains at least *prima facie* the vexatious question of objectivity that necessarily arises when theology moves beyond the stage of meaning, where theory serves to control meaning, into the stage where the converted self is foundational reality (in Lonergan's terms).

This new stage of meaning is admittedly a much more complex context for theological development and assessment. However, as Lonergan would persuade us, the development is not at the price of objectivity. In Lonergan's terms the objectivity of human knowing resides in the process of self-transcending intentional subjectivity itself.[58] Correlatively, transcendental (or meta-) method, by its very nature critical and self-correcting, itself offers the means of verification of its results. As we have seen here, the resultant new meanings may be confirmed, at least partially, by examining the coherence of any particular development with other developments in the field and in related fields. Although undoubtedly a more complicated theological context it is also a richer one, the fruit of a fuller range of authentic subjectivity attending to the data of revelation and experience. In effect what we have demonstrated in our study (again adumbrating the emerging context for theological development) is the occurrence of an ever fuller subjectivity being integrated into the theological enterprise. Far from sacrificing any objectivity, this development promises ever closer approximations to the objective truth of God's self-communication in Christ.

[58]Lonergan, *Method in Theology* 265, 292, 338.

Summary

In summary the interconnection of Trinity and paschal mystery is to be strongly defended and heartily commended on the following grounds:

In terms of its methodology:

1. Its legitimacy is fundamentally grounded in its status as a valid interpretation of the biblical data.

2. It represents an attempt to *interconnect* the central mysteries of Christian faith, a theological technique endorsed and encouraged by Vatican I.

3. It responds to a broad theological consensus in the Latin tradition concerning the need to modify traditional Latin approaches to trinitarian theology.

4. It represents an attempt to respond more adequately and appropriately to contemporary sensibilities and exigencies.

5. In its shift from substance-fashioned to more relational and personalist categories it has resonances in contemporary developments in neo-Thomist thought in which relationality is retrieved as equally primordial with substantiality.

6. In its shift from system to data it finds resonances in postmodern philosophical thought.

In terms of the verifiability of its thematic advance:

1. While attempting to achieve a fuller and more nuanced statement of trinitarian theology it does not contradict the traditional teaching of Latin trinitarian theology.

2. A high degree of convergence emerges across remarkably different methods of approach to the interconnection.

3. This development in trinitarian theology shows considerable convergence with traditional Eastern trinitarian theology and soteriology.

4. Parallel developments are to be found in contemporary Protestant and Orthodox trinitarian theology.

In terms of its yield for doctrinal development:

1. In situating trinitarian theology in the context of the paschal mystery it firmly grounds an understanding of the mystery of the Trinity in the events of salvation history and expresses that understanding in soteriological terms.

2. In explicating the mystery of the Trinity in terms of love and in employing more relational and personalist categories it meets the contemporary exigency that theology be expressed in a more existentially meaningful fashion.

3. It challenges the hegemony of the classical psychological analogy as it has been applied in the scholastic and neoscholastic tradition, and in particular its intellectualist bias, and effectively heralds a radical reconsideration of the balance of knowing and loving in the analogy as traditionally explicated.

4. A more nuanced understanding of the divine attributes emerges that addresses a deep dissatisfaction in contemporary culture—theological and philosophical as well as "everyday" culture—with classical philosophical notions of the immutability and impassibility of God.

5. It responds to contemporary theological concerns in relation to the distinction between the immanent and economic Trinity without abandoning the distinction.

Further questions and future possibilities for trinitarian theology

A number of possible future directions for further development of this new treatment of trinitarian theology also present themselves:

1. The integration of critical biblical scholarship in relation to the paschal mystery

In a methodological shift from doctrinal or philosophical starting point to the biblical data each of our four authors has situated trinitarian theology in the context of the paschal mystery of Jesus Christ. However, while a return to the biblical data is a characteristic and determining feature of our authors' trinitarian theologies, critical biblical scholarship plays at best a minor role in these revelation-centered theologies. Further prospects for this new development in trinitarian theology will no doubt emerge as theology appropriates the insights from the burgeoning field of biblical scholarship in this area, and indeed contributes to them by stimulating the imaginations of exegetes themselves.[59]

[59]See, for example, Raymond E. Brown, *The Death of the Messiah: From Gethsemane to the Grave: A Commentary on the Passion Narratives in the Four Gospels*, vols. 1 and 2 (New York: Doubleday, 1994), and Moloney, Francis J., *Belief in the Word: Reading John 1–4.* (Minneapolis: Fortress Press, 1993); idem, *Signs and Shadows: Reading John 5–12* (Minneapolis: Fortress Press, 1996); idem, *Glory Not Dishonor: Reading John 13–21* (Minneapolis: Fortress Press, 1998), examples of the critical scholarship that is becoming available.

2. *The integration of a wider range of biblical data*

The incorporation of the wider field of the biblical data as it emerges in contemporary critical biblical scholarship will also contribute to this kind of trinitarian theology. Recall, for example, that this interconnection of the Trinity with the paschal mystery and a concentration, to some degree at least, on the resurrection as the Father's act of generation of the Son contributed to a tendency to emphasize the biologically-generative image of Father and Son and correlatively to de-emphasize the image of intellectual emanation of God and Word. Clearly there is much more in store for trinitarian theology as it attends to the full range of the larger gospel narrative and its witness to Jesus' relationship to the Father and the Spirit.

David Coffey's exploration of the mystery of the Trinity from the vantage point of the baptism-anointing of Jesus is an example of what is to be gained when theology attends to the broader range of biblical data.[60] On the basis of this particular aspect of the biblical data Coffey proposes an alternative model of the trinitarian relations that he variously labels the "bestowal," "mutual love," or "return" model, as a complement to the traditional Latin trinitarian paradigm, the "procession" model. Where the "procession" model (the psychological analogy) begins with the essential unity of God and posits the distinctions on the basis of the nature of the processions, Coffey's model begins with the distinctions between the persons and moves toward the personal unity of the Trinity based on the mutuality of love between Father and Son, that being the Holy Spirit. As a complement to the Latin procession model based on the productive and constitutive origin of the persons Coffey's mutual love model thus emphasizes the interpersonal relationship of the persons rather than their constitutive relationship. His theology too shows a high degree of convergence with Eastern Orthodox theology. Here also the pneumatological dimension of trinitarian theology emerges with remarkably renewed vigor. In Coffey's work, which Ralph Del Colle describes as "a mature Spirit-Christology in trinitarian perspective, one which (as he admits) pushes beyond the boundaries of neo-scholasticism"[61] we also find a trinitarian theology that is more responsive to the data of biblical salvation history and strives to account for aspects of salvation history that are not well expressed in the traditional Latin model of the inner-trinitarian relations.

---

[60]Coffey, *Grace: The Gift of the Holy Spirit. Faith and Culture* 2 (Sydney: Catholic Institute of Sydney, 1979); idem, "The Pre-Existent and Incarnate Word" in *Faith and Culture: Contemporary Questions* (Sydney: Catholic Institute of Sydney, 1983) 62–77; idem,"The 'Incarnation' of the Holy Spirit in Christ," *Theological Studies* 45 (1984) 466–480; idem, "A Proper Mission of the Holy Spirit," *Theological Studies* 47 (1986) 227–250; idem, "Our Return to God through Christ in the Spirit," *Compass* 23 (1989) 33–36; idem, "The Holy Spirit as the Mutual Love of the Father and the Son," *Theological Studies* 51 (1990) 193–229. For a discussion of Coffey's theology see Del Colle, *Christ and Spirit: Spirit Christology in Trinitarian Perspective* (New York: Oxford University Press, 1994), especially 91–140.

[61]Del Colle, *Christ and Spirit: Spirit Christology in Trinitarian Perspective* 6.

3. The challenge of a feminist critique

One cannot but note the lack of awareness of issues of gender in reference to God that is evident in our authors' works. Certainly in Durrwell we find a preponderance of "feminine" images for the Holy Spirit as womb, fertility of God, the "maternal" divine person.[62] Nevertheless, at best such a tack is hardly adequate to a feminist critique. At worst it tends to reinforce a genderization of the divine persons and to impose a "gender-matrix" onto the Trinity, which is precisely what is under challenge, and rightly so.

Admittedly most of the works before us were written before the emergence of this movement in contemporary theology. However, with feminist consciousness now so urgent and pressing an aspect of contemporary theology the development must be prepared to face a feminist critique. It is a simple fact that one can no longer uncritically refer to God or the persons of the Trinity by means of the masculine gender. Reference to the first person of the Trinity as Father is particularly problematic. The critical question at this point is how a trinitarian theology built by reflection on the paschal mystery of Jesus Christ is to respond constructively and with integrity to the feminist critique.[63]

Here a theology and ontology of love such as that intimated by Lonergan[64] and developed by Kelly[65] offers new possibilities. To the degree that such a theology refocuses our perception of God in terms of Being-in-Love a number of the difficulties are attenuated, even averted. A new context for trinitarian theology emerges, together with new symbols and categories for a richer imagining of the divine mystery, one that is more sensitive and responsive to what are legitimate gender concerns.

4. Implications for theological education

In terms of theological education it is only fitting to insist that this way of approaching the mystery of the Trinity, grounded in the biblical data and in the human experience of salvation, should precede and have priority over the more abstract and a-historical way of approach of the traditional trinitarian theology. In order of treatment of the mystery, it should be presented first to theological students, as indeed was suggested by Vatican Council II:

[62]Durrwell, *HSG* 151–155.

[63]See for example Catherine LaCugna's article "The Baptismal Formula, Feminist Objections and Trinitarian Theology," *Journal of Ecumenical Studies* 26 (1989) 235–250. In an attempt to construct an alternative set of trinitarian names Elizabeth A. Johnson suggests Spirit-Sophia, Jesus-Sophia, Mother-Sophia (*She Who Is: The Mystery of God in Feminist Theological Discourse* [New York: Crossroad, 1992]). It is interesting to note that Johnson's feminist methodology takes the experience of the Spirit as the starting point for trinitarian reflection. See also "Review Symposium," *Horizons* 20 (1993) 324–344.

[64]Lonergan, "Christology Today: Methodological Reflections" in *A Third Collection* 93–94.

[65]Kelly, *The Trinity of Love*, especially 250–255.

The following order should be observed in dogmatic theology: let biblical themes be treated first, then what the Fathers of the church (both east and west) have contributed to the faithful transmission and explanation of the revealed truths, followed by the later history of dogma, including its relation to the general history of the church. Then, in order to throw the fullest light possible on the mysteries of salvation, let them learn through speculation guided by St. Thomas to enter into them more deeply and see how they are interconnected, to recognize how they are present and active in liturgical celebration and in the whole life of the church.[66]

May such an approach lead students, not only in their minds but in their hearts, in the very concrete realities of their lives, into the paschal mystery of life and love and ever more deeply into the ever glorious mystery of the Trinity, this mystery of love. As Augustine, introducing *De Trinitate,* says: "For nowhere else is a mistake more dangerous, or the search more laborious, or discovery more advantageous."[67] My own assessment of this recent discovery in theology is that this new approach to the mystery of the Trinity is indeed advantageous, very much so, although the search for both writer and reader remains a strenuous and painstaking one. As for the mistakes, the assessment of our study and its intrinsic value, these must be left to the ongoing conversation that theology has come to be.

---

[66]*Decree on the Training of Priests (Optatem Totius)* 16, in Austin Flannery, o.p., ed., *Vatican Council II. Constitutions, Decrees, Declarations* (Northport, N.Y.: Costello, 1996).
[67]*DT* I.5.

Selected Bibliography

Augustine. *De Trinitate*. CCSL 50, 50A. Turnhout, Belgium: Brepols, 1968. English: *The Trinity*. John E. Rotelle, ed., The Works of Saint Augustine: A Translation for the 21st Century. With Introduction, translation, and notes by Edmund Hill. New York: New City Press, 1991.

Babini, Ellero. "Jesus Christ, Form and Norm of Man according to Hans Urs von Balthasar," *Communio* 16 (1989) 446–457.

Bauckham, Richard. *The Theology of Jürgen Moltmann*. Edinburgh: T & T Clark, 1995.

Brito, Emilio. *La Christologie de Hegel: Verbum Crucis*. Translated by B. Pottier. Bibliothèque des Archives de Philosophie Nouvelle 40. Paris: Beauchesne, 1983.

Buckley, James J. "Balthasar's Use of the Theology of Aquinas," *The Thomist* 59 (1995) 517–545.

Catão, Bernard. *Salut et rédemption chez S. Thomas D'Aquin: L'acte sauveur du Christ*. Théologie études publiées sous la direction de la Faculté de Théologie S. J. Lyon-Fourviére 62. Paris: Aubier, 1965.

Clarke, W. Norris. "What is Most and Least Relevant in the Metaphysics of St Thomas Today?" *International Philosophical Quarterly* 14 (1974) 411–434.

_____. *The Philosophical Approach to God*. Winston-Salem, N. C.: Wake Forest University Press, 1979.

_____. "To be is to be self-communicative: St. Thomas' view of personal being," *Theology Digest* 33 (1986) 441–454.

_____. "Fifty Years of Metaphysical Reflection: The Universe as Journey" in *The Universe as Journey: Conversations with W. Norris Clarke*. New York: Fordham University Press, 1988, 49–92.

_____. "The 'We Are' of Interpersonal Dialogue as the Starting Point of Metaphysics," *The Modern Schoolman* 69 (1992) 357–368.

_____. "Person, Being and St. Thomas," *Communio* 19 (1992) 601–618.

_____. "Thomism and Contemporary Philosophical Pluralism," in Deal W. Hudson and Dennis W. Moran, eds., *The Future of Thomism*. Notre Dame, Ind.: University of Notre Dame Press for American Maritain Association, 1992, 91–108.

_____. *Person and Being.* The Aquinas Lecture, 1993. Milwaukee: Marquette University Press, 1993.

Coffey, David. *Grace. The Gift of the Holy Spirit.* Faith and Culture 2. Sydney: Catholic Institute of Sydney, 1979.

_____. "The Pre-Existent and Incarnate Word," in *Faith and Culture: Contemporary Questions.* Sydney: Catholic Institute of Sydney, 1983, 62–77.

_____. "The 'Incarnation' of the Holy Spirit in Christ," *Theological Studies* 45 (1984) 466–480.

_____. "A Proper Mission of the Holy Spirit," *Theological Studies* 47 (1986) 227–250.

_____. "Our Return to God through Christ in the Spirit," *Compass* 23 (1989) 33–36.

_____. "The Holy Spirit as the Mutual Love of the Father and the Son," *Theological Studies* 51 (1990) 193–229.

Connor, Robert A. "Relational Esse and the Person," *American Catholic Philosophical Quarterly Annual.* A.C.P.A. Proceedings 65 (1991) 253–267.

_____. "The Person as Resonating Existential," *American Catholic Philosophical Quarterly* 66 (1992) 39–56.

Cousins, Ewert. "A Theology of Interpersonal Relations," *Thought* 45 (1970) 56–82.

Crowe, Frederick E. *The Lonergan Enterprise.* Cambridge, Mass.: Cowley Publications, 1980.

_____. *Appropriating the Lonergan Idea.* Edited by Michael Vertin. Washington, D. C.: Catholic University of America Press, 1989.

_____. "Rethinking God-With-Us: Categories from Lonergan," *Science et Esprit* 41 (1989) 167–188.

_____. *Lonergan.* Outstanding Christian Thinkers Series. London: Geoffrey Chapman; Collegeville: The Liturgical Press, 1992.

Daurio, Janice. "Toward a Theology of Desire: The Existential Hermeneutic in the Soteriology of Sebastian Moore," *Downside Review* 106 (1988) 195–232.

Del Colle, Ralph. *Christ and Spirit: Spirit Christology in Trinitarian Perspective.* New York: Oxford University Press, 1994.

de Lubac, Henri. "A Witness of Christ in the Church: Hans Urs von Balthasar," in *The Church: Paradox and Mystery.* Translated by James R. Dunne. Shannon: Ecclesia Press, 1969, 103–121.

de Margerie, Bertrand. *The Christian Trinity in History.* Studies in Historical Theology 1. Translated by Edmund J. Fortman. Petersham, Mass.: St. Bede's Publications, 1982.

Denzinger, Heinrich, and Adolf Schönmetzer, eds. *Enchiridion Symbolorum: Definitionum et Declarationum de Rebus Fidei et Morum.* 32nd ed. Freiburg: Herder, 1963.

Doran, Robert M. "Psychic Conversion," *The Thomist* 41 (1977) 200–236.

_____. *Subject and Psyche: Ricoeur, Jung, and the Search for Foundations.* Lanham, Md.: University Press of America, 1980.

_____. *Psychic Conversion and Theological Foundations: Towards a Reorientation of the Human Sciences.* Atlanta, Ga.: Scholars Press, 1981.

_____. "Psychic Conversion and Lonergan's Hermeneutics" in Sean McEvenue and Ben F. Meyer, eds., *Lonergan's Hermeneutics: Its Development and Application.* Washington, D. C.: University Press of America, 1989, 161–208.

_____. *Theology and the Dialectics of History.* Toronto: University of Toronto Press, 1990.

Dunne, Thomas A., and Jean-Marc Laporte, eds. *Trinification of the World.* Toronto: Regis College Press, 1978.

Dupré, Louis. "Hans Urs von Balthasar's Theology of Aesthetic Form," *Theological Studies* 49 (1988) 299–318.

_____. "The Glory of the Lord: Hans Urs von Balthasar's Theological Aesthetic," *Communio* 16 (1989) 384–412.

Durrwell, François-Xavier. *The Resurrection: A Biblical Study.* With an Introduction by Charles Davis. Translated by Rosemary Sheed. London: Sheed and Ward, 1960.

_____. *In the Redeeming Christ.* Translated by Rosemary Sheed. London: Sheed and Ward, 1963.

_____. "Lamb of God," *New Catholic Encyclopedia.* Washington, D. C.: Catholic University of America, 1967.

_____. "Theology of Resurrection of Christ," *New Catholic Encyclopedia,* 1967.

_____. *The Mystery of Christ and the Apostolate.* Translated by Edward Quinn. London: Sheed & Ward, 1972.

_____. "Mystère pascal et Parousie: L'importance sotériologique de la présence du Christ," *Nouvelle Revue Théologique* 95 (1973) 253–278.

_____. *L'Eucharistie: sacrement pascal.* 3d ed. Paris: Éditions du Cerf, 1980.

_____. "Liminaire: La Pâque du Christ selon l'Écriture" in *La Pâque du Christ, Mystère de Salut: Mélanges en l'Honneur du Père Durrwell.* Paris: Éditions du Cerf, 1982, 9–13.

_____. *L'Esprit Saint de Dieu.* Paris: Éditions du Cerf, 1983. English: *Holy Spirit of God: An Essay in Biblical Theology.* Translated by Benedict Davies. London: Geoffrey Chapman, 1986.

_____. *Le Père: Dieu en son Mystère.* Paris: Éditions du Cerf, 1988.

_____. *L'Esprit du Père et du Fils.* Paris: Médiaspaul, 1989. English: *The Spirit of the Father and of the Son.* Translated by Robert Nowell. Middlegreen: St Paul, 1990.

_____. "Pour une Christologie selon l'Esprit Saint," *Nouvelle Revue Théologique* 114 (1992) 653–677.

Fallon, Timothy P., and Philip B. Riley. *Religion and Culture: Essays in Honor of Bernard F. Lonergan, S. J.* Albany, N.Y.: SUNY Press, 1987.

Fletcher, Frank. "Exploring Christian Theology's Foundations in Religious Experience." D.Theol. diss. Melbourne College of Divinity. Melbourne, 1982.

Fortman, Edmund J. *The Triune God: A Historical Study of the Doctrine of the Trinity.* London: Hutchinson, 1972.

Gregson, Vernon. *Lonergan, Spirituality and the Meeting of Religions.* Lanham, Md.: University Press of America, 1985.

Gregson, Vernon, ed. *The Desires of the Human Heart: An Introduction to the Theology of Bernard Lonergan.* Mahwah, N.J.: Paulist, 1988.

Gunton, Colin E. *The Promise of Trinitarian Theology.* Edinburgh: T & T Clark, 1991.

_____. *The One, the Three and the Many: God, Creation and the Culture of Modernity.* Cambridge: Cambridge University Press, 1993.

Hall, Douglas C. *The Trinity: An Analysis of St. Thomas Aquinas' Expositio of the De Trinitate of Boethius.* Leiden: E. J. Brill, 1992.

Hankey, W. J. *God in Himself: Aquinas' Doctrine of God as Expounded in the Summa Theologiae.* Oxford: Oxford University Press, 1987.

Hart, Kevin. *The Trespass of the Sign: Deconstruction, Theology and Philosophy.* Cambridge: Cambridge University Press, 1989.

Henrici, Peter. "Hans Urs von Balthasar: A Sketch of his Life," *Communio* 16 (1989): 306–350.

_____. "The Philosophy of Hans Urs von Balthasar" in David L. Schindler, ed., *Hans Urs von Balthasar: His Life and Work*. San Francisco: Ignatius Press, 1991, 149–167.

Hill, Edmund. *The Mystery of the Trinity*. Introducing Catholic Theology. London: Geoffrey Chapman, 1985.

Hill, William J. *The Three-Personed God: The Trinity as a Mystery of Salvation*. Washington, D. C.: Catholic University of America Press, 1982.

Jansen, Henry. "Moltmann's View of God's (Im)mutability: The God of the Philosophers and the God of the Bible," *Neue Zeitschrift für Systematische Theologie und Religiöse Philosophie* 36 (1994) 284–301.

Johnson, Elizabeth A. *She Who Is: The Mystery of God in Feminist Theological Discourse*. New York: Crossroad, 1992.

Jüngel, Eberhard. *The Doctrine of the Trinity: God's Being is in Becoming*. Translated by J. C. B. Mohr. Edinburgh: Scottish Academic Press, 1976.

_____. "The Relationship between 'economic' and 'immanent' Trinity," *Theology Digest* 24 (1976) 179–184.

_____. *God as the Mystery of the World: On the Foundation of the Theology of the Crucified One in the Dispute between Theism and Atheism*. Translated by Darrell L. Guder. Grand Rapids: Eerdmans, 1983.

Kay, Jeffrey. "H. U. von Balthasar, Post-Critical Theologian?" *Concilium* 141/6 (1981) 84–89.

Kehl, Medard, and Werner Löser, eds. *The Von Balthasar Reader*. Translated by Robert J. Daly and Fred Lawrence. Edinburgh: T & T Clark, 1985.

Kelly, Anthony. *The Trinity of Love: A Theology of the Christian God*. New Theology Studies 4. Wilmington, Del.: Michael Glazier, 1989.

_____. (Kelly, Tony) *Touching on the Infinite: Explorations in Christian Hope*. Blackburn: Collins Dove, 1991.

_____. (Kelly, Tony) *An Expanding Theology: Faith in a World of Connections*. Newtown, N. S. W.: E. J. Dwyer, 1993.

_____. "The 'Horrible Wrappers' of Aquinas' God," *Pacific* 9 (1996) 185–203.

Kelly, J. N. D. *Early Christian Doctrines*. Rev. ed. New York: Harper and Row, 1960, 1965, 1968, 1978.

LaCugna, Catherine Mowry. *God for Us: The Trinity and Christian Life*. New York: Harper Collins, 1991.

_____. "The Baptismal Formula, Feminist Objections and Trinitarian Theology," *Journal of Ecumenical Studies* 26 (1989) 235–250.

_____. "The Trinitarian Mystery of God" in Francis Schüssler Fiorenza and John Galvin, eds., *Systematic Theology: Roman Catholic Perspectives* 1. Minneapolis: Fortress, 1991, 149–192.

Lafont, Ghislain. *Structures et méthodes dans la Somme théologique de Saint Thomas d'Aquin*. Paris: Desclée de Brouwer, 1961.

_____. *Peut-on Connaître Dieu en Jésus Christ?* Cogitatio Fidei 44. Paris: Éditions du Cerf, 1969.

_____. *God, Time and Being*. Translated by Leonard Maluf. Petersham, Mass.: St Bede's Publications, 1992.

Lamb, Matthew, ed. *Creativity and Method: Essays in Honor of Bernard Lonergan, S. J.* Milwaukee: Marquette University Press, 1981.

Loewe, William P. "Encountering the Crucified God: The Soteriology of Sebastian Moore," *Horizons* 9 (1982) 216–236.

Lonergan, Bernard J. F. *Insight: A Study of Human Understanding.* New York: Harper & Row, 1957.

_____. *De Deo Trino I. Pars Dogmatica and II. Pars Systematica.* Rome: Pontifical Gregorian University, 1964.

_____. *Verbum: Word and Idea in Aquinas.* London: Darton, Longman & Todd, 1967.

_____. *Method in Theology.* New York: Seabury, 1972.

_____. *Philosophy of God, and Theology.* Philadelphia: Westminster, 1973.

_____. *A Second Collection: Papers by Bernard J.F. Lonergan, S.J.* Edited by William F. J. Ryan and Bernard J. Tyrrell. London: Darton, Longman and Todd, 1974.

_____. *The Way to Nicea: The Dialectical Development of Trinitarian Theology.* Translated by C. O'Donovan. London: Darton, Longman & Todd, 1976.

_____. *A Third Collection: Papers by Bernard J.F. Lonergan, S.J.* Edited by Frederick E. Crowe. New York: Paulist, 1985.

_____. *Collection.* Collected Works of Bernard Lonergan 4. Edited by Frederick E. Crowe and Robert M. Doran. 2d rev. and augmented ed. Toronto: University of Toronto Press for Lonergan Research Institute of Regis College, 1988.

_____. *Understanding and Being.* Collected Works of Bernard Lonergan 5. Edited by Elizabeth A. Morelli and Mark D. Morelli. 2d rev. and augmented ed. Toronto: University of Toronto Press for Lonergan Research Institute of Regis College, 1990.

Löser, Werner. "Being Interpreted as Love: Reflections on the Theology of Hans Urs von Balthasar," *Communio* 16 (1989) 475–490.

MacKinnon, Donald M. "Some Reflections on Hans Urs von Balthasar's Christology with Special Reference to Theodramatik II/2 and III" in John Riches, ed., *The Analogy of Beauty: The Theology of Hans Urs von Balthasar.* Edinburgh: T & T Clark, 1986, 164–174.

Marion, Jean-Luc. *God Without Being: Hors-Texte.* Translated by Thomas A. Carlson. With a Foreword by David Tracy. Chicago: University of Chicago Press, 1991.

Marsh, Thomas. *The Triune God: A Biblical, Historical and Theological Study.* Maynooth Bicentenary Series. Blackrock, Co. Dublin: Columba Press, 1994.

Mascall, E. L. *The Triune God: An Ecumenical Study.* Oxford: Blackwell, 1986.

McCarthy, Michael H. *The Crisis of Philosophy.* Albany, N. Y.: SUNY Press, 1990.

McCool, Gerald A. "An alert and independent Thomist: William Norris Clarke, S. J." in Gerald A. McCool, ed., *The Universe as Journey: Conversations with W. Norris Clarke.* New York: Fordham University Press, 1988, 13–47.

_____. "The Tradition of St. Thomas since Vatican II," *Theology Digest* 40 (1993) 324–335.

McDade, John. "Reading von Balthasar." *Month* 20 (1987) 136–143.

_____. "The Trinity and the Paschal Mystery," *Heythrop Journal* 29 (1988) 175–191.

_____. "Catholic Theology in the Post-Conciliar Period" in Adrian Hastings, ed., *Modern Catholicism: Vatican II and After.* London: SPCK, 1991, 422–443.

McEvenue, Sean E., and Ben F. Meyer, eds. *Lonergan's Hermeutics: Its Development and Application.* Washington D. C.: Catholic University of America Press, 1989.

McGregor, Bede, and Thomas Norris. *The Beauty of Christ: An Introduction to the Theology of Hans Urs von Balthasar.* Edinburgh: T & T Clark, 1994.

Merriell, Donald Juvenal. *To the Image of the Trinity: A Study in the Development of Aquinas' Teaching*. Toronto: Pontifical Institute of Mediaeval Studies, 1990.

Meyendorff, John. *Byzantine Theology: Historical Trends and Doctrinal Themes*. London: Mowbrays, 1975.

Meynell, Hugo A. *The Theology of Bernard Lonergan*. American Academy of Religion Studies in Religion 42. Atlanta, Ga.: Scholars Press, 1986.

_____. *An Introduction to the Philosophy of Bernard Lonergan*. 2nd ed. Toronto: University of Toronto Press, 1991.

Moltmann, Jürgen. *The Crucified God*. Translated by R. A. Wilson and John Bowden. London: SCM, 1974.

_____. *The Trinity and the Kingdom of God: The Doctrine of God*. Translated by Margaret Kohl. London: SCM, 1981.

_____. "The Unity of the Triune God," *St. Vladimir's Theological Quarterly* 28 (1984) 157–171.

_____. *History and the Triune God*. Translated by John Bowden. London: SCM, 1991.

_____. *The Coming of God: Christian Eschatology*. Translated by Margaret Kohl. London: SCM, 1996.

Mooney, Hilary A. *The Liberation of Consciousness: Bernard Lonergan's Theological Foundations in Dialogue with the Theological Aesthetics of Hans Urs von Balthasar*. Frankfurter Theologische Studien 41. Frankfurt: Josef Knight, 1992.

Moore, Sebastian. *The Crucified is No Stranger*. London: Darton, Longman and Todd, 1977.

_____. *The Fire and the Rose are One*. London: Darton, Longman and Todd, 1980.

_____. "For a Soteriology of the Existential Subject" in Matthew Lamb, ed., *Creativity and Method: Essays in Honor of Bernard Lonergan, S. J.* Milwaukee: Marquette University Press, 1981, 229–247.

_____. "Death as the Delimiting of Desire: A Key Concept in Soteriology" in Steven Kepnes and David Tracy, eds., *The Challenge of Psychology to Faith*. New York: Seabury, 1982, 51–56.

_____. *The Inner Loneliness*. London: Darton, Longman and Todd, 1982.

_____. *Let This Mind Be in You: The Quest for Identity through Oedipus to Christ*. London: Darton, Longman and Todd, 1985.

_____. "The Communication of a Dangerous Memory" in Timothy P. Fallon and Philip B. Riley, eds., *Religion and Culture: Essays in Honor of Bernard F. Lonergan, S. J.* Albany, N.Y.: SUNY Press, 1987, 237–241.

_____. *Jesus: Liberator of Desire*. New York: Crossroad, 1989.

_____. "Jesus the Liberator of Desire: Reclaiming Ancient Images," *Cross Currents* 40 (1990) 477–498.

_____. "'Author's Response.' Review Symposium: Sebastian Moore's *Jesus Liberator of Desire*. Three perspectives by Stephen J. Duffy, Elisabeth Koenig and William P. Loewe with Author's Response." *Horizons* 18 (1991) 93–129.

_____. "Four Steps Towards Making Sense of Theology" *Downside Review* 111 (1993) 79–100.

Moss, David. "Costly Giving: On Jean-Luc Marion's Theology of Gift," *New Blackfriars* 74 (1993) 393–399.

Nicolas, Jean-Hervé. *Synthèse dogmatique de la Trinité à la Trinité. Avec Préface par Cardinal Ratzinger*. Paris: Beauchesne Éditions Universitaires Fribourg Suisse, 1985.

Oakes, Edward T. *Pattern of Redemption: The Theology of Hans Urs von Balthasar.* New York: Continuum, 1994.

O'Callaghan, Michael C. *Unity in Theology: Lonergan's Framework for Theology in Its New Context.* Washington, D. C.: University Press of America, 1980.

O'Donnell, John J. "The Doctrine of the Trinity in Recent German Theology," *Heythrop Journal* 23 (1982) 153–167.

_____. *Trinity and Temporality: The Christian Doctrine of God in the Light of Process Theology and the Theology of Hope.* Oxford: Oxford University Press, 1983.

_____. "The Trinity as Divine Community: A Critical Reflection upon Recent Theological Developments," *Gregorianum* 69 (1988) 5–34.

_____. *The Mystery of the Triune God.* Heythrop Monograph Series 6. London: Sheed & Ward, 1988.

_____. "Truth as Love: The Understanding of Truth according to Hans Urs von Balthasar," *Pacifica* 1 (1988) 189–211.

_____. "In Him and Over Him: The Holy Spirit in the Life of Jesus," *Gregorianum* 70 (1989) 25–45.

_____. "Hans Urs von Balthasar: The Form of His Theology," *Communio* 16 (1989) 458–474.

_____. *Hans Urs von Balthasar.* Outstanding Christian Thinkers. London: Geoffrey Chapman; Collegeville: The Liturgical Press, 1992.

O'Hanlon, Gerard F. "H. U. von Balthasar and De Deo Uno—A New Tract," *Milltown Studies* 5 (1980) 115–130.

_____. "Does God Change?—H. U. von Balthasar on the Immutability of God," *Irish Theological Quarterly* 53 (1987) 161–183.

_____. "The Trinitarian God: Towards a New Ireland," *Irish Theological Quarterly* 55 (1989) 99–124.

_____. *The Immutability of God in the Theology of Hans Urs von Balthasar.* Cambridge: Cambridge University Press, 1990.

_____. "The Legacy of Hans Urs von Balthasar," *Doctrine and Life* 41 (1991) 401–407.

_____. "The Jesuits and Modern Theology—Rahner, von Balthasar and Liberation Theology," *Irish Theological Quarterly* 58 (1992) 25–45.

O'Meara, Thomas F. "Grace as a Theological Structure in the Summa theologiae of Thomas Aquinas," *Recherches de Théologie ancienne et médiévale* 55 (1988) 130–153.

O'Regan, Cyril. "Von Balthasar and Thick Retrieval: Post-Chalcedonian Symphonic Theology," *Gregorianum* 77 (1996) 227–260.

Pannenberg, Wolfhart. *Systematic Theology* 1. Translated by Geoffrey W. Bromiley. Grand Rapids: Eerdmans, 1991.

Principe, Walter H. "The Dynamism of Augustine's Terms for Describing the Highest Trinitarian Image in the Human Person," *Studia Patristica* 18 (1982) 1291–1299.

Rahner, Karl. "Remarks on the Dogmatic Treatise 'De Trinitate,'" *Theological Investigations.* 4. Translated by Kevin Smyth. Baltimore: Helicon Press, 1966, 77–102.

_____. *The Trinity.* Translated by Joseph Donceel. London: Burns and Oates, 1970.

_____. *Foundations of Christian Faith: An Introduction to the Idea of Christianity.* Translated by William V. Dych. New York: Crossroad, 1987.

Ratzinger, Joseph. *Introduction to Christianity.* Translated by J. R. Foster. New York: Seabury Press, 1969.

_____. "Concerning the Notion of Person in Theology," *Communio* 17 (1990) 439–454.

Remy, Gérard. "Une Théologie pascale de l'Esprit Saint," *Nouvelle Revue Théologique* 112 (1990) 73–741.

Rende, Michael L. *Lonergan on Conversion: Development of a Notion*. Lanham, Md.: University Press of America, 1991.

Roberts, Louis. *The Theological Aesthetics of Hans Urs von Balthasar*. Washington, D. C.: Catholic University of America Press, 1987.

Saward, John. *The Mysteries of March: Hans Urs von Balthasar on Incarnation and Easter*. London: Collins, 1990.

Scheeben, Matthias J. *The Mysteries of Christianity*. Translated by Cyril Vollert. London: B. Herder Book Co., 1947.

Schindler, David L. "Norris Clarke on Person, Being, and St. Thomas," *Communio* 20 (1993) 580–596.

Schmitz, Kenneth L. "The God of Love," *The Thomist* 57 (1993) 495–508.

Scola, Angela. *Hans Urs von Balthasar: A Theological Style*. Grand Rapids: Eerdmans, 1991.

Stanley, David Michael. *Christ's Resurrection in Pauline Soteriology*. Analecta Biblica Investigationes Scientificae in Res Biblicas 13. Rome: Pontifical Biblical Institute, 1961.

Studer, Basil. *Trinity and Incarnation: The Faith of the Early Church*. Edited by Andrew Louth. Translated by Matthias Westerhoff. Edinburgh: T & T Clark, 1993.

Tanner, Kathryn E. *God and Creation in Christian Theology: Tyranny or Empowerment?* Oxford: Basil Blackwell, 1988.

Tanner, Norman P., ed. *Decrees of the Ecumenical Councils*. 2 vols. London: Sheed & Ward, 1990; Washington, D. C.: Georgetown University Press, 1990.

Thomas Aquinas. *Summa Theologiae*. 60 vols. Edited by Thomas Gilby. London: .Blackfriars, 1964–1966.

Thompson, John. *Modern Trinitarian Perspectives*. New York: Oxford University Press, 1994.

Torrance, T. F. *The Trinitarian Faith*. Edinburgh: T & T Clark, 1988.

Tsirpanlis, Constantine N. *Introduction to Eastern Patristic Thought and Orthodox Theology*. Theology and Life 30. Collegeville: The Liturgical Press, 1991.

von Balthasar, Hans Urs. *The Way of the Cross*. London: Burns & Oates, 1964.

_____. *Love Alone: The Way of Revelation: A Theological Perspective*. Edited by Alexander Dru. London: Burns & Oates, 1968.

_____. *Elucidations*. Translated by John Riches. London: SPCK, 1975.

_____. *Theodramatik. III, Die Handlung*. Einsiedeln: Johannes Verlag, 1980.

_____. *First Glance at Adrienne von Speyr*. Translated by Antje Lawry and Sergia Englund. San Francisco: Ignatius Press, 1981.

_____. *Pâques: Le Mystère*. Translated by R. Givord. Paris: Éditions du Cerf, 1981.

_____. *The Glory of the Lord: A Theological Aesthetics. I, Seeing the Form*. Edited by Joseph Fessio S.J. and John Riches. Translated by Erasmo Leiva-Merikakis. San Francisco: Ignatius Press, 1982.

_____. "The Descent into Hell," *Chicago Studies* 23 (1984) 223–236.

_____. *Life Out of Death: Meditations on the Easter Mystery*. Translated by Davis Perkins. Philadelphia: Fortress Press, 1985.

_____. *Theologik. II, Wahrheit Gottes.* Einsiedeln: Johannes Verlag, 1985.

_____. "On the Concept of Person," *Communio* 13 (1986) 18–26.

_____. *Prayer.* Translated by Graham Harrison. San Francisco: Ignatius Press, 1986.

_____. "Death is Swallowed up by Life," *Communio* 14 (1987) 49–54.

_____. *Dare We Hope "That All Men Be Saved"? With a Short Discourse on Hell.* Translated by David Kipp and Lothar Krauth. San Francisco: Ignatius Press, 1987.

_____. *Theo-Drama: Theological Dramatic Theory. I, Prologomena.* Translated by Graham Harrison. San Francisco: Ignatius Press, 1988.

_____. *The Glory of the Lord: A Theological Aesthetics. VII, Theology: The New Covenant.* Edited by John Riches. Translated by Brian McNeil. San Francisco: Ignatius Press, 1989.

_____. *Credo: Meditations on the Apostles' Creed.* Translated by David Kipp. New York: Crossroad, 1990.

_____. *Theo-Drama: Theological Dramatic Theory. II, Dramatis Personae: Man in God.* Translated by Graham Harrison. San Francisco: Ignatius Press, 1990.

_____. *Mysterium Paschale: The Mystery of Easter.* Translated with an Introduction by Aidan Nichols. Edinburgh: T & T Clark, 1990.

_____. *Theo-Drama: Theological Dramatic Theory. III, Dramatis Personae: Persons in Christ.* Translated by Graham Harrison. San Francisco: Ignatius Press, 1992.

_____. *My Work: In Retrospect.* San Francisco: Ignatius Press, 1993.

Waldstein, Michael. "An Introduction to von Balthasar's The Glory of the Lord," *Communio* 14 (1987) 12–33.

Weinandy, Thomas G. *Does God Change? The Word's Becoming in the Incarnation.* Still River, Mass.: St. Bede's Publications, 1985.

_____. "The immanent and the economic Trinity," *The Thomist* 57 (1993) 655–666.

_____. *The Father's Spirit of Sonship: Reconceiving the Trinity.* Edinburgh: T & T Clark, 1995.

Willis, W. Waite, Jr. *Theism, Atheism and the Doctrine of the Trinity: The Trinitarian Theologies of Karl Barth and Jürgen Moltmann in Response to Protest Atheism.* Atlanta, Ga.: Scholars Press, 1987.

Zizioulas, John D. *Being as Communion: Studies in Personhood and the Church.* With a Foreword by John Meyendorff. Crestwood, N.Y.: St. Vladimir's Seminary Press, 1985.

_____. "The Church as Communion," *St. Vladimir's Theological Quarterly* 38 (1994) 3–16.

Index

Printed in the United States
23946LVS00005B/139-342